Don't Worry, Be Happy!

A memoir of hope, humour and survival
from Hitler's Germany to Mugabe's Zimbabwe

Ursula la Cock

Don't Worry, Be Happy!
A memoir of hope, humour and survival from Hitler's Germany to Mugabe's Zimbabwe

by Ursula la Cock
edited by Kim Kimber

Text & images © Ursula la Cock, 2025

Every reasonable effort was made to track down the copyright holders for all content used in this publication. Please contact us if you become aware of any copyrighted material used inappropriately.

Some of the terminology and opinions used in this memoir reflect the time depicted; we have tried to strike a balance between retaining expressions which could now be considered offensive, and over-sanitizing retrospectively.

All rights reserved. No part of this document may be reproduced, copied, distributed, transferred, modified, or transmitted, in any form or by any means, electronic or mechanical, including photocopying, recording, or by any information storage or retrieval system, without the prior written permission of the copyright owner; nor can it be circulated in any form of binding or cover other than that in which it is published and without similar conditions including this condition being imposed on a subsequent purchaser. In no event shall the author or publisher be liable for any damages caused in any way by use of this document.

Published by Ōzaru Books, an imprint of BJ Translations Ltd
Street Acre, Shuart Lane, St Nicholas-at-Wade, BIRCHINGTON, CT7 0NG, UK
https://ozaru.net

First edition published 27 February 2025

ISBN: 978-1-915174-08-6

Contents

Part 1: MY YOUTH 7
1. Allenstein (1925–1928) 7
2. Oestereiden (1928–1932) 11
3. Preußisch Görlitz (1932–1936) 13
4. Brückendorf (1936–1942) 16

Part 2: THE WAR YEARS 28
5. Duty Year (1942) 28
6. Berlin (1942) 30
7. AEG 34
8. Berlin (1943) 35
9. Berlin (1944) 42
10. Berlin (1945) 46
11. Escape from Berlin (June/July 1945) 63
12. Raven (1945–46) 69
13. Lüneburg (1946–1950) 73
14. Will 81
15. Hamburg (1950–1953) 87
16. England (1953–1955) 96

Part 3: RHODESIA 102
17. Salisbury (1956–1959) 102
18. Divorce 107
19. Johnny 110

Part 4: SOUTH AFRICA 115
20. Johannesburg (1959–1964) 115
21. Linmeyer 117

Part 5: SOUTH WEST AFRICA 125
22. Windhoek (1964–1968) 125
23. Mick-Mick the meerkat 126
24. Valerie the baboon 128
25. Another divorce 131

Part 6: RETURN TO RHODESIA 133
26. Park Meadowlands (1968–2008) 133
27. Death of a husband 135
28. Nedbank 136
29. Ronnie 139
30. Eve 141
31. Neville 142

32.	Dogs	150
33.	Karl	160
34.	Flower clubs	164
35.	Birth of Zimbabwe	167
36.	Visit to Germany	169
37.	Banking	172
38.	Retirement	174
39.	Alexa	176
40.	My Mother	180
41.	Life under Mugabe	181
42.	Farmers	184
43.	Deterioration	186
44.	Birds	195
45.	Hyperinflation	199
46.	John and Eve	204
47.	Neville's last days	207
48.	Life after Neville	212
49.	Passports	215
50.	Cars	217
51.	Rising costs	219
52.	Health	226
53.	Leaving Zimbabwe	229
Part 7: NEW BEGINNINGS		**235**
54.	Oxted (2008–2010)	235
55.	Kingston (2010–2025)	240
56.	Afterword	246
Other publications from Ōzaru Books		250

List of illustrations

Main family members mentioned in the text..6
Main locations in Germany..6
With Mother, about two years old...8
Aunts, uncle, and lots of cousins..9
With Mother and Father, about two years old...10
First day at school: two snapshots from 1930..12
Names no longer seen on maps..13
Georg, Ursula and Gerhard in Pr. Görlitz, 1933..15
Father and Mother playing music...18
With Father's motorbike...20
Georg, Gerhard, Norbert, Heinz, Ursula and Gelda in Brückendorf, 1940....22
Soldiers billeting en route to Poland, August 1939......................................26
Mother, Norbert, Father and Ursula..28
My identity card..30
Christmas 1942..32
In coach near Allenstein..33
Peter, 1943...37
Allenstein, 1944..43
With Father in his police uniform, 1944...46
The train ticket which was never used, 1945...52
Friedenau cellar..54
Friedenau attic...58
Order from Hitler, 22 April 1945..59
Irene Dimanovsky, abducted 1945...61
Riding, c. 1946...75
Major Geoff Thomas..77
With Will in Berlin...82
Will, Dec 1949..83
Portrait by Will..86
With Will, 1951...88
Christel and Norbert, 1952..92
At Norbert's with Mother & her boyfriend Paul, and sister; Xmas 1952 95
MV *Durban Castle*...100
En route to South Africa, Dec 1955...101
Park Meadowlands...102
Park Meadowlands 'swing-bed'...105
Picnic, 1957...111

Johnny with his sister Baps, and Eve & Ronnie 112
Driving from Rhodesia to Johannesburg 113
Eve and Ronnie outside the house in Bezuidenhout Valley 115
House on the *kopje* in Linmeyer 117
Johnny digging on the *kopje* 119
Sputnik 121
Snow! June 1964 122
Eve and Ronnie with Chummy and Cheeky 123
Mick-Mick the meerkat 127
Nedbank company car, 1983 138
Ronnie on his motorbike 140
Ursula, Neville and Eve at the Coq d'Or 143
At Victoria Falls with Eve and Karl 145
Neville and Lassie 151
With Neville 152
Cheeky, Bobby, Lassie and Charlie 153
With Charlie the Chow Chow 154
Bathing Cindy 155
Ian Smith at a dog show 156
Bobby in hat and scarf 157
Marina with The Hulk 158
Dogs in the garden 159
Playing the accordion 162
Winning a cup at the Hatfield Flower Show 165
With Mother, Tante Lene and Gerda in Berlin 171
The family in Oxted 177
Alexa and a few of her teddy bears 178
Admiring flowers with Alexa 179
Fibian in the garden, 1997 183
The Park Meadowlands lounge: plants everywhere 193
Inflation hits 500,000,000,000% (Metro) 200
Counting the zeroes on banknotes 201
Garden party at Park Meadowlands 202
Enjoying the garden 203
Bricks of banknotes 204
Queuing for petrol in Harare, March 2006 204
John and Karl at the Balancing Rocks near Harare, March 2006 205
At Victoria Falls 206
Max 213

Arrival at Gatwick, 28 Dec 2008 234
Avril (former neighbour), Ursula, Eve and Lana 246
Revisiting Poland 247
Original birth certificate 248

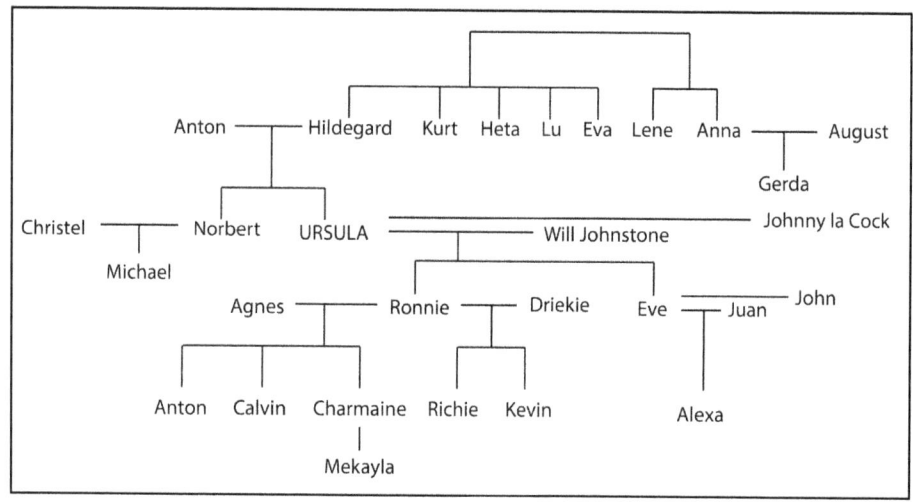

Main family members mentioned in the text

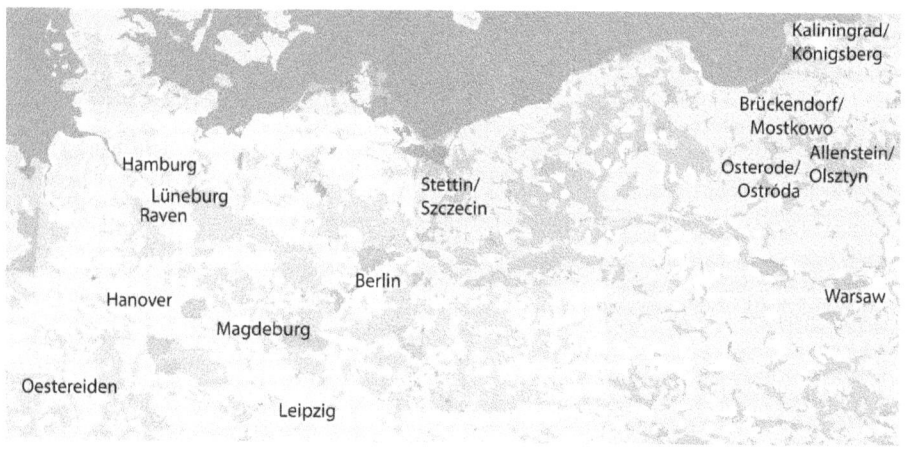

Main locations in Germany

Part 1: MY YOUTH

1. Allenstein (1925–1928)

When I started to write about my experiences during the Second World War, I had no intention of writing anything more than that. I did not write with the aim of being published, only for my children and grandchildren to learn more about their origins. Eventually, I got carried away and started documenting my life after the war. Then I thought maybe they would also be interested in what happened before that, so I wrote about my youth. However, I must warn you I have lived a long life and might repeat some stories or forget certain details. Still, I hope you will find what I have to say interesting.

So, here goes.

On 27 February 1925 I saw the world for the first time, or rather the world saw me, as I have no recollection of that time, of course. I was born in Allenstein, East Prussia, Germany. Let me tell you a little more about East Prussia, which most people have probably never heard of.

East Prussia was a province in the east of Germany, surrounded by Poland and Lithuania, and just about bordered by Russia. That was when I was born. After the Second World War it was divided between Poland and Russia. The part I was born in, Allenstein, now belongs to Poland and is called Olsztyn. Sometimes I wonder whether that now makes me Polish.

East Prussia had changed their nationality a few times over the centuries. Every time there was a war it changed hands to the winner and, as a result, many of the older generation spoke a kind of Polish language with a German dialect. It was thought that anybody with a name ending in "-ski" was of Polish origin, and when Hitler came to power a lot of families changed their name. Domanovski into Domanshöfer etc.

My grandfather's name was Magdalinski, but he would never change his name, not even for Hitler. However, my grandparents still spoke "Masurisch" (a cross between Polish and German) with each other, especially if they did not want us children to understand what they were saying. Naturally, we soon learnt some swear words in Masurisch. Masuren used to be in East Prussia, and it is a beautiful area with many forests and lakes. East Prussia had no industries; it was an agricultural country. Perhaps that is why they were hardly ever hit by air raids during the war but, unfortunately, towards the end of the war, they were the first ones to be occupied by the Russians, who really took their fury out on the poor population.

I know my paternal grandfather was a farmer, but do not know much about my maternal grandfather. I just know he owned and ran a restaurant a few kilometres from Allenstein. It was situated on the shore of a lake and, as a result, was very popular. It was a family outing venue with rowing boats, swimming etc. They also held events there, such as dance evenings, parties and weddings. The name was Lykusen[1], and some people may remember it.

With Mother, about two years old

---

[1] More precisely, the restaurant was called Seestern, but in a district called Lykusen, later renamed Likusen (1938-45) and now Likusy

My mother said the reason she got married at a young age (eighteen) was to avoid the hard work she had to do at the restaurant. In those days, people had large families to provide them with cheap labour. There were enough Magdalinskis around. My grandfather must have been married before as my mother had two stepsisters, Tante Anna and Tante Lene. She also had three sisters, Tante Heta, Tante Lu and Tante Eva, the youngest and the most spoilt. There was also a brother, Kurt, who of course received a better education. I believe there was another brother who was killed in a motorcycle accident. My grandmother used to tell us she watched him dying for two days in great agony.

Aunts, uncle, and lots of cousins

Back row: Mother, Tante Lene, Tante Lu, Tante Heta, cousin, Onkel Horst, Gerhard, Ursula
Front row: Norbert and other cousins

Well, my mother, Hildegard (my father affectionately called her Hildchen), was physically the strongest of the brood, and it was up to her to offload the beer barrels and scrub the kitchen table. She informed me that the table was so large she had to climb on top to scrub it.

When she saw Anton, my father, in his smart police uniform, it was love at first sight. My father was, what you would call, a village cop. They were deeply in love all their lives.

With Mother and Father, about two years old

I am not sure where in Allenstein I was born. My grandfather must have made a good profit from the restaurant, as he bought two blocks of flats. One in Königsberg[2], the other at Kurzestr. 4 in Allenstein. The property in Allenstein had eight flats, and my grandfather occupied two of them which he had converted into one – well, he needed a lot of space with all those children, who by then had mostly flown the nest, but they never ran out of occasions to get together for a "big bash". In between, my grandfather occupied a flat in the Bahnhofstrasse, which is about my first recollection of Allenstein.

---

[2] Now Kaliningrad (and part of a Russian exclave)

2. Oestereiden (1928–1932)

My first memory, however, takes me to Oestereiden, Westphalia, a village somewhere between Cologne, Dortmund and Düsseldorf; a long way from East Prussia. Why my parents chose this place to live, I do not know. My father must have found a good posting there.

They were not too well off. My mother never worked. Oh, sorry, she did work for one day (so she told me). That was when she was a widow. But found it too hard, and she said she was earning enough in pension in those days, even when sleeping. She loved her beauty sleep. "Should I get up?" she'd say. "No, let me go back to sleep and earn more money."

My mother was quite a character. When we got up to mischief as kids, she even encouraged us. She once gave us some bedsheets to play "ghosts" in the street to try to scare people.

One day, when I was older, we were sitting on a bench in a park, when a gentleman came past, raised his hat and said, "Good morning." She smiled back and answered, "Good morning to you, too." I asked her if she knew the chap. She said, "I did not know him before, but I know him now." She used to call me *Kalte Anna* at times, saying I was too cold. She was quite a pretty woman and there was always a twinkle in her eyes when she met a man; she would later tell me stories about her doctor visiting regularly, as they had become pretty intimate.

When I was sixteen, we once went to a dance in Lykusen given by the *Wehrmacht* (army). One chap started dancing with my mother, another one with me. After a couple of dances, her partner danced with me and asked me if it was true that the lady he had been dancing with was married. Diplomatically I said, "If she says so, it must be true." He went back to my mother. Next time when he swapped partners again, and danced with me, he asked if it was true I was the daughter. I said, "Yes, I am, and her husband is sitting right next to her." I never saw two soldiers vanish so quickly.

However, back to my time in Oestereiden.

As I mentioned, money was scarce and so, therefore, were toys. When I was about four years old, my parents gave me a doll, which I hated. I always wanted a teddy bear, which I never got. So, the poor doll was put next to my bed. I never even looked at her. I preferred to play with the toys my father made. There was a puppet on a string that he'd cut out of cardboard and painted to look like a policeman. It worked fine. But my favourite was a little wagon, which my father had made out of an old cigar box (he smoked cigars all his life). This cigar box had four wheels made from empty spools (compliments of my mother's sewing machine). A piece of string finished my "wagon" which I pulled around most of the time.

This brought me to my love of flowers. I used to go next door, where there was a big meadow with cows grazing and, once in a while, even a doe would show up. How exciting! There I would pick tiny flowers in the grass, like white stars, and load them on my little wagon. I do not remember what my mother did with them.

There were rabbits running around the meadow and my father told me that to catch a rabbit you had to throw salt on his tail. Well, there was me chasing the rabbits around the meadow with a spoonful of salt in my hands.

My memory of plants is so vivid, I could take you today to the meadow where the marguerites (daisies) bloomed, the quarry where the wild bush roses grew and to the neighbour's garden, with a most impressive "snowball tree".

I also loved horses and went to a small farm, where they allowed me to sit on a horse while they cleaned out the stables. They had a huge chestnut tree. Those shiny brown nuts made lovely beads.

I was just five when my school years started.

In 1930 my brother Norbert was born. I resented him. For a start, he was the reason I saw my father cry, when the ambulance took my mother to hospital. I can still see him standing by the window. Also, I was no longer the centre of my parents' attention. I tried to ignore him.

Well, there I was, off to school, with my satchel on my back. I do not remember much of those years, but I can recall that I was one of the few pupils who could already read a book, before I began school.

First day at school: two snapshots from 1930

I made friends with a Chinese girl. Her parents must have been very well off. She lived in such a big place, it seemed like a castle to me. She had the most beautiful selection of books, and I never forget the one about a "family" of clocks. There were clocks with faces and legs and arms and stories about them. Later, my friend hid the book every time I came so that I would spend more time with her.

3. Preußisch Görlitz (1932–1936)

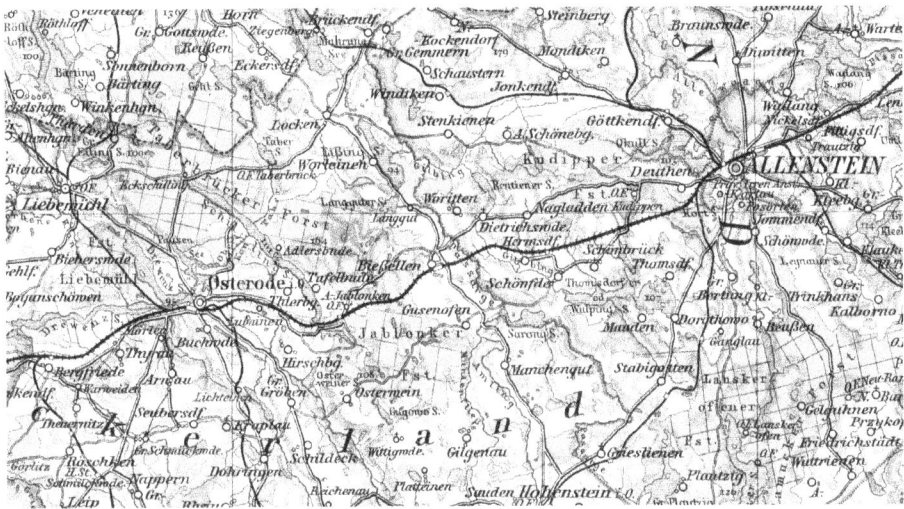

Names no longer seen on maps

Görlitz bottom left, Osterode to its northeast, Brückendf mid-top, and Allenstein to the right

I was about seven years old when we moved to Görlitz[3], a small village in East Prussia near the Polish border in the area of Osterode[4]. My mother had missed her family and wanted to move closer to them.

This was a tiny village with about 300 habitants, but as it was at the Polish border it had two village policemen and three customs officials.

There were about two dozen children at school, spanning eight years of school classes, with the result that the teacher had a job to manage all the different ages at the same time. I felt superior, as I already knew more than anybody else thanks to my previous school. The children's parents were mostly employed on a huge estate

---

[3] Now Gierłoż
[4] Now Ostróda

farm, run or owned by some rich landlord, whose children, of course, went to boarding school.

I received a few hidings (I was caned on my hand), one of which made me very proud. There was a very poor boy in the school, always in rags, who was the target of the older children. When the teacher was not in the class, one of these big bullies was in charge and anybody misbehaving had their name chalked on the blackboard. Out of spite, they always put his name on the board. I promptly got up and wiped it off, but they put it back on. After a while they got tired and wrote my name instead. I did not mind, as it was all in a good cause. My teacher was more upset, as he was friendly with my parents and promptly went across the road to apologize to them for having to cane me.

I no longer had my little wagon, but went for long walks instead. The forest started only about 100 metres from our house. I loved it, with the beautiful dark path of special Christmas trees. I often wondered who had planted them. There was also a long row of silver birches, shining from a distance. I learned later that, hundreds of years ago, all of these trees had been planted by a rich aristocrat.

In winter, I used to get the village boys to pull me around on my tobogganing sledge. I do not think they did it because they liked me, but rather out of respect for my father, who was after all a policeman. In the forest the trees would be beautifully laden with snow. I loved to get the boys to pull me up a small hill, and then I went downhill on my own, whereas the poor boys had to slide down on their backsides and pick me up at the bottom of the hill. I do not remember any girls being about.

Once, when I was about ten years old, the boys had got hold of a cigarette, and we were taking turns to have a puff at it. Suddenly, my father appeared on the horizon. I did not want him to see me before I'd had a good mouthwash at home, so they all made a ring around me, me hiding on the ground. Respectfully, they greeted my father.

When I got home, I tried my best to get rid of the smell, but my father must have noticed something anyhow. That evening, he took me into his office and offered me a cigarette. He said I was now old enough to make up my mind about smoking. Naturally, I was most embarrassed and would not touch the cigarette and did not smoke again until I was about 30 years old. (I was then working for a tobacco company and the free cigarettes were too tempting.)

There was a girl in our school who I believed might have a learning disability. She sat next to me and often peed her panties. Unfortunately, she also had some uninvited guests crawling around in her hair. Our teacher noticed and, as I was sitting next to her, they gave me a checkup. In fact, he just grabbed me and took me home to my parents, who were naturally shocked. It was agony to get rid of them, washing with special soap that stunk to heaven. Then a tight tooth comb was pulled through my hair. They succeeded eventually. At least this girl was then moved away from me.

It was at this point that I got my first dog – a cute curly-haired Dachshund. I loved him to bits. I named him "Putzi" and most of my future dogs had that name. Unfortunately, he had one bad habit: catching chickens in the neighbourhood (we did not have any). The neighbours complained, and my father, being a policeman, had to do something about it. It was impossible to train him (the dog, not my father), so one day my Putzi was gone. They told me they had given him to a forester who lived a few kilometres away. I was heartbroken. Even a year later, my mother once found me crying in bed. "I want my Putzi," I sobbed, but I never saw him again.

When my two cousins, Gerhard and Georg, came for the school holidays, we played army games. A big hole was dug in the garden for our defence, and we made bows and arrows out of willow trees and string. No guns or pistols were needed as presents under the Christmas tree; we had more fun making the weapons ourselves. We spent hours carving the bark off the branches for our arrows and spears. Georg was about the same age as me and Gerhard a year older. We were very fond of each other, even in later years.

Georg, Ursula and Gerhard in Pr. Görlitz, 1933

I mentioned before that we were not well off, especially now there was also my brother Norbert to provide for. So, for years, every Christmas my parents took us to town to a shoe shop, blindfolded us and made us try on shoes. At Christmas, we found them under the Christmas tree, and then we could see what the shoes looked like.

I still liked books. The school had a small library (comprising around 300 books). My favourite was a huge religious book containing all the stories from the Old Testament. I found this most interesting, with the stories about Solomon and his wise judgement (read it up, it's worth it) and Sodom and Gomorrah, never mind Adam and Eve and the snake in paradise. But it was mainly the illustrations that fascinated me. Beautiful prints.

I was born a Catholic but was never very aware of it. My grandparents went to church every Sunday, my mother and father about once a month, and me, well, only when I had to. However, I was never really one for religion, for reasons that I will explain later.

4. Brückendorf (1936–1942)

Well, back to my little village. It was about five kilometres from the nearest bigger village and eleven kilometres to the nearest station. When I was eleven years old my parents decided it was time for me to go to high school, and my father asked for a transfer. This brought us to Brückendorf[5], in the district of Osterode, about 30 kilometres northwest of Allenstein.

Brückendorf had about 2000 inhabitants. It even had a pub, a bank, a butcher, bakery, you name it. However, the nearest suitable school was either in Osterode by bus or Allenstein by train. My parents settled for Allenstein High School. My grandparents still lived there, also Tante Lu, who was now married and living in a large flat near the station. (It had a garden centre next to it – most important.) However, the nearest station from our village was about one kilometre away: Gamerki Wielkie. No problem, my mother had an old bicycle and off I went.

You may think one kilometre is not very far, but it is when you are late and the train overtakes you in the last 50 metres. Most of the train drivers knew us students and waited patiently for us to throw our bikes into the railway yard. It was a different story in winter when the temperature was always below zero. The snow lasted from November to early April, sometimes May, but at times the temperature sank to 40 degrees below zero. I can still see myself on the road to the station, with the wind blowing into my face, freezing my ears and bringing tears to my eyes.

---

[5] Now Mostkowo

When the weather was that bad, my grandparents offered to take me into town, which was a relief.

We were the famous travelling students (or do you call them scholars?), always getting into mischief. We were three girls with four boys in the next compartment. Somehow, we managed to drill a hole between the compartments. At the early stage we just passed insults, like so-and-so is an idiot etc.

Once, I was brave enough to go next door and get the four boys to hold a piece of string. I said, "I just wanted to see what it looks like to hold four oxen on a string." Naturally, things like that led to fights. I loved the fights – with the boys, of course, never with the girls. On two occasions the conductor had to come and separate us – luckily, otherwise I would have missed my station. One time, I did miss my stop and had to walk home a long way. I suppose that cooled me off. As we got older, and some students left, the boys moved in with us, but that is another story.

We had monthly season tickets, which we sometimes forgot to renew. No problem! When the conductor came round, we just scratched around for our tickets and waited for some of the other girls to pass on theirs. At the station, the ones without a pass just went out and got a platform ticket – and me, a policeman's daughter! Now, I ask you, would you consider that a sin? What about little white lies, should they be confessed? We were frequently reported to the school authorities. We treated it as a joke.

When we enrolled in the school, I was a little bit behind the others with my knowledge. I had not learnt much at that small school in Pr. Görlitz, and had a lot of catching up to do. I believe my teachers told my parents that I was so far behind I should go back to an elementary school for one year. With a great deal of persuasion, they gave me another chance and I made it through. After that it was plain sailing. I usually ended up amongst the top three scholars.

Apart from the exams, I liked school. I got on well with most teachers, especially the male ones, whom I used to tease, asking them questions about their beautiful wives etc.

We had one teacher who was quite fond of me. When he asked us a question, and we raised our hands, he let me speak. But eventually he saw no point in asking me, as I always knew the answer. The result was that I got bored and behind with my learning. One day, when he asked me a question, I, of course, did not know the answer, and I did not pay attention again, as I thought I had had my turn already. The next time he asked me (obviously to give me a chance to make up for my previous failure), I again did not know the answer. Unfortunately, the third time he asked me, it was about something they had learnt in my "missing period". There I was, really stuck. He got extremely cross, gave me a black mark in his famous big report book, and made me stand outside in the corridor. I cried bitterly and did not even stop when I was called in again.

They were in the process of telling jokes, so I stopped crying for a moment and said I knew one. I got up and told my joke (I could repeat it here, but it would be lost in translation), sat down and carried on sobbing. Consequently I still got a good mark, and even that "black mark" in the schoolbook disappeared.

I was also popular with my music teacher, for my piano playing, not my singing. People always said, "Please, just play the piano." I would have loved to have been able to sing. My mother had such a beautiful voice. She played the piano as well as the accordion, and my father the violin. I can still hear the music, lying in bed with my parents playing and singing next door.

Father and Mother playing music

I had learnt to play the piano when I was about seven years old while staying with my grandmother, who made me take lessons for two months. I learned the basics, but mainly how to read sheet music, after that I was on my own. When I went to high school my mother enrolled me with a music teacher in Allenstein, but all he wanted me to play was "Etudes", running up and down the scales – how boring! I preferred playing the latest hit songs. I started skipping classes and gave up after four months. Then I only went there to pay for my lessons, until my mother found out. That was the end of my musical education. The trouble with me is that I am a "Jack of all trades, master of none". I lose interest after a while.

But back to Brückendorf. We had a big house and a fair-sized garden. With my love of flowers, I can remember exactly where the lilacs bloomed, the jasmine, with the beautiful perfumed blossom, the peonies, the bleeding heart and roses. My father had a large vegetable garden. My only interest was picking the ripe fruit of apples, cherries and various berries. We had two rows of asparagus. First thing every morning, we had to check where the soil was breaking and the tips peeking out. We had to dig deep to get out the whole stem. These were beautifully white. It took me a long time to discover that one could also eat green ones.

The forest was just behind the station, with a couple of beautiful lakes and areas where lilies of the valley and violets grew. Along the railway lines, lupins ran riot.

Once a year a shooting competition was held – "*Schützenfest*" – no hunting, not much actual shooting either, but a lot of drinking beer. It was held at one of the lakes and the wives would row out on a boat to amuse themselves. One year, they overloaded the boat, and it sunk before they could get started. It was quite a picture. Luckily, the boat was at the edge and the water was only a couple of feet deep. Their husbands had a good laugh.

There was a river, Passarge[6], two kilometres from our house. It was not very wide but quite turbulent. As it was not deeper than one and a half metres it was perfect for my father, who could not swim. I can still see him standing in the river, wearing sunglasses and a straw hat, with his beloved cigar in his mouth. When we asked him once how he had passed the twenty-metre swimming test at police school, he said he had stayed in the shallows and kept one foot on the ground.

Well, that describes my father. He had a wonderful sense of humour. He was always telling us jokes, which he unfortunately never finished as halfway through, he would be laughing too much. It didn't really matter, as we would laugh with him. In winter, he used to warm up the feather eiderdowns for us on a huge tiled stove and drop them on our bodies, waiting in bed.

When the war came and meat was in short supply, he used to push it round his plate and, at the end of the meal, would say, "Oh, I have forgotten to eat my meat, and now I am full." Then he would give it to my brother – after all he was a growing lad. I never fancied meat, only meatballs and chicken. I did not miss out on much, as we could only afford to have meat on Sundays. It was so scarce that we refused

---

[6] Now Pasłęka

to share it, and if someone pitched up during our meal, we quickly hid the plates under the bed and pretended we had just finished.

The rest of the week was divided between fried potatoes with fatty bacon and eggs and milk soups (my mother made her own noodles). There were vegetables from the garden and plenty of fruit. The apples were stored all through the winter, laid out in the attic. Potatoes were stored in a big hole in the garden, covered with straw and soil. Every house had a cellar to keep food cool. There was no fridge for us.

My mother excelled in baking. Her cooking was good, I suppose, but then we never had that much food to cook. (My speciality was and still is fried potatoes with scrambled eggs.) That was a meal we had nearly every second day as a main meal, but there was always "speck" (a fatty bacon) with it.

Somehow, we managed to have cake from time to time and home-baked bread. Now that was delicious. My mother could not bake quickly enough. As soon as it came out of the oven, we got stuck in. It was so hot we had trouble holding it. The bread was always served with margarine and home-made jam. I am surprised we did not get sick. At family parties, my mother was always roped in to bake the cakes which were usually stored in the cellar. My cousin, brother and I spent some time in the cellar sampling the cakes.

With Father's motorbike

Every couple of months or so my parents held a party, which was not my kind of thing, but Norbert used to hide behind the settee in the lounge and listen to them all night (or until he was discovered). Halfway through the parties, it was the turn of the "Eggerländer March", which was played on a gramophone. My father used to lead the "conga". There he was, with his cigar in his mouth, carrying the record player, leading people in a polonaise dance around the house and garden.

About four in the morning, it was coffee time. The coffee grinder was nailed behind the door of the pantry and couples took turns to go and grind the coffee (in the dark, of course). About seven in the morning was breakfast time and after that everyone retired.

There was not much crime in the country. I think in the whole time I knew him, my father only arrested one person. He had a problem with members of the public if they were high up in the Nazi Party. He once got into trouble for reporting one of them (something to do with not complying with regulations, like dipping cattle during an outbreak of disease). This chap was going to report my father to the higher Nazi authorities, which might have landed him in a labour (concentration) camp. How dare my father accuse an innocent Nazi boss? Well, my mother used her charm on them and sorted it all out. It ended in a big booze-up, and they became quite friendly afterwards.

My father was very helpful around the house. He was always the first one to rise and light our iron stove in the kitchen. He would make the breakfast and shout up the stairs, "Come and get it." He even did the washing, which was quite an involved affair. There was no washing machine. A big kettle was heated up in an outhouse and the washing boiled. (This happened every second week.) Just stirring the washing was a job. After rinsing, the washing was squeezed through two hand-operated rollers and then hung on the washing line, mostly by my father. He used to go to the fence first to make sure nobody was coming, run back and hang a few items on the line and back again. Can you imagine catching the policeman of the village doing such undignified tasks? In those days, German men were not normally domesticated. It was considered beneath them to do women's work. But my father maintained that if he helped my mother, she would have more time for him. What love!

I do not know much about my father's ancestors. Only once did we visit his parents on the farm in Tollak, a small village in East Prussia. I only saw my grandmother briefly through the door. She was lying in bed, I never found out why.

Having been brought up on a farm, it always surprised me how little interest my father had in horses. My father could have had a police horse if he'd wanted to. We even had a stable. How I would have loved riding his horse, but he said he was no good at riding. He said (tongue in cheek) he had tried a few times, but got up on one side and promptly fell off the other.

I mention all this to show how influenced I was by the image of my father. To me, he was the ideal husband and, all my life, I was looking for someone like him.

My mother, Hildegard, was twelve years younger than my father and quite pretty. Unfortunately, I did not take after her in that respect; my brother Norbert was the one with good looks. The only nice thing about me – I was told – were my eyes. Once, as a joke, my father said he would not mind having another daughter if she would take after my mother.

My mother liked to be made-up. She was good at flirting, and there was always a mischievous glint in her eyes. She was very popular, and the men adored her, especially when she started to sing.

Georg, Gerhard, Norbert, Heinz, Ursula and Gelda in Brückendorf, 1940

When I got older, my mother told me not to call her *Mutti* but instead Hilde, in order to pretend I was her younger sister. In later years, I looked more like her older sister; I was never interested in my appearance. She spent a lot of time getting her beauty sleep, which I found such a waste of time. For me, the days were, and still are, never long enough to waste in bed.

I think I always considered my mother more a friend (and she was a good friend with whom I could talk about anything), whereas my father maintained a fatherly figure. I was never a very affectionate person, but I really loved him. He was my idol!

When he was forced to punish us children, it always hurt him more than us. He used to go sobbing to my mother and excused himself for having to do this. The few times I got a hiding usually related to my brother. Norbert always got into mischief and had the habit of blaming me for it. For instance, he loved salami sausage, I did not. So, he helped himself to a big chunk, but insisted on me trying a tiny bit. Just to get rid of him, I took it. When we were found out, we both got a hiding, as he insisted I had shared the sausage with him. (Well, salami was something precious in those days.)

Once I started school in Allenstein I used to get one *Reichsmark* a week as pocket money. There was a bakery on the way to school that sold broken cake pieces in a paper bag for one *Pfennig* (penny). But most of my money was spent on tiny toy horses. They may have been made from clay and painted but were really lifelike, with soldiers riding on their backs. Luckily, these were removable. When I was fourteen my parents gave me a barrack for Christmas, and I could then take the soldiers off and put them to bed.

One day, I came home and all my soldiers were gone, never to be found again. When in later years I visited my brother, he confessed that he had played with them that day. They were "shot" and he buried them in the garden and forgot all about them. It rained and after that he could not find them any more. (Believe it or not, I have at last found some toy horses for sale to put on my shelf again.)

Otherwise, Norbert and I did not have too many problems with one another. We lived in different worlds. He liked his sport, and I liked my books. When my mother told me to take my nose out of a book for a change and do some dusting about the house, I usually stood in the middle of the room, duster in one hand, book in the other. When I heard my mother coming, the book vanished, and she would find me vigorously swinging the duster.

I think, in a way, my brother was fond of me. In the last year of the war, after they had seen me off at the station, my father wrote to tell me that on the way home Norbert had lagged behind. When my father looked round, he found Norbert wiping the tears out of his eyes.

Well, it is time I get round to the "boys". I was eleven years old when we moved to Brückendorf and my best friend became Irene. Her father owned a dairy, where we used to snack on cheese while it was still being processed.

Irene liked to role-play, pretending we were getting married. She called herself "Mrs Rilke", taking the name of a boy in the village she liked, whom I had yet to meet. I could only think of a boy I had admired in our previous village. He was the son of the wealthy landowner, and his name was Günther Prange. I thus became "Frau Prange".

However, the first time I saw Irene's "husband" I fell in love. His name was Gerhard and just thinking of him brings tears to my eyes even now. He was my first love, and sometimes I think the only love in my life.

Gerhard's father was a teacher in the next village. Every Saturday, Gerhard came to our village to attend Hitler Youth meetings. He was the leader of their troop, and each week they would march past my window. He was very good-looking and on top of that wore a Hitler Youth uniform. I have been a sucker for men in uniform all my life. So, there I was every Saturday hiding behind the curtains, trying to get a glimpse of the tall, dark and handsome Gerhard.

Although Gerhard was only one year older than me, he appeared much more grown up, especially when he started going about with "Eva". Eva was the daughter of the owner of the local pub, quite a big place, with a large hall, which has fond memories for me – a few dances and especially a play that was laid on for a Christmas event. It was not so much the performance as the rehearsals leading up to it. My role was being the "wife" of Gerhard and I thought then, "Now I've got you!" He was supposed to give me a kiss during the play, and I was looking forward to that, but he refused and said he would do it only at the actual performance. He never did. I know I might not have been that pretty, but I was not that ugly either. (I was about fourteen by then.)

During rehearsals, I had fun with the boys, who would lay planks up to the stage and ride up on bicycles. I was brave enough to sit on the handlebars. This went well... except for the day we only got halfway up and fell off. I caught my leg on a nail protruding from the stage and had quite a big tear on my leg. Probably trying to be brave in the eyes of the boy I secretly admired, I just stuck a plaster over it and forgot all about it. After a couple of weeks my mother started sniffing around me. "What is that horrible smell coming from your leg?" My leg was rotting. The doctor was called. He scraped it out and put in a few stitches. Well, at least I now had a scar to put proudly in my passport. Could that have been what put Gerhard off?

Back to Eva. She was my age but very pretty. I did not have much contact with her as she went on the bus to school in Osterode, but I talked to her from time to time. In company, she was very aloof and hardly spoke. She sat there with a mysterious smile on her face – Mona Lisa style. I think that got the boys' interest;

they wanted to find out more about her. By contrast, I was too open and always talked too much. I still do.

Poor Irene did not stand a chance and neither did I. Over the next two years, Gerhard was seen with various other girls, but I was not in the running. My mother, who had watched me peeping through the windows to get a glance of Gerhard marching by, started teasing me. She said to me, "Don't worry. One day Gerhard will get tired of all the other girls, and it will be your turn."

Gerhard also went to school in Allenstein, but probably stayed mostly with relatives in town. He used to come home for the weekend and I tried to catch him on the same train home. Not much luck there either. (Do I sound like a stalker?)

After the stage performance, Gerhard at least started to greet me in the street, and when I was fourteen, my mother invited him to my birthday party. At long last I had him in my "den". He singled me out at all the party games we played and once I found myself hiding with him in the same wardrobe. At last! He gave me a little kiss, and that was the beginning.

It was, by then, a few months before the start of the Second World War, and all of a sudden, a great many soldiers turned up, taking accommodation in local houses. The place was milling with military. We still had no true thought of war, as they told us they were going on manoeuvres in the "Rominter Heide" close to the border. So, after a few days of excitement, we waved them goodbye as they marched past and carried on with our business. My business was Gerhard.

Then in September 1939, the invasion of Poland began and we were truly at war, although I do not think anybody was particularly worried. After all, German troops had just marched into the Saarland[7] and occupied Austria[8], so it did not seem that serious. And after four weeks the war was over, and we went back to normal life.[9]

Gerhard's father had a car (I think the only one for ten miles around). Sometimes they took Gerhard to the station and gave me a lift, too. Eventually, Gerhard started commuting daily on "my" train. He often came on his bicycle and gave me a lift on the handlebars. What bliss! Also, by now the boys on the train had moved into our compartment; our war with them was over. A different generation had started; now we were holding hands, albeit hidden by coats. Ursula was in love.

We went ice skating on the lakes in the forest, playing ice hockey with branches off the trees and a couple of frozen horse "apples" (dung). Once we hired some horses and a sleigh from a farmer and a crowd of us went for a ride through the

---

[7] In 1935, after a plebiscite voted to rejoin Germany
[8] The *Anschluss*, in 1938
[9] The *Blitzkrieg* meant that by 5 October 1939 the Polish Army had been defeated

forest. I had to sit on my boyfriend's knee, due to lack of space (what luck!) and I held my father's "gramophone" on my lap. The roads through the forest became very narrow, the sleigh turned over, and we all tumbled into the snow. Yet no one was hurt. The snow in East Prussia would be about a metre deep at times.

Soldiers billeting en route to Poland, August 1939

Gerhard and I went to the cinema and held hands; nothing could beat that ecstasy. I might have forgotten his face, but I remember his hands. I can still see them. Rather pale and with a few black hairs at the back.

When I was sixteen, he was called up. We met for the last time in Allenstein at my aunt's place. She discreetly went off and left us alone. It got rather steamy, but I hesitated to go all the way. Maybe I should have? He wrote a few letters from his training school about 100 kilometres away and asked me to visit him. I did not think this was proper. After all, I was still going to school and had my reputation to consider. Maybe he got fed up with my inexperience, and he stopped writing. A year later I met him once in our village when he was on leave, and he apologized and said he had been stupid. I was too proud to accept his apology and walked away. Afterwards, I could have kicked myself, of course. He was even in Berlin for six months at the same time as me, but we never made contact again. However, I never forgot him.

In the meantime, life at the school carried on. I noticed a few shops showing the "Jew" signs and two lovely girls of Jewish origin suddenly vanished from school. We did not think anything about that, assuming their parents had just decided to send them to another school. In my grandfather's block of flats there was an old Jewish couple living on the floor above them. One day, they also vanished. I had liked them and often visited them and ate their "Matzen". I just remember the flat being repainted.

I was puzzled by not being able to buy music by Jewish composers like Mendelssohn, and if you bought an album that had some of their pieces in the book, the pages were glued together so you could not play them. Still the penny did not drop. I had heard of concentration camps, which were simply called labour camps; I thought they were just for minor criminals. Nobody spoke publicly about it, and I think that is why most Germans were ignorant in that respect. Those inside could not speak out; those who got out would not dare.

As far as books were concerned, many that I liked to read had vanished from the market. Comic books had been banned long ago, perhaps because they were foreign? Hitler did what he liked with us, but most people were happy. He succeeded in bringing down the unemployment rate – nobody was starving. No wonder there was no unemployment, they were busy building the "autobahn" and employing people in factories, manufacturing ammunition.

Part 2: THE WAR YEARS

5. Duty Year (1942)

The war was drawing closer and our school was requisitioned for wounded soldiers. We gathered every morning outside the school and went into the forest, about a mile away, found a glen and started lessons. Lots of fun.

I finished my school education, passed my exams and entered the *Pflichtjahr*[10], a year of community service ordered by Göring. Everyone leaving school had to either join a household for one year or enter an army camp for half a year.

Mother, Norbert, Father and Ursula

Before Father was sent to Norway

My father decided that an army camp was not a safe place for a young girl and enlisted the help of a friend, who ran a farm in Warglitten[11], about six kilometres from Osterode, in East Prussia. It was light work. My main concern was looking

---

[10] From 1938 it had become compulsory for women in Nazi Germany to complete a 'duty year' to address the shortage of skilled workers in the country

[11] Now Warlity Wielkie

after their six-year-old boy and laying the table. For other work, they had a Ukrainian woman who did the cleaning and cooking.

One time, they were short of labour on the farm and needed the Ukrainian woman to help with the harvesting. I had to do the housework. It took me two hours to wash the kitchen floor. I had used too much water, and it took all that time to mop it up. I also had to cook for the twenty French prisoners of war they had on the farm, a huge pot full of mostly turnips. They usually ate at 7 p.m. Half an hour later, they brought the full pot back to the kitchen and asked me to eat it. Well, my cooking days were over. Luckily, the farmer's wife had done the rest of the cooking. The Ukrainian woman came back, and we carried on as usual.

Another job of mine was to look after their Dachshunds. This I really enjoyed. They had a few and used to breed them. I had just arrived there when a litter was born, and I promptly wanted a puppy. I had to pay for it. My wages were ten German *Reichsmark* a month, and they charged me 50. In other words, I worked for five months just to pay for my puppy, but I did not need money otherwise: everything else was free.

The lady of the house was hardly ever there, as she was always at meetings. I hardly saw her. The farmer was very friendly and often had a few drinks with the warden of the twenty prisoners in the evening.

One day, his nephew came to visit, and they invited the two of us for a drink. Boy, did I get sloshed! Eventually, I went outside and spewed up over the parapet onto a heap of coals. The next morning, I was very embarrassed and went outside to get rid of my "evidence" on the coal. The farmer came out and said to me, "Don't worry about cleaning up." His nephew had already done that as he had used the same spot. His nephew said, however, he could not understand where the peas had come from, as he had not eaten any that night.

The farm was adjacent to a forest with a small lake. In summer, people came to swim there. Someone told me how nice it was to swim naked in the moonlight, and one night I did just that. Nobody was watching, I hope. But it was a lovely feeling.

After six months I found a job in Berlin. I left my puppy with my parents. They did not have him for long, as here was another dog chasing – this time – my father's ducks. He had a pair of grown ducks and seven ducklings. One of them did not grow. So, there were his siblings marching in front of him, all in a line and little "Antek" (my father called him that) trying to keep step with them. When he got behind, he sped up to catch up with the rest of them and carried on in step again. He was so cute and my father loved him dearly. Then came "Putzie", the Dachshund, and no more "Antek". So, my father got rid of "Putzie". I cannot blame him.

6. Berlin (1942)

The war had now been going on for three years. As far as East Prussia was concerned, not much had changed. There were a few shortages here and there, and we heard about some bombing in the west of Germany, but East Prussia remained untouched.

As I said before, I was completing my Duty Year. I still have my identity card (*Kennkarte*), issued at that time, with my picture and profession "*Pflichtjahrmädel*" and an official stamp with the swastika on it.

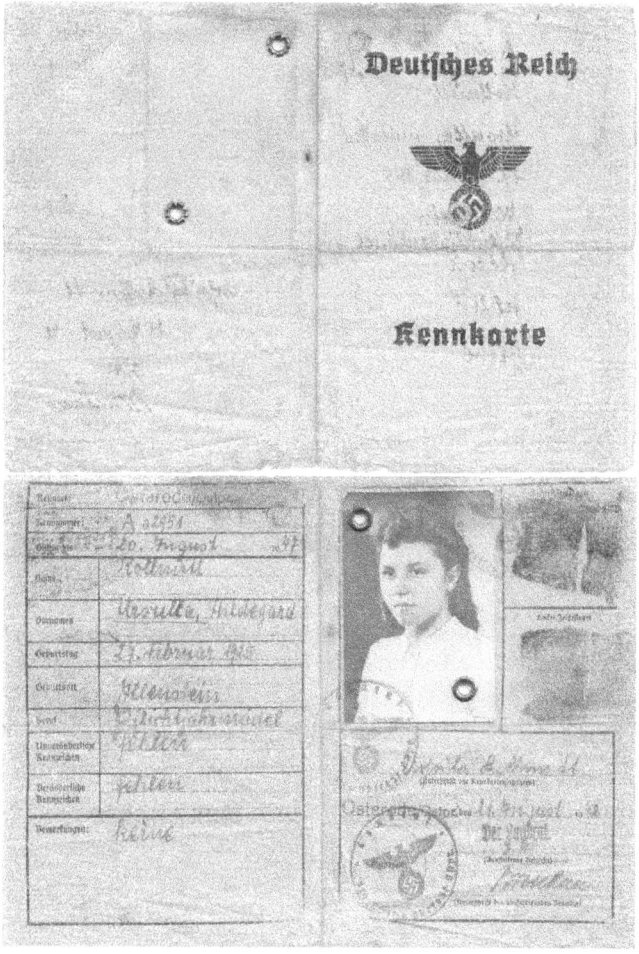

My identity card

In theory valid in the Reich until 1947

While I was working at the farm, I saw an advert in a newspaper. AEG, an electronics company in Berlin was looking for girls to be trained in laboratory work. Free accommodation was offered along with a generous allowance, more like a salary to start with. I had always pictured myself in a laboratory, but perhaps working more with humans. We had not had the means for such farfetched education, but this was something close enough to it.

I was accepted and gave in my notice. Normally, I would not have been allowed to break off my Duty Year. However, the new job involved research concerning navy equipment: special "valves" designed for night vision, so that target ships would not realize they were being observed. In those days, the experiments were top secret, but today, anyone can use similar equipment for night photography. Due to its importance for the war effort, I was exempted from my Duty Year and packed my suitcase.

My mother would not let me go on my own and, perhaps also to assess the new situation, she came with me. She had lived in Berlin for a year, when I was around two years old, but was still a bit lost when we arrived. I, on the other hand, had already studied the map of my route and by the time we reached our destination, she accepted that she need not have come with me, as I knew the place better than she did. Anyhow, we arrived and the first thing we passed on the way was a funeral procession. Was this a bad omen? Let's be optimistic and take it as a good sign.

AEG provided me with accommodation at a clubhouse, next to the River Spree, which was closed down during the war years. I was very excited, as I expected something with beautiful furniture, but no such luck. What was obviously a big hall, had been partitioned off into four rooms, separated by wooden partitions halfway up the ceiling. The furniture consisted of wooden bunks, primitive furniture and all in a sparse, military style. There were about four of us to a room. Our partition had a small wood burner in the corner, which came in handy in winter. We had a communal kitchen downstairs, but the wood burner was good enough to boil water for coffee.

Eventually, I organized an old tin coffee can from some distant relatives in Berlin and this was shared by us all. I discovered when I came home one day that it was burnt out, as someone had used it to boil their serviette. I could see it was a serviette as it still had the pattern at the bottom. (In those days we used old-fashioned napkins.) I was pretty cross, as things were getting scarce in Berlin and so was my money. However, we had the use of a kitchen downstairs with eight gas stoves and pots were provided – not that I did much cooking, I waited for my mother's "care parcels".

But life was great. We had a beautiful view of the river and access to it. Unfortunately, it was then winter. Still, we had a free telephone (very important when you are a young girl) and enough freedom to roam the city. The older girls were given accommodation in single rooms in the attic. We were the young chicks, we stuck together and made good friends.

We had a long way to travel each day as our clubhouse was in Oberschöneweide, a suburb in the southeast of Berlin, while our workplace, Reinickendorf, was in the north.

First, we took the tram to the station, then changed trains in Ost Kreuz to Reinickendorf. From there we took another tram from the station to the factory and still had another ten minutes' walk. It took two hours, and we worked from ten until six, so we got home very late. If we wanted to go "out on the town" we went directly from work to the centre of the town.

I was rather lonely in Berlin and hated the first few months. My mother had introduced me to a cousin of my grandmother. At least she had four sons, who helped to alleviate the boredom. Eventually I found other interests. A school friend of mine had a cousin in Berlin whom I had already met in East Prussia. When he came to Berlin on leave, he invited me along with his girlfriend to his mother's house in Spandau, although this did not turn out very well, as my blind date did not show up.

Christmas 1942

Tante Eva's husband, Tante Heta, Grandfather, Georg, Norbert, Grandmother, Gerhard, Ursula and Onkel Georg

I used to spend most holidays at home with my family. Christmas 1942 came and it was time to get the train home to Brückendorf. Here let me translate a few lines from my father's letter. "I have already ordered a special sleigh from Richter, the guest house owner, along with his best horses. The local squire offered his stage coach, nothing's too good for our precious daughter. We cannot let our star walk from the station. The snag is that everyone wants to come along to pick you up and there may not be room for you. So, we are tying a small toboggan to the back for you".

In coach near Allenstein

Well, we had a good time and also visited my grandmother in Allenstein. There I met the brother of my aunt's boyfriend, who impressed me very much. Every time I met an attractive man, I lived in hope that it would work out, but no such luck with this one.

Back in Berlin, life went on. Now and then there would be an alarm, but as nothing happened it was usually ignored. I went to theatres like the Scala and the Metropolitan, or visited the Wintergarten.[12] I was on my own, no boyfriends – I did not have time for them. Who was I kidding? Nobody asked me.

We had a full programme at our "school": physics, chemistry, maths, drawing and workshop. One of our main teachers was Dr Eckhardt, who was twenty-nine

---

[12] A world-famous variety theatre near the Zoological Gardens, also offering dining; it was destroyed by bombs in 1944

years old and a bachelor. The older girls ran their heels off after him. Our drawing teacher, Nadolle, started every class with, "In the beginning God created the middle line." Mister Barre taught us how to handle a chisel and hammer. At one stage I had to do a drawing of a screw to the micro millimetre. I got very good marks for that one. Physical training classes were instructed by Mr Reuss who had the athletic figure to go with his job. Dr Eckhardt often visited the clubhouse, flirting with the older girls. We chicks did not count.

7. AEG

Our work was war research. The laboratories were busy developing and improving ultra-red (or was it infra-violet?) valves for use in night work, mainly for ships. We had to learn everything from scratch. My first job was in the hothouse, where the sediment was "cooked" in special glass cases and everything had to be absolutely sterile. I only had to wash the floor once and made such a mess of it, they soon transferred me to another department!

One of my chick friends was working on another stage of development, which was to "roast" previously prepared valves (that resembled huge light bulbs) in a special oven whose temperature went up to about 1000 degrees. Nothing was automatic in those days, and one person had to watch the oven for nearly an hour. She started reading a book, fell asleep, and the oven blew up. She was OK, but the oven had a big crack in it.

I was not much better. We learned from the glassblower how to "melt" and pull the valve from a vacuum construction made purely from glass that was mounted on the wall, with glass funnels leading all over the place. When the valves were ready, they had to be pulled away from the contraption by gently melting the glass funnel outside the valve and pulling. The first time I did it by myself, I managed to pull the whole thing off the wall. I was really upset, but the master blower said he would fix it and keep it our secret. I was not so lucky when I dropped an ampere meter worth 1000 *Marks* – a lot of money in those days – but I was soon forgiven.

I don't think we did much learning as we were always up to mischief, like drawing extra rations for 96% proof alcohol (not methylated) for our experiments. You can imagine what happened: we sometimes added some to our coffee. I once offered some to my boss, who took one look at me and said I better get home, which suited me, as it was early. I went to the cinema and slept through the film.

Another time, Paula, who later become a very good friend of mine, had been "sunbathing" in a room that was meant for other work on the "valves". It had an ultraviolet lamp for use in some experiments, but she used it to tan her face. She had gradually increased it from half a minute to two. On one occasion, I had to work with her in that room. In order not to get too much of the ultraviolet rays, I positioned myself about two metres behind her. Little did I know that the distance made no difference, and my poor skin cooked for two minutes. I had serious sunburn the next day, my skin blew up with a big crust over it, and I was sent home.

After a couple of days, I got bored and went to the cinema. Who would see me in the dark as long as I sat in the first row? They showed one of my favourite films with Heinz Rühmann. It was called *Quax, the Crash Pilot*. I laughed so much the skin cracked all over my face. Anyhow, after that it was just a matter of peeling it off until it revealed beautifully smooth skin.

Once a gang of girls turned up and, for some reason, they had to clean the factory floor as punishment. They said they were ballet girls, but I think they were prostitutes. They were beautifully made-up, like dolls. The work did not faze them, and they went about their job cheerfully. I wonder what happened to them.

I had no experience of a proper air raid, whereas the rest of the gang coming from Dresden or Hamburg had a lot to tell. One evening, we were enjoying our supper when the sirens went off. Nobody took any notice until the shooting began. In the distance we heard bombs falling and our "Flak"[13] guns started firing at the bombers. Splinters from their ammunition echoed on the pavement. The nearest air raid shelter was about eight minutes away. I think I beat them all to the coal cellar under the house. There we sat on the coal, a mass of trembling girls. I thought this would be my last day on earth. My thoughts went through my life and I started thinking of all my sins… I noticed something shining in the ceiling and thought it was an iron beam, so I sat under that, feeling a little safer.

After an hour, one of the braver girls went upstairs to get a candle, and I discovered that I had been sitting under a glass window. After that I calmed down: fate had meant to be kind to me. I was even brave enough to go to the front door. In the distance we could see the fires. There was a soldier, the son of the house ward, standing with us. We talked, and he kept writing to me when he went back to the front. When his letters turned into love letters, I broke it off.

8. Berlin (1943)

It was now March 1943, and I decided to take lessons in tap dancing near the zoo[14]. It was great practising in the washrooms of the clubhouse. One day, in the middle of our lesson, the air raid sirens sounded. There was a cellar under the house, and we emerged three hours later to see the whole area lit up by fires. The

---

[13] *Flug-Abwehr-Kanone* = "aircraft defence cannon"

[14] The zoological gardens, founded in 1844, and their station serve as a common reference point in Berlin – not to be confused with the *Tierpark* zoo in the eastern side of the city, which only opened in 1955

Gedächtniskirche, a monumental building of Berlin, looked like a silhouette against the fiery sky. A church clock rang the twelfth hour. It sounded ominous. That night, it took us four hours to get home (usually three quarters of an hour). The trains were interrupted as some lines had been hit by bombs, and we had to walk a long way to the next connection.

It was around this time that I received an invitation from my "boyfriend's" mother to visit them in Hamburg, as their son was on leave. Now, I must come back to their son. His name was Aube and I had met him in Brückendorf at the beginning of the war. He was then one of a few students sent to our village for a brief training course in agriculture. I met him while walking with my friend Irene along the Passarge River. He invited us to a student ball they had arranged in the village hall. He was a good dancer – I think that was all I liked about him. However, my mother was very impressed with him. Most likely this was because he was studying engineering. To me, he looked a bit geeky, and when the girls pulled my leg and said he had flat feet, I was really put off.

Yet my mother kept pushing, as he had managed to get under her skin. On the whole I kept him at a distance, but after he left to go back to university I did answer his letters. There is a German proverb, "*Papier ist geduldig*". Not easy to translate, it's something like 'paper feels nothing'. So I wrote back, and when I got to Berlin his mother invited me round. However, at the last minute I received a telegram saying he was now in the *Wehrmacht* and could not get leave. He gradually gave up on me. Not even his marriage proposal could tempt me and boy, there were not many such offers in my life.

Anyhow, one day, as I had nothing planned, I decided to take in a show in the city, and on the way home I met someone that would stay in my life for a good while.

I was standing on the platform at Station Zoo. I had just missed a train, and it was a while until the next one. On the other side of the platform, waiting for a train in the opposite direction, stood a young lieutenant. He kept looking in my direction. What cheek! He came closer and walked a few times up and down. Checking me out? He was not bad looking, and as mentioned before, I always had a thing for men in uniform. By the time the train arrived, he was standing next to me. I was a bit embarrassed. I only had a second-class ticket, and officers usually travelled first class. The first-class coach happened to stop in front of me and I took a chance and jumped in and he followed. I felt a bit uncomfortable about my invalid ticket and stayed near the door in case I saw the inspector coming. It was quite a long ride and my lieutenant was getting a bit fidgety; he probably couldn't understand why I was not sitting down on such a long journey.

At last, we got to my station Oberschöneweide, and as I walked down the steps he asked me for directions to the train to Spandau, which was over an hour's ride away, on the opposite side of town. I directed him, he thanked me and walked away, and I thought that was the end of it, feeling rather disappointed. When I got out of the building, he appeared next to me and said that after following me so far it was rather stupid to go home without having made my acquaintance, and he offered to see me home. He did not know that a tram ride was still to come. Well, we talked and when we got to the clubhouse, we stopped opposite where there was a small park and a bench to sit on. We talked a lot of nonsense, but arranged to meet again.

Peter, 1943

He told me the next day he had fallen asleep on the journey home and woke up still on the train, in a siding somewhere outside the station. I had arranged to meet him after my tap-dancing class. He said his name was Peter, and I had always liked that name, although it turned out this was only short for his surname Peterson, and his real name was Johannes, which I did not like at all. He came from Peine, a small town near Hannover, and was attending an officers' school in Döberitz – part of West Berlin not far from where the Olympics had been held. I was surprised and happy he turned up, and he must have thought quite a lot of me to do those long journeys between my accommodation and his.

Well, we were standing on the platform again, and someone sang a German song. Words like "Kiss, please kiss me, before the last train comes, and I must get home". So we did. We were in touch all the time. If he could not see me, he phoned. Once, when I did not have time for him, I discovered the next morning a rose pushed through the letterbox with a note saying "I love you". I was very impressed. We forgot about the war and air raids, which at that stage were more concentrated on other big cities. We went out often to cabarets and cafés. He brought me flowers, once even two bunches, one of tulips and one of lilacs – he said he could not make up his mind, so he got both. Is that not impressive? This must be love. We spent hours on the bench outside the clubhouse, sometimes we even had our sandwiches there.

It was now the end of March. The war went on. I had not yet lost any relatives or friends to the war, nor had any of them lost property. Food was rationed – that did not worry me much. We were served one hot meal at work and my parents looked after me. East Prussia was an agricultural country and there was plenty of food to eat, especially if you lived in a small village as we did, with 2000 inhabitants, surrounded by farms. The salami came rolling in the post and the rationed bread was sufficient for me. It was perhaps selfish to be pleased that the bombs had not hit Berlin too much.

However, on 31 March 1943 we woke up to the sound of sirens. Usually, we did not take too much notice, but the news over the radio (illegally obtained, of course) stated that hundreds of bombers were heading for Berlin. We decided to go to the official air raid shelter, a factory that also belonged to AEG. We were not there long when we felt the earth shaking and trembling. Not too close, we thought, but then someone said a bomb had come down into the Spree, near our clubhouse. It turned out to have fallen into the river just next to our house. When we arrived back and went upstairs, we found the furniture all over the place. There was a big hole in the wall behind my bed and my friend Ruth's wardrobe had settled nicely on my bed for the night. Strangely, my wardrobe was untouched.

There was nothing else to do but pack up what we could and look for a temporary place to stay. For me, this was with my mother's distant cousin. The next day, our firm offered us various private accommodations scattered around the city. I found a room in the Prinzlauerstrasse, which was only two train stops away from the station, Reinickendorf. The room contained a bed, a wardrobe and a chair along with the usual washstand that came with most rooms. There was no immediate air raid shelter nearby, but there was a large cellar, which had one side halfway out of the ground. I shall never forget the first raid when my landlady hopped around my room in her nightshirt. I had a job to calm her down and get her to the cellar. The mood down there was not much better. A lot of prayers were said, and the other tenants were all in a state of shock. I felt very brave in the face of this tumult, but there was much more to come.

I had lost contact with my darling Peter, but he managed to find me and was very cross that I had not contacted him. We had a bit of an argument, after all it was only two days since I arrived, but we soon made up. However, he also had bad news to convey. His training was complete and in a few days he would be going to fight the war. Where, he did not know, or would not tell me.

The day before he left, his fellow officers gave him a great send off. I could not believe it when I found them dancing on the table, as they usually behaved so superior. Peter left, but it was only a couple of days later when his letters rolled in. And that was more or less what happened between us till the end of the war. He wrote the most poetic love letters and I tried my best to return the same.

We had to sit for our first tests at work, and I did not do too badly. Peter wrote to tell me that he had landed in Geldern in the Netherlands, which was better than the Russian front, and I went home for Easter. I went to look up my old school and the teachers fell over themselves to greet us, although one of them said we had been the naughtiest class he had ever come across. The school was now free of soldiers again. While I was still at home, Peter wrote to say he was on the way to the Russian front, which upset me greatly, as we were not getting good reports about that place. It appeared the war was not going too well for the *Wehrmacht*.

A month later, our laboratory section was transferred to the factory in Oberschöneweide, where we used to take shelter when we lived in the clubhouse, but it was further to get to work again. On the other hand, it was nearer to the town centre. It was handy and suited my activities. Every Monday and Thursday I would take typing lessons. I never knew at that stage how handy that would become in my later life. My father had sent me a spare portable typewriter so I could practise. I was just learning how to type numbers when we were bombed out again. When I arrived for my lesson, there was nothing left of the building. I took everything in my stride. On Tuesdays, I joined some philosophical evenings and on Wednesdays, extra lessons in French.

We had learned French at school; it was a must. English too was compulsory. I had studied English at school for six months but could not stand my female teacher with her mouth full of teeth saying, "How do you do?" My father encouraged me to give it up; he could not see the point and did not think I would ever need that language in my life. Boy was he wrong there! The French we learnt at school was very boring – just verbs and tenses and reading historic lines. I wish they had taught us how to make conversation, as I am sure I would have been more interested.

On Friday, I had my exercise classes, and after my tap-dancing studio also got bombed, I took part in something I have to translate as a cross between gymnastics and ballet. Well, that place did not last much longer either and was eventually bombed out. On Saturday, I met Paula (one of the "seniors" when I was in the "Kindergarten" at the clubhouse). We used to go to the Olympic Stadium, where we played tennis or visited the indoor swimming pool. The first time I went with her she took a long time in the shower, and told me to go ahead. I did not know my way around, and she said, "Just go through there to the door opposite the hall," which I did. When I opened the second door, I got a first-class view of naked chaps in the showers. I was very embarrassed. They, of course, thought it was a great joke and told me to come on in. Was my face red! Damn Paula!

We trained for a German sports medal, starting with the bronze. We had various subjects to choose from. I took running, jumping and throwing, where I chose to throw balls. I did not have a problem with the first two, but I just could not throw the ball far enough. I think it was something like 21 metres. I nearly gave up with my test until, one day, the wind was blowing in the right direction and I reached a couple of metres past the target. I therefore qualified, but never received my medal as by then things had gone haywire. Between my activities and going out with various chaps, I did not have much time left.

There are some beautiful lakes around Berlin and wonderful lidos, which was a great opportunity to meet people – I mean boys, naturally! I went along with Paula, who was very attractive and used to reel them in.

Then there were school friends, relatives and their friends. The men were all in the army and if they passed through Berlin, they dropped in. As previously mentioned, I was especially fond of my cousin Gerhard (not to be confused with my first great love). Gerhard (II) and I had a lot in common, and we literally made great music together. I played the piano and he sang. He was the only man I could talk to openly, and we wrote to each other from time to time. If he had not been my cousin, it would have progressed further. To me, cousins were taboo. I found out later that he carried a torch for me all his life. After I had met him again with his wife in later years, I noticed that he appeared ill at ease to come near me for some reason, but his eyes never left me. He passed away a few years ago.

We managed to have a good time in between air raids. After a while, one did not take much heed of the bombings any more. At least I didn't. Sometimes we walked like zombies into the cellar in the middle of the night and forgot the next day what had happened the night before. I was still in Prinzlauerstrasse, not far away from my mother's relatives. One day, a great many bombs fell in between their flat and mine, and after we got the all clear I went to check on them. It was in the middle of night and the skies were red all over town. I had to make huge detours around fallen and burning buildings. I did not stop on the way and hurried on. To my relief, their block of flats was untouched, and we were all just happy to be alive.

It was getting more and more difficult to get a train home to East Prussia during the holidays as they were few and far between. We were lucky to be able to find a standing place. Once, some soldiers pushed me in through the window, as it was impossible to get in via the door. Trains were mostly full of soldiers going on leave or travelling back to the front. One time, a couple of soldiers asked me where I came from. When I told them I came from East Prussia, they said they found the East Prussian girls "*stur*". Something like "behind the times" or "pig-headed". They said they had given a girl from there a swig of alcohol out of their bottle and she just became "*sturer*". I told them they should have tried three or four swigs – that would have loosened her up! It was always great to be home. Firstly, there was no shortage of food, and secondly, there was always someone on leave.

In October 1943 a friend from East Prussia sent me a letter telling me that his cousin Heinz (whom I had met in Berlin, where his mother lived) had been wounded and was in a hospital in Allenstein. He said he had four wounds, one in the shoulder, his left hand, jaw and leg. I assumed it must have been splinters from a grenade. At Christmas, I went home, and we had a good get-together with his relatives and mine. Heinz told us he did not have a pass to go out, but the doctor had said it was OK for him to leave for a few hours. When we saw him, we realized that he had exaggerated, as there was not much wrong with him. My father, always ready for a lark, connected a microphone to the radio and spoke from next door. He then gave a good imitation of a radio voice, saying they were looking for Lieut. Bähre who had gone AWOL. Poor Heinz kept stuttering that the doctor had said it was OK. Shortly after that he came on leave to Berlin and we had a party at his mother's flat in Spandau.

My date was a second lieutenant, with a very imposing figure, but his face was slightly scarred from splinters. Paula grabbed him, of course. I brought along some 98% proof alcohol "organized" from the lab at work, and we made a lovely egg flip liqueur. Paula had put ash into the boys' glasses to make them drunk, but they must have noticed and swapped them. So, in the end we drank our own concoction. You can imagine the result: I had to make for the bathroom. In those days, baths were always left full of water.[15] I was sitting on the edge waiting for Paula to finish and did not spot that my dress was hanging in the water. It was made from some funny

---

[15] Presumably in case the supply failed (and water was needed to put out fires, to drink, or for hygienic reasons) – see similar concerns later in Zimbabwe

material, perhaps seersucker. Anyhow, it shrank and crept up my bum. It was most embarrassing going back to the boys, but we found them fast asleep.

9.　Berlin (1944)

In the meantime, multiple love letters arrived from Peter, my "fiancé". As this had been arranged by post, I never really knew if I should consider myself engaged or not. He had just asked for my hand in one of his letters, and even wrote to my parents to ask permission. I do not know if he ever asked his own parents. I kept some of his letters, but they would be impossible to translate. They were so poetic, and I don't think anybody would be interested. At the beginning of 1944 I did not hear from him for a while and did not know what happened to him. One minute I was worried, and the next I was upset in case he had given up on me. Usually, the reason I did not hear was because he would be moving to another destination and had no access to the post. This did not stop me from having a good time and taking advantage of getting out and about. There were no dances any more, but cafés and restaurants were open.

So far, nothing drastic had happened to my relatives or friends. Whatever occurred during the war, most of the time, I felt I had not asked for it and, therefore, it had nothing to do with me. I found wars every wasteful – I can understand killing in passion, but not killing someone you don't know and have no feelings for. I always suggested that they should have put Stalin and Hitler in a boxing ring to just fight it out between themselves.

We never heard bad news over the radio, and all seemed fine. Neither my family nor friends knew the reality of the concentration camps. We knew that labour camps existed for offenders; something less serious than prisons. Goebbels told us beautiful stories on the radio, and who were we to know they were fairytales? By the time I got to Berlin, I'd never met any Jews. Even if I had, I would not have known the difference. After all, they are the same as us.

4 March 1944 was Gerhard's birthday – remember my first and only love? It was on this day that my mother wrote to tell me that he had been seriously wounded, and just a week later I heard from her that he had died. I was distraught, threw myself on the floor and had a real tantrum. One thinks "if only, if only, if only…" I consoled myself with Peter and his letters.

After I came back from the Easter holidays at my parents' home, I got a room with an elderly couple in Karlshorst, which was nearer to work. Sometimes in winter when there were no trams, I walked. I really liked that old couple; they must have been in their 70s, but still held hands. Even in their flat he would open the door for her and let her go in first. I always say it is the little things that mean a lot, more than a bunch of flowers.

Shortly afterwards, Karlshorst was seriously hit by bombs. There were more factories around and a military camp nearby. I had been in town and saw the mess when I came home. Miraculously, our building was untouched while everything around was in ruins and in flames. Luckily, my couple were away on a short holiday at the time.

Allenstein, 1944

Life carried on with its ups and downs. Paula talked me into taking part in a Red Cross training course for auxiliary workers, purely for being on standby. Apart from the lectures that we went to, we were invited to watch an operation in the clinic, probably to get us used to the sight of blood.

The first operation was for a hernia, which was not too bad. The doctor made a small incision and stuffed everything back again. Paula had teased me; she called me a little mouse (she was a head taller than me) and said she bet that I would faint. However, when the doctor made the first cut, she had already fainted. The second operation was for a gallstone. He cut the poor man open, then there was a lot of muttering going on amongst the doctor, assistants and nurses, and they just sewed him up again. Afterwards, the doctor told us that he'd found the patient was riddled with cancer and had only a couple of months to live. There was no point in putting him through the stress of an operation. I was very upset over this.

We felt quite proud walking around in white coats and using masks etc. I found this far more interesting than physics. The next operation, it was my turn to faint. It was a breast cancer operation. The cut went from the armpits to the waistline. I could take that, but then the doctor looked round for a dish to put the cut-off breast in, and as the nurse was not on hand quick enough, he threw the whole lot on the floor. The sight of this flesh slithering across the tiled floor was too much for me, and I passed out.

We were on duty for emergencies, but were never called out. Every so often we had cinema duty, which was great. We just watched the film and luckily nothing ever happened. I do not know how I would have reacted if it had. I would have probably panicked.

In July 1944 a rumour spread that they were cancelling trains to East Prussia. (That reminds me, sometimes we were on duty at the station dishing out coffee to the passing trains full of soldiers coming or going to the front, which was always quite entertaining.) Anyhow, I had some leave due and quickly made my way home. It was an eight-hour ride and the train, as usual, was packed with soldiers. What a contrast to see all of them going out in good spirits to the front. They never looked as cheerful when they returned.

We decided to visit my aunt in Osterode. As usual, I received a great welcome. While the men were out the air raid alarm went off. It was unusual for my mother and aunt to go into a panic, but this occasion was different. They wanted to rush to the cellar, but never made it: they were too busy chasing each other off the seat in the bathroom.

"Hildchen, get off. I've got to go again."

"Hurry up, Hetchen, I've got to pay another visit myself."

All that time I was lying on the couch listening to the news which said there was a navigation plane flying over. By now I was a veteran, and I didn't even bother to get up.

As usual, we had to wait three hours before the train could enter the station when I returned to Berlin, as the air raid alarm was on.

A week later, I found out that Heinz, the cousin of my schoolfriend, had been killed. He was the one my father had teased on my last visit home. I immediately went to visit his mother in Spandau. There was not much I could do. It had only been a few months since the episode with the swapped ash-drinks. Things were now getting serious.

Once I was at the underground station when the siren went off. People tried to get up the stairs, which were totally packed. They then tried walking up the downwards escalator. I remember this poor man who tried to beat the flow. He was nearly at the top when his energy ran out, and I can still see him sitting on the steps, coming all the way back down again.

On one occasion I visited Paula, who also lived in a flat in Karlshorst. As the alarm went off, some people went to the public air raid shelter about 200 metres away. Others, like Paula and me, settled to stay in the stairwell on the ground floor. Paula said we should perhaps make a dash for the air raid shelter, but the Flak started shooting, and splinters resounded once more on the pavement. I was far too scared to risk the run, and just as well. A bomb came down, we felt the earth shake, and an air raid warden came past and said a bomb had fallen directly onto the shelter. Of over 200 people, only a handful survived. I have been told that more civilians were killed at home than soldiers in the war.

Nobody wants war, except a few fanatics, but the nation has to follow their leader, especially when they have so much power. There was no option for people. As a village policeman, my father often had trouble with farmers who had made it in the Nazi Party. They never followed his instructions: they were gods above it all.

The signs of war were now everywhere – even in cafés. I remember once they must have had an outing for wounded soldiers. They were mainly wounded in the face. I remember looking at a handsome officer from one side, only to find that when he turned his head the other side was missing entirely. Another one only had one eye where his cheek had been. It was really horrible.

In November, I found nice accommodation in a villa on the other side of Karlshorst. It had two rooms, one with a stove, and my own bathroom. To me that was wonderful. It was on the first floor. There was only one other bedroom which belonged to the landlord, and I mostly had the place to myself.

I had not heard from Peter for a while, but a few weeks later his sister wrote to tell me that he had been taken prisoner on the Western Front. In a way I was glad;

he was safe and in American hands, not Russian. He soon wrote to me afterwards and was apparently doing well.

With Father in his police uniform, 1944

I wanted to go home for Christmas. It was a struggle to get a ticket, but eventually I made it. What a sad Christmas it was. Of course, I did not know at that stage that it would be the last time I saw Brückendorf, and also the last time I saw my father. The Russians were close to the East Prussian border, but we brainwashed people believed the radio reports claiming that Hitler had it well in hand, and the Russians would never actually get that far. Still, there was an ominous silence over the country, and we did not find anything to laugh about any more.

10. Berlin (1945)

Back in Berlin, in January, I was feeling pretty frustrated at not having a proper boyfriend nearby. Letters were fine, but not enough. I went out here and there with a few chaps, but nothing serious.

Although I have been trying to follow my diary while writing this book, I have made shortcuts and written mainly from memory. There was, however, one particular entry that I will try to translate.

15/1/1945. Last night, the alarm went off as usual. We sat in the cellar and followed the flight path of the enemy planes on our special radio station. "The bulk of the fighter planes are making for the west and there are only a few planes left in the east of Berlin". I breathed a sigh of relief... and then it really started. It sounded as if a train was rattling past in the air, and I heard the bombs falling and shaking the ground. My heart started beating furiously and I held my breath. I was prepared for the worst. I felt something hitting the ground, then a second of stillness, and then the detonation. I ducked instinctively. The house was shaking. I started breathing again and waited for the next one.

The next one blew away all protection from the windows. We had strengthened them with sandbags, but both the window and its bags fell into the cellar. The house lights went out, but through a gap in the window I could see light from numerous fires. It sounded as though a tornado were whirling around the house, and I also heard fire burning. We were not sure if it was our house, but were too scared to go outside. More bombs were falling, but slowly they receded. I sighed in relief and we went upstairs.

There was not much of the roof left, and I stepped over roof tiles, but at least our house was not on fire. When I came to my room, I felt glass under my feet and got hold of some matches. It was chaos. The window frames were lying in the room, the built-in wardrobe was not built-in any more, my beautiful lamp was in splinters. In the bathroom, there was a big hole in the wall. Still, it could have been worse.

I spent the next day cleaning up the mess, and someone put the windows back in, but it took days to clear away the dust. The mine had dropped about 100 metres from our house. Twenty houses were down in the neighbourhood, but life went on as usual.

On the 17th of the month the first news filtered through that the Russians had reached East Prussia, and were starting a massive strike. On the 19th, the Russians were only about 100 kilometres from my parents' village. Till then, I had not seriously worried about my parents, but now I started to do so, and hoped that they had left in time.

I began to have nightmares. I dreamt my parents were lying in a cellar and gradually moving in the wrong direction. I dreamed about a train with a lot of dead people lying under it.

I heard on the 22nd that the Russians had entered Allenstein, less than 30 kilometres from Brückendorf. I could not stop thinking about my family. I was also wondering whether my brother was with them, as he should be in boarding school by now.

On the 26th, I dreamt I saw my mother, looking very old, and my father very pale. But they said they were OK and I saw my mother was in Berlin.

On the 27th, the doorbell rang at six in the morning, and I knew it was them. I cried with joy as my mother and brother Norbert stood at the door. Not my father, however. Here is the story of their journey.

On Saturday 20 January, they were told to get ready for the great trek, and they left that night. My mother packed as much as possible and spread the packages around the wagons of various farmers, drawn by horses. My father did not want to go with her: he said he was a policeman and had to wait for the order to leave. Little did he know that all his superiors had already legged it.

Their first aim was to reach a railway station at Mohrungen[16], about twenty kilometres away, but as the wagons were all fully loaded most people walked, including my mother and Norbert. It was heavy going. It was the middle of winter and the snow was lying thick. It took them a whole day to reach Mohrungen. They spent the night in their wagons, rested as well as they could, and decided to carry on the next day to the Baltic. From there they had been told ships were taking people to the west of Germany. Some wagons had already left during the night.

But by now my mother had had enough: she hoped to get a train instead. They grabbed a suitcase and a large wicker basket full of meat, unfortunately wrapped in old clothes – new ones would have been better. The other packages were already gone. Maybe thrown off the wagons.

They were told the last trains had left; there was, however, a train standing there, especially for those people who worked on the trains. My mother used her charm and succeeded in getting a place in the corridor. It was not long before someone got out an accordion and my mother started singing; after that they even got seating. There was plenty to eat and drink on the train, and they helped themselves to anything left on the platform at the various stations. As luck would have it, the train went all the way to Stettin[17], north of Berlin, where they caught another train to Berlin. They stayed with us for quite a while, and I felt as if I was the mother, and they were my children.

I heard from a girlfriend, Irmgard from Allenstein, that their family had made it via Königsberg by boat. It was only later that I heard a great many stories about people getting stuck and ships being sunk, or about people from the trek giving up and returning home. Tante Heta got a lift with a military truck, together with my uncle, who was in the police like my father. When the Russians occupied the rest

---

[16] Now Morag
[17] Now Szczecin

of Germany, they fetched him for questioning and she visited him once, managing to speak to him through a barbed wire fence. She never heard from him again.

My grandparents on my mother's side, who lived in Allenstein, also made it out. I heard later from my grandfather that while they were waiting at the station, there was an air raid. They hid in a cellar, and my aunt threw herself under a lorry for protection. After the all clear, they saw about twenty people lying dead on the platform, so they had a narrow escape but made it to the North Sea.

In Berlin, my mother and brother experienced their first serious air raids. Norbert had his head in my lap and his fingers in his ears. To them, it must have seemed really bad. We therefore decided to head for the bunker every time. It took about five minutes. They usually left before me, while I stayed to open all the windows, to equalize air pressure and avoid breakage. If it started getting serious, I could make it in three minutes, overtaking them on the way.

Air raids were happening daily now; it could be any time of the day but mostly at night. We just had to put up with it and were glad to be alive. We still went to the bunker, but I was always in a hurry to get home afterwards, and used to leave as soon as we heard the pre-'all clear' siren, which meant the bombers were on the way out.

One day, I had just got home and was busy closing the windows when I saw "Christmas trees" in the sky. That's what we called the flares shot down from the planes to illuminate a certain area ready for bombing. At the same time, the sirens sounded full alarm. I grabbed my briefcase with my photo albums – the only thing I used to take to the bunker. I was rushing back when, looking around, I fell into a crater that had been made by a mine some time ago. It was about two metres deep, and I tried to scramble out of it, but it had filled up with all kinds of things over time. There was an old perambulator clinging to my skirt, and all sorts of other items. In my panic, I could not make it out. So, I resigned myself to my fate, sat down, placed the briefcase on my head, stuck my fingers into my ears and closed my eyes tightly. No bombs fell nearby, but Flak splinters were all around. When the all clear sounded again and things grew a bit calmer, I managed to find a way out and returned to my room. After this incident, I decided to head for the bunker during air raids and wait it out until the all clear.

My mother was really suffering, and it was not just the air raids. She was not accustomed to queuing three hours for a pound of turnips, having been used to the good life in East Prussia. Meat was rationed and hardly in existence. So, she volunteered to be evacuated from Berlin to the countryside, and left on 22 February. At the station she found out that her cousin in Berlin was also going, and they managed to stay together, ending up in a little village named Raven about twenty kilometres from Lüneburg. My mother and my brother ended up on a farm. They had one big room and also got their meals there. In return, they had to help on the farm or in the kitchen. There was no payment, but free lodging and food was all they needed.

I made new friends in Karlshorst and soon had a couple of men chasing after me. It was something to help to take your mind off the war. Around that time, I heard from Peter that he was a prisoner of war in Colorado, USA, and doing fine. I think he was better off than us.

I also heard from my father, somewhere on the way to Danzig[18]. When he heard the Russian canons coming nearer, he gave up waiting for an order to leave. He took his bicycle and tried to get to Elbing[19]. He managed to get there after travelling three days through snow and cadging a lift here and there. He met people from the village who had given up and were on their way back home. My father was overtaken by a military vehicle packed with his superiors. They did not even stop. These were the people that had been dancing at the parties my mother used to give in Brückendorf. When my father got to Elbing he heard that the Russians were at the edge of the town. He carried on for another 30 kilometres towards Danzig. He was worried about my mother and brother, and there was no way to let him know they were safe. I received another postcard from him in March, where he wrote that the *Wehrmacht* had picked up all stray men to fight the Russians. That was the last time we heard from him – we never found out what happened.

Three sisters of my mother got out and, together with my grandparents, they all settled near Lübeck in a holiday place by the sea. The fourth sister (Tante Anna) had about six children and stayed where she lived, in East Prussia.

I heard later that she had taken Polish nationality, together with her family. My family came from near the Polish border, and the older generation still spoke Polish (especially when they did not want us kids to understand).

The air raids continued and often when I came home I found pieces of the house missing. It was especially bad one day towards the end of February, when the sirens went off while I was at work. We were pretty shaken up. The lights went off and there was no water or gas. They had no electricity even to sound the sirens, so they blew whistles instead, or drummed on empty cooking pots to warn people of any imminent trouble.

My twentieth birthday arrived on 27 February, but there was really nothing to celebrate. Even so, someone managed to get hold of a bottle of wine, and it got quite lively. A few days later, a girl from work came to me crying about the fight she had had with her father, and I gave her a good lecture on how precious parents were. I told her how when I was sixteen, I had received a hiding from my father

---

[18] Now Gdańsk
[19] Now Elbląg

one Christmas because I'd lost my temper. We only had six nuts each for Christmas, so I cherished mine. Norbert finished his first and then started on my plate. When my father said, "Well, give him one," I emptied the whole plate over my brother, saying he might just as well take the lot. My father chased me and I ran out into the snow, hoping I'd catch pneumonia, which of course I did not. I hid in the pigeon loft, but my father found me and belted me with a washing line. But I forgave him. I still loved him.

It was the middle of March when the authorities requisitioned a number of people from our factory to dig trenches outside Berlin. The girls from the laboratory were first in line, and we worked from 8 a.m. to 4 p.m., digging and gathering branches to disguise the trenches. The weather was beautiful, and we enjoyed being in the open – especially the tea breaks and lunch from a mobile canteen. We were praised for our efforts, but it was fun for us. Nobody missed us in the laboratory. We did not think much of the food itself. "Potato soup" – except we could not find any potatoes in the soup. "Meat" – what is that? We dug out the bunkers and helped to build barricades.

Naturally, it was a dirty job, and we must have looked very dishevelled when we returned to the factory. One day, when we had just returned from our expedition, we got off the truck at the factory and a German man passing asked us, "You Russkis?" We must have really looked scruffy. How degrading. This man was most surprised when we spoke German and told him we were German. He shook his head and mumbled something like, "What is the world coming to, when German woman have to do such dirty work?" Luckily, we had showers at work.

On 4 April we were at work, when we heard rumbling in the far distance, as we had done for a few days. The front was getting closer.

We did not do much work anymore and just fooled around. We took off to go out shopping or left early. My boss often stayed in the laboratory late at night, and we learned he was experimenting with our "valves". There was a park opposite the factory along the Spree and my boss used to watch courting couples through these special devices. The courting couple would not know they were being observed. Naughty, naughty!

My boss was quite a character, and we used to tease him. My friend and I used to go to a sauna in town once in a while. My boss asked if it was true that everyone walked around in the nude, mixed sexes and all. We confirmed that to him, and a few days later he stormed in and called us liars. Of course, they did not mix. Otherwise, the nude bit was true amongst the women. It takes a bit of time to bare all even in front of them, but it was wonderful. First we had a hot bath, then into the steam room, and after that into a room with hot air. And lastly, another dip into the big bath with lovely hot towels afterwards.

The air raids were now a daily occurrence, every night and sometimes during the day as well. We got used to the "Christmas trees", and I spent a lot of time in the air raid shelter. We still had our fun in between. I met a few other chaps on the way to the front, which was drawing ever closer. Looking back, they were fine, but of no real interest to anybody. When the electricity supply stopped, we could not follow events on the radio any more.

My mother and brother were safe on the farmhouse in Raven, and I would have dearly loved to join them. We heard the Russians were on the outskirts of Berlin and had really hoped that the Amis[20] would get there first. We learned later that the British and American troops stopped fighting a long way from Berlin. Some arrangement with Russia…

We were not allowed to leave work as that was regarded as treachery. Also, one had to have special permission from the *Wehrmacht* to board a train. On the 18th, my mother sent me a telegram, begging me to come. She and my brother were visiting other refugee relatives in Lütjenburg, a seaside resort near Lübeck.

I still had my pass stating that I was from East Prussia and, pretending I was a refugee, I got my train ticket. We closed for the weekend, and I was convinced that by Monday the Russians would be there, as they were coming in our direction.

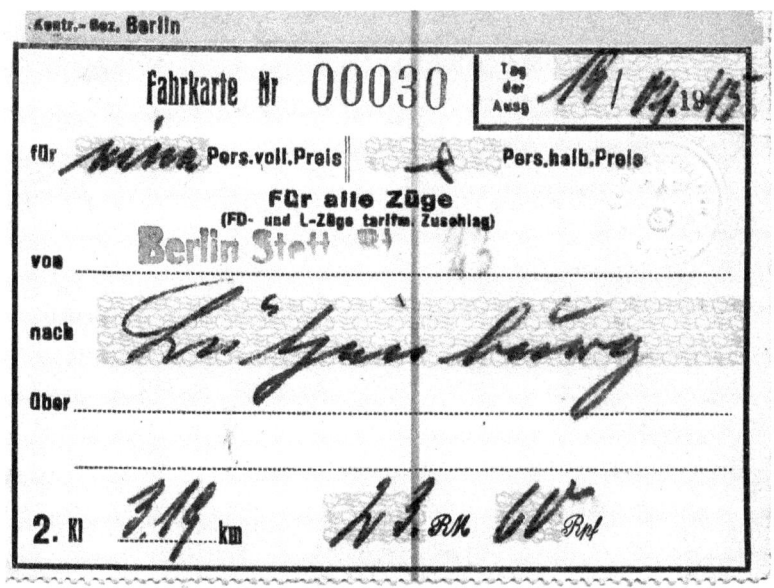

The train ticket which was never used, 1945

---

[20] Americans

I packed my suitcase and on 20 April I went to catch the town train to get to the departure station. The local train was packed, and I spent most of the time near the floor. But there was no reason to hurry. The lines outside Berlin had been destroyed by bombers, so no trains were running anyway.

I thought of walking, but decided to leave my heavy suitcase with the mother of one of my friends. She lived in Spandau not too far away, and was surprised to see me. She did not look too happy either. I thought things over during the night and decided it would not be good if I was overtaken by the Russians in the open. I had relatives, Tante Lene, another sister of my mother, who lived in Friedenau in the south part of the city with her husband, her daughter Gerda who was a year younger than me, and a son who was over twenty but had the brains of a six-year-old. Family is family. I had visited them a couple of times before, and they took me in with open arms.

The block of flats they lived in had a reinforced cellar, and we had several bunk beds available. We had blankets and usually slept through the night unperturbed by the air raids. Tante Lene did her best to feed us.

The next day we heard about big sales in town and I went to the bank to fetch some of my savings. This is just to point out that at that stage, most things were still running smoothly. I had saved since my parents gave me a savings book on my sixth birthday, and all my life until I retired I put a little money monthly into my account.

On the 23rd we heard the Russians had reached Karlshorst and taken over. We went to the shops to get more rations, but the shops were closed and people started to plunder. Not far from our flat, we saw an old soldier hanging from a lamppost. He was old, somewhere around 70, grey-haired and bearded. I will never forget that picture. I still see him hanging, pathetically, with a cardboard sign hanging from his neck saying: "Here I hang because I was too much of a coward to fight for my *Vaterland*" (fatherland). From my window I watched the planes coming past and saw them releasing bombs which flew underneath the plane for a short distance, looking like pencils, till they curved and fell. Well, as long as I could see them there was no danger for us.

The next day, we heard that there were sacks of potatoes stashed in a shed near the station in Friedenau. Everyone helped themselves. Uncle August, Tante Lene, Gerda and I rushed for our share. It was a big barn, with sacks of dried potatoes stacked around the wall and people shoulder to shoulder pushing each other out of the way. Some succeeded in getting the sacks down, but could not get them out as everyone was trampling on the sacks.

I was lucky. I was leaning against a sack and my uncle quickly heaved it onto my shoulder. Then I had to get outside, which seemed impossible. Suddenly, the big barn doors were closed. The police had arrived, armed and with dogs. Panic broke out as people thought they might light the barn and roast us alive. The panic gave those inside strength, and everyone pushed at the door, which gave way and fell outwards, with me falling in front of a policeman. He had his pistol out and threatened to shoot me if I did not take the sack back. Luckily, my uncle, being in the customs service, knew the chap and whispered something in his ear. After that, the policeman turned away from me and concentrated on someone else. It was serious, some women were running around with blood pouring down their legs from dog bites.

Friedenau cellar

Over the next few days we "organized" some grain and coal. We had a coffee mill and from morning till night we took turns grinding the grain through the mill with a handle. Tante Lene baked bread with it, and we were rationed one dry slice a day. And boy we were looking for the biggest one. The dried potatoes she cooked and made dumplings.

We lived on that for a few weeks. No meat or fat, not even salt. The shops were empty. We went to one nearby and found the door broken open. Flour, sugar, jam, eggs etc. spread all over the floor and trampled in. There were broken bottles everywhere – so much for that.

We also had to look for water. There were public pumps in some streets, but the queues were a mile long. My uncle said he knew about a pump with no queue. Why? It was in the line of fire of the Russian artillery. I did not want to go, but my cousin was game, and I followed reluctantly. Planes were offloading in the distance, and they were shooting near the pump. We watched and noticed the next one go 100 metres further away, and another 100 metres, then back again. My uncle waited until the shots fell near the pump. After the dust cleared, a soldier appeared, like out of the clouds, dirty and going somewhere. We rushed to the pump, hoping the next shots would be 100 metres away, quickly fetched the water and made it back. I felt sick with relief.

As they were shooting all around it, we all stayed in the cellar and brought our meagre food supply down. It was 27 April. For hours, it had been very quiet, no shooting, an ominous silence. One of the men went up and said there was a big Russian tank outside the flat in the street. And the first Russians were descending the stairs to the cellar.

We knew then the war was over for us, but the worst was yet to come. I always said, rather three years of air raids than three days under the Russians.

The first thing they did was relieve us of our watches. "*Uri, Uri*" – we soon learnt that word[21]. They bundled us together on the first floor, where we lived in one room. Through the window, we saw the tank with the canon pointing at us. We thought that was it. One went into the cellar to look through the suitcases. Apart from the watches, they were very partial to cameras.

I tried to make myself inconspicuous. It did not help. Then one Russian pointed his rifle at me and said, "*Frau komm*" (woman, come). These too were words we often heard in the next few days. He threatened me with the rifle and pulled me down the stairs to the entrance of the cellar. I begged him to leave me alone, but he just grinned and approached me. I gave him a push, and he fell against a big plank of wood leaning against the wall opposite. The plank fell over and when it reached the floor it sounded like a shot. The people in the room upstairs heard it and thought he had shot me. They started screaming and pandemonium broke out. The Russian got such a fright he took off. What luck!

---

[21] Probably a Russified plural of the German "*Uhr*"

The propaganda had not been exaggerated in this respect. The rapes started, and there was no use trying to make yourself look ugly. From seven years old to seventy, it made no difference. We heard about women being shot for refusing, and in the block next door I saw a father making a coffin for his daughter out of old boxes. Another man was shot when he stood in front of his wife. The Russians found alcohol, and when drunk I do not think even their superiors could control them.

These were the advance troops, the fighting forces, and they had to make way for the next lot. They left in a hurry, and the next day the occupation troops arrived. They chased us all out of the flats. We thought they would send us to Siberia, but they said, "Just go ten kilometres." We found out later that they needed our block to install a communications centre, which turned out to comprise one room, one soldier, and a couple of telephones.

We started walking. My aunt said she had a friend in the next street who lived in another block of flats with a good, large cellar. As usual, we found all the tenants in the cellar. They were very friendly until my aunt pointed out that our young girls should go to the back row, out of sight. They protested and said we had to stay in the front. That's when we discovered why they were so pleased to see us. Apparently, the Russians had been busy pulling out the women all night and raping them upstairs in the flats. In the corner lay a young girl of about eleven sobbing and crying her eyes out.

Two Russians came into the cellar and started to search our suitcases. My uncle had to explain to them how to work his camera, and while they were busy, I grabbed my cousin's hand and pulled her up the stairs. When the Russian started to follow us, my aunt got into their way, and we made it to the street. In Berlin, they have big round advertising pillars everywhere, and we hid behind them.

We waited ten minutes. Nobody came out. I edged cautiously nearer the glassed entrance, and there I saw my uncle standing at the bottom of the flight of stairs. At the same time my aunt came down the stairs alone, sobbing. There had been two of them, one a Mongolian, and they had taken turns raping her. My uncle consoled her, saying, "Better you than the young girls." When he had tried to get in front of her, they had just booted him down the stairs.

We did not hang around and kept walking with the flow of other people, all seeking new accommodation. A few streets away, we found a block of flats where only the cellars were still intact. Other people were already occupying some of the cellars, but there were plenty of them.

We lit a candle and found a cellar that had everything. A couple of beds, chairs, a table and even a stove. We found coal in another cellar and cupboards full of groceries. One cellar was like a chemist's store. We helped ourselves to some soap. Well, if it was not us, it would be the Russians.

We even found a hidden hole behind the shelves, through to another cellar with more beds. Here we felt safe for the night. There was another door to the outside, but that was safely locked – or so we thought. We heard later that some of the other refugees had given us away, when the Russians were after their wives, and told them about the young blood under their nose. They banged on the wall and broke it open, shouting at us, "We knocking, you not open." They looked us over and went away. We felt relieved, but they came back after dark. My uncle had gone in search of water, but he would not have been able to help us anyhow.

They held a pistol to our breasts and pulled us out of the cellar. Gerda vanished with one, together with another young soldier of about fifteen. The one in uniform pulled me into an empty cellar. There was no furniture, so he threw me on the floor and fell on top of me. The gun was in his hand. I have often heard women saying they would rather give their lives, but it is different when you have a pistol touching your breasts. The young soldier stationed himself near the door and watched the whole process, grinning.

I made a last effort to save myself by telling him I had syphilis, but he only grinned and reached in his pocket for a packet. I felt numb and stunned. It was soon over. Luckily, he did not bother to give the young soldier a turn, but had the cheek to say, "*Auf Wiedersehen.*" When I got into the passage, my cousin came towards me, crying bitterly. It had been a longer ordeal for her as there had been two of them.

A couple of weeks later, when things were a little quieter, Tante Lene, Gerda and I went to a clinic. It had been specially set up for similar cases and everyone got an injection "just in case". When we got there, there were 40 women in front of us; by the time we left I counted 80 behind us.

We did not hang around for a repeat performance. My uncle came back from a fruitless water expedition and told us that he had spoken to the sergeant occupying the telephone "centre" in their block of flats, who had said it was OK for us to return. He would make sure nothing happened to us again. He even gave my uncle a loaf of bread, something we had not seen for weeks.

There was still a lot of coming and going in our flat, but usually we could threaten them with the sergeant downstairs. Once, one told us to come and my uncle said he would get the commandant. This young chap said he was the commandant, at which point my uncle showed him his little finger and said he was that small a commandant. He got embarrassed and left. Another came and said the commandant had told him to fetch me to come and peel potatoes. I told him to bring the potatoes to me and I would peel them. They were not quite so aggressive by then – probably running short on alcohol – and he vanished.

Once the sergeant came looking for my cousin. My uncle said he had had enough, and he might just as well shoot him first. The sergeant was impressed and, shaking his head, left.

1 May came, which is a big Russian holiday, and we knew the vodka would be flowing. In the afternoon, a few Russians came up and were searching through the rooms. Gerda and I had had enough. While they were busy in another room, we grabbed our shoes and on tiptoes made it out of the flat. We went up the stairs, but on the third floor all the rooms were burned out, so we made for the attic above. I was hoping the burnt out flat would put them off, but just to be on the safe side, we got hold of a ladder and climbed up to a second attic and pulled up the ladder.

Friedenau attic

We watched the celebrations from the attic. Half of the roof was missing and we had a good view. There was no end to that night. Short of fireworks and rockets, they made do with shooting their pistols up into the air all over the place (I hope it was only in the air), and for further entertainment they started a few fires. My aunt brought us bedding and bread every day, which continued to be provided by the sergeant.

We spent a few days there. We did not know what was happening with Germany. We had no communication and did not even know if the war was over. We had plenty of time for reflection, and I could not understand what had gone wrong. Why were they still fighting when there had not been any hope for such a long time? Most of the people I knew were killed in the last month of the war. It was all so senseless.

What a pity the plot to kill Hitler on 20 July 1944 had failed. They shot everyone that had taken part,[22] who were obviously the ones that had any brains left. No wonder the whole army had lost their minds. Why did everyone follow this fanatic?

Why had they fought to the last man? I think they had no option. I heard they burnt down the house of some people who had hissed at the white flag. Or those soldiers who were shot if they turned around and tried to flee. I had seen some of them: youngsters as young as eleven and a grandfather of 70. They had put a gun in their hand in the last few days of Berlin to defend the city. Even if they had no gun, they had to find some weapon. They called it the *Volkssturm*, the People's Army, and they had no option but to fight.

Führerbefehl.

An die Berliner Bevölkerung!

Merkt Euch, jeder, der die Maßnahmen, die unsere Widerstandskraft schwächen, propagiert oder gar billigt, ist ein Verräter! Er ist augenblicklich zu erschießen oder zu erhängen! Das gilt auch dann, wenn angeblich solche Maßnahmen im Auftrag des Gauleiters Reichsminister Dr. Göbbels oder gar im Namen des Führers befohlen werden sollten.

gez. Adolf Hitler

22. April 1945

Order from Hitler, 22 April 1945

"To the people of Berlin! Anyone who spreads or approves actions that weaken our resistance is a traitor, and to he shot or hanged on the spot, even if such actions are allegedly ordered in the name of the Führer or on behalf of Gauleiter/Minister Göbbels!"

---

[22] In fact some were hanged

We ventured down from our attic on 4 May. There were rumours that Goebbels had hanged himself, Hitler had gone down fighting, and Göring had run off. Well, it was all wrong, and eventually we found out that Hitler and Eva Braun had shot themselves and that Goebbels and his family had taken poison. This was not the way out for a "fighter". It was a little quieter in the streets, with not so many Russians about but still enough. It scared me when there were shots fired through the night.

My uncle supplied us with water from a pump about 100 metres away. He got a bit tired when there were two young able-bodied girls lounging around and said it was time we helped. I did not trust this business in the street and painted a few wrinkles on my face, put on some implausible clothes with many layers and limped through the streets. I pulled my face down and pretended to be an idiot. My aunt and uncle were laughing hysterically, but it helped, as nobody came near me. I heard later that they were a bit scared of idiots.

We also had some funny moments. I was looking out of the window one day – behind curtains, of course – and saw a Russian soldier taking photographs of his friend. He merrily pressed the trigger but had the lens facing his stomach. Another story we heard was of a German boy going past on an old bicycle showing off the "look no hands" pose, holding both arms in the air. A Russian soldier came past on a brand-new bike and stopped the youth. He persuaded him to swap bikes, in order to get this wonderful hands-free bike. The German boy did not wait for the results and made off quickly!

They also did not know what to make of our bathrooms. Some peed into the sink and washed in the toilets. They usually used the corner of a room for other business. They all had shaved heads and looked awful to me, except for the officers, who mostly had a full head of hair. When I look now at pictures of Russian people, I see them looking quite different, like normal people.

On 8 May, we heard it was amnesty day and everyone wondered what would happen next. Someone had to pay. I thought of my beloved East Prussia and wondered how the people were faring, those who had stayed behind.

My brother had made contact with one of his friends in Brückendorf and heard various stories. The parents of two twins, about ten years old, were dead. They had stayed behind as they spoke fluent Polish and hoped to get away with it. The invaders had hanged the father, while the mother died of typhoid. A sister, Irene, had been my best friend but was never heard of again, after the Russians abducted her. Another girl in the village about my age was raped over twenty times and died. So, I could still consider myself lucky. A Polish aunt eventually took over the dairy and looked after the two children. In Berlin, I heard that the old couple I had stayed with in Karlshorst, who were still so in love with each other, had committed suicide before the Russians came. They were not the only fatalities.

Irene Dimanovsky, abducted 1945

The war had been lost, and at what price? Millions of people dead – some 80 million, we have been told, and this all because of one man. I never took much interest in Hitler. He was a figure on top and leading the country. What difference does it make, king or queen, or the leader of any country? People elected him: in Hitler's case I believe over 90%. Surely, they must have known what they were doing, and they must have thought him competent to become leader. For the rest of my life, I never bothered about politics, and I never voted for anyone. I would not want to be responsible for making the wrong decision.

I am now much older, and hear and see more on TV about Hitler and the time of the Nazis than ever before. I am starting to take notice of what happened, and only now do I find out what really happened during that time.

I see films on concentration camps, and I am shocked. I never heard anybody in our family talk about it, and I doubt they knew anything. I hear of the air raids in England and the destruction of many European countries, historical buildings and people's possessions. They, like my parents, did not only lose a home and all their achievements, but their homeland as well. The land I was born and lived in until I went to Berlin is now Polish. I do not even know now if I was born in Germany or Poland.

Well, what is the difference? I do not hate anybody, and I am mostly at home in my new cosmopolitan town of Kingston, where you rub shoulders with all nationalities. I would not consider myself a very patriotic person. I've had a German passport, a British passport, a Zimbabwean passport, even a South African one, not all at the same time, of course. I always kept my British nationality, though. Just as well.

Maybe the war made me that way. The three years in Berlin and the time of the Russian occupation left me slightly numb at the time and blunted my feelings. The bad times are somewhere in the back of my mind and I remember only the good. I have maintained the ability to see the funny side of things. A few years ago, I met an official in Zimbabwe I had met four years earlier. I told him I recognized him, and he asked what made me feel so sprightly at my age. I told him my motto is: "Don't worry – be happy".

Back to Berlin. It was the middle of May and I decided to pay Karlshorst a visit, check out my flat and fetch a couple more items. My job was finished, and I had only one thing in my mind now, to get to my family in Raven. There were no trains going as yet, so I had to bide my time.

With no trams or other transport to Karlshorst, I decided to walk the sixteen kilometres. I had to cross a river where the bridge had been destroyed, probably by our own soldiers. They had put up a provisional bridge, and lodged against the destroyed bridge I saw the body of a Russian woman in uniform, floating in the water. She must have been there some time as her body was very bloated. Nobody bothered.

Shortly before Karlshorst, I was stopped by Russian soldiers who wanted me to come to the camp and peel potatoes for the commandant. Well, I had heard this before, and told them to get lost. I found out that with a bit of cheek, one got further with them. They left me alone.

I found out that everyone in Karlshorst had survived. They confirmed that the Russians had got to them two days after I had left, and there were the usual tales about raping and plundering.

My record player and my typewriter were gone. Luckily, I had taken my photo albums with me, as the Russians were very partial to any photographs. I never had much else, but they were untouched. The people in the house were fine, and one chap already had a job with the town council. Yes, things were starting, or at least trying, to get back to normal – not that things would ever be really normal again. They even had light, gas and water and I felt like staying, but there was a Russian camp nearby, and I did not want to take any chances.

I got back to my aunt's place the same day, on foot. As my job in the laboratory had come to an end, I had to go to the employment office to look for work. Marvellous how fast the authorities became established. Anyone who appeared to be clean, i.e. had not belonged to the Nazi Party, was privileged. But the only work they had for me was clearing rubble, and I was not that desperate yet.

11. Escape from Berlin (June/July 1945)

On 4 June, I made an effort to get to the west. I walked as far as Potsdam, found there were no trains, and decided to go back. Fortunately, I got a lift in a lorry. The cinemas were open but only showing Russian films, better than nothing even if I could not understand a word. Sometimes they brought a German film for children. Mostly fairytales, and I had heard enough of them from Hitler. There was even a variety performance and I found people were laughing again.

I was getting a bit bored and despondent. I decided to walk back to Karlshorst. I found out that with a lot of detours one could get a tram here and there and succeeded in finding one halfway. Travelling through the city, I saw that there was really not much left standing. I was especially upset going through the *Tiergarten* park adjacent to the zoo, and discovering that a great many animals had perished.

I met a young girl on the train, and she told me that she was on the way home to Burg, which was right next to the border from East Germany to the West. I thought this was a chance to get to my family, and she said she would help me get across, as she had good connections. I took her to my aunt's place, packed a few things, got a couple of sandwiches from my aunt and off we went. (Yes, food was becoming available on ration cards, not much, but some.) We got a lift on a vegetable lorry to Werder and found a goods train to Burg. We were in a cattle train, sitting at the door with our legs dangling outside. Great fun.

It was 19 June and my new friend, Gisela, took me to spend the night with some of her friends. I had started to get a little suspicious about Gisela, fears that were confirmed when we arrived at a house at the back of some flats in a weird looking alley. When they opened the door for us, there were a few girls, and they told Gisela to "push off". However, I think when they saw me, they relented and said we could spend the night there. Just as well, as it was evening and there was a curfew from 10 p.m. until 5 a.m. the next morning. Anybody found in the street was in danger of being shot.

They even gave us a meal which consisted mainly of horse meat. I have eaten horse meat since then which was not bad fried or roasted. But this was just fat and comprised something unidentifiable; nor did I want to enquire too closely. I found out about Gisela's "connections" with the Russian commandant, which amounted to her being the girlfriend of some Russian soldier. Mind you, he did work for the commandant. It appeared he was not the only one she befriended. All I wanted was for her to get me across the border. I needed a pass from the Russians to do that. Not at her price, however.

The next day, she told me to stay put while she went out to make an arrangement with the "commandant" to get me the pass. With the girls gone, I went out exploring and found nearby a school occupied by a number of refugees waiting for a chance to get across the border. I spoke to a chap in the yard who lived with his parents in the front of my current abode. He told me not to go near the refugee camp as it was full of pests crawling all over you. He and his family offered for me to stay with them until I found the opportunity to move on. I said I would wait to see what news Gisela brought. All the girls arrived loaded with food, and I was really hungry. When I asked Gisela for a piece of bread, she told me to go and sleep with the commandant and earn it myself. I think she was very disappointed with me not going "their way".

I was thinking of the school opposite, which looked like a gypsy camp, and decided to take up the offer of the people in the front house. Of course, there had been no more mention of Gisela getting me across the border. I thought of giving up and returning to Berlin, but it turned out one even needed a pass to get on the train to Berlin. To get the pass would take time, and the people I was staying with offered to let me stay a bit longer.

That day they were going to some farms to do a bit of "fencing", in other words taking some useless articles from the house to trade for horse meat. It succeeded, and the mother made a stew that night which I enjoyed, although I could not get the sausage down.

Next I went to the town office to apply for my travel pass. While in the waiting room I saw an actor I had seen on the stage in Berlin, Jupp Hussels[23], passing with a picture under his arm. He seemed quite at home with the officials there. It appeared that artists and doctors were exempt from prosecution for having been a Nazi, whereas otherwise around us the prosecution of former Nazis carried on.

I did not get my travel pass yet, but managed to get ration cards for two days; 500 grams bread, 50 grams meat and 25 grams fat, which I shared with the people I was staying with.

On the way back, I passed a swimming stadium and saw a lot of German girls flirting with the Russians. So, there was no need to "confiscate" women any more. I also went to a fortune teller who declared that I would reach my family in four weeks, and that my fiancé would come back, but that we would be splitting up.

I heard that it was very hard to get across the border. When caught, you were locked up if they did not shoot you first. I spoke to an elderly woman who said she knew how to get across the river, which was now the border. Apparently there were men who would risk getting you across in a rowing boat. I thought I would give it a try and the two of us started walking towards a small village by the river. Just as we caught sight of the first house of the village, we ran into a Russian border control. I stood still, but the woman with me started running back. The Russians asked me where I was going, and I told them a fabricated story of having met a farmer in town who had offered me a job. They asked me who the farmer was, and I told him the farmer had told me to go to the third house on the right. (I was hoping there were three houses in the street.)

I might even have got away with it, but the woman with me confessed our intentions. They took us back to a house they were using as a military post, and said they had to send a rider (on bicycle) to the commandant in the city, to find out what to do with us. They separated us and put us in two different rooms, and the chap with me put on a gramophone record. He offered me a meal, but I refused to eat unless the other woman joined me. To my surprise, he let her. We had a great plate full of soup and a big slice of bread. After about two hours they let us go, but back to Burg. I even had the cheek to ask him for the rest of the bread, which he gave us.

Apparently we had been lucky, as we found out later that the previous night the Russians had kept some women "prisoners" in the cellar and raped them.

It was late, but a woman living nearby offered us a place to stay for the night. I even gave her my precious boots in payment. These boots had a bit of a history. I had left them in Spandau with my friend's mother, where I had stayed the night on the way to my aunt before the Russians arrived. When afterwards I went to collect

---

[23] German cabaret artiste and actor who later took up painting

them, my friend's mum, who was quite feisty, told me a Russian female soldier had taken them when they searched the house. But she had gone to one of the commandants (a female) and managed to get back my boots. I suppose she gave up listening to my friend's tirade.

We thought to have another go at the river the next day but saw there were a number of Russians about and decided to give up. On the way back to Burg, we came across three chaps working to fix a locomotive, which was standing on a siding. They succeeded and offered us a lift back to town.

In the meantime, I had managed to get my travel pass, so we made for the station. There were no trains until the next morning, and the five of us joined the overcrowded waiting room. The Russians came and looked us over, and one came to me with the potato peeling story. I told them to bring the potatoes and I would peel them in the waiting room. By then I had learnt how to deal with them, and they left me alone.

In the middle of the night, a couple of soldiers came in to check our passes. Apparently, one had to have permission to stay out at night, which of course I did not have. A chap sitting next to me saw me fidgeting and when I told him I did not have a pass he pulled six of them out of his pocket. He gave me one with the name of Paul. The Russians looked at it and said "charrasho", which means OK. Obviously they could not even read.

We decided to return to Berlin, fetch more provisions, and meet in a day's time to try again to get across the border. I went to Karlshorst for some of my things and noticed that the Americans had taken over part of the west, including my aunt's place. Karlshorst remained under Russian control.

When I arrived at our meeting place, my new friend Jupp was not there, so I walked again to Potsdam and got a train to Burg. I got hold of Jupp's friend, who had stayed behind with some of our luggage. Jupp pitched up eventually but did not want to go any further. We managed to talk him into coming with us and on the 24th we were on our way. However, in the meantime the border had been adjusted, and was now about twenty kilometres further from the river. We first had to get to Magdeburg which was the first town about six kilometres beyond the river.

Crossing the river was no longer a problem, and we arrived in Magdeburg at eleven at night, which was after curfew. A Russian stopped us, but we persuaded him to let us go with the help of some tobacco. We now had to get inside quickly, but it took us a long time to find a house still standing amongst the ruins. By that time, we had already gathered quite a few people on the same mission. We found a block of flats intact and knocked on the door, but nobody came. In desperation we started hammering the door. At last, a woman from the first floor let us sleep there, on the floor and in the stairwell. I got no sleep that night, and had to step over sleeping bodies to get to the toilet.

At seven the next morning we were at the station, where Jupp and his friend split up to go in different directions. The rest of us got on the train for a short distance. That was as far as the train would go, and still some distance from the border. A horse-drawn cart gave us a lift, but it was another five kilometres to the border. We went to the *Autobahn* to see if we could get a lift across, but there were only American trucks and cars, and the soldiers just pulled faces at us. We heard about a small village right at the border and walked on, trying to avoid Russian patrols. Once we had to wade through a small rivulet, of course barefoot.

We made it to a village near Helmstedt. It consisted of only a few houses, but the courtyards were packed with about 1000 people, all with the same idea to cross the border. Apparently, one could only manage that at night. I think it was officially not allowed. I noticed that during the day there were a few Russians around with grim faces. I asked one Russian standing guard if we could get across. He was very friendly and told us to come back at night. At that very moment a Russian officer came past, and the guard raised his rifle at me, shouting, "Back, back!" Once the officer had gone, the guard said to me, "Now we can talk again."

About eleven that night, we heard handcarts rolling towards the border barrier. No curfew here. When I came to the barrier, one of the guards asked me what I had to offer to get across. The only thing I could think of was a ring my mother once gave me, with two little diamonds and one sapphire. "OK," the guard said. "How many in your family?" I looked round and about eight people had gathered around me. I told him they were all my family, and he let us through. We were told to go straight for 50 metres and then turn right.

We had only gone a few metres when a railway worker (who must have had a special pass to cross) told us not to go to the right, as he had seen some Russians in the bushes waiting for women, but to go straight on, which we did. After about 200 metres, the road started turning to the left. It was dark, and we were afraid we would land back in the East Zone. There was a stone building in the field. No roof. We camped under the stars and waited for dawn. The morning came and we could see Helmstedt. We crossed the field and went to the station, to catch a train to Braunschweig. On the platform, I saw my first British soldiers. They took no notice of us, and were carrying no weapons. What a relief!

There were no trains to Lüneburg, my next destination. I was exhausted and went to the Red Cross, hoping to find a vacant bed for a few hours. On the way there I passed a butcher's shop and, would you believe it, they were selling sausages. As I eyed them hungrily, the butcher came outside and asked me if I came from "the other side". When I confirmed this, he said, "I bet you are starving?" I could only nod; my mouth was full of water. He took me inside and cut off a slice of sausage, and I burst into tears.

I was not so successful at the Red Cross. No room for me, only for women with children. I had been hoping for a meal and a few hours' sleep. No such luck. As I stepped outside, I saw a German driver getting into an American car and asked if he was going to Lüneburg. He was not, but offered to take me to the *Autobahn* to try for a lift. As usual, there were mostly British military vehicles streaking past. Some German trucks passed intermittently but refused to stop. After a while, an army convoy came past, and all the trucks had to stop at the side of the road. There were dozens of hitchhikers, and we all made for the nearest truck and just climbed on, without asking permission. My lorry was carrying salt sacks to Lüneburg.

By late afternoon there was no other transport available, so I decided to walk as far as I could and, if necessary, perhaps sleep on a farm. On the outskirts of Lüneburg, a private car overtook me and the driver offered me a lift. He did not go directly to Raven, my destination, where my mother and brother had found accommodation, and when he stopped it looked like nowhere. I was worried he might have evil intentions, but he told me about a shortcut to cut the distance by half: if I went through a farm there would be another road on the other side. I could see the farm and, as I arrived, it was packed with British soldiers who had put up quarters there. They were sitting in the yard, drinking beer and having a good time.

I tried to explain to them where I wanted to go, but did not get far with my three words of English. I found out later from the farmer's wife where my family was staying that my mother had fared much better. She explained that when the first British soldiers arrived at their farm, they had wanted to remove the radio. My mother must have given everyone the impression that she understood English, so the farmer's wife called her over. My mother pointed at the radio and said, "You!" before rolling up her sleeves, producing a fist and saying, "I!" They laughed so much, they just took off, without the radio.

Anyhow, the British soldiers indicated that they were going to get someone to translate. They offered me a seat and a beer. After the long journey and sitting on the salt sacks, I was very thirsty. I would have drunk water, but they offered beer and I finished the glass in one go. I could have finished a barrel and when they offered me another one, I drank that too, not thinking of the consequences. Eventually, a twelve-year old German boy came and asked what I wanted. I asked for directions to Raven, but I think by that time I had trouble understanding German. One of the soldiers said he knew the way and offered to show me. We tried to talk to each other; by the time we managed to get one phrase together we were nearly in Raven.

When the village was in sight, the soldier stopped and explained (via sign language) that it would be better if I did not arrive with a British soldier. I only realized then that I had been making conversation, of sorts, with a British soldier, i.e. the enemy. I also had heard that "fraternization" was then still forbidden, and so I said goodbye to the soldier, whose name was Len.

I arrived at the farm unexpectedly. My mother was in the kitchen helping the farmer's wife, my brother flirting with the farmer's daughter. All was rosy and the reception overwhelming. There were a lot of tears shed for unexpected joy. It was lovely to be surrounded by family again, and we had a lot to talk about. Naturally, a bed was found for me, although all three of us had to share one room. It was by then 28 July.

12.   Raven (1945–46)

They were very well-organized for parties. There was a *Schützenhaus* in the woods: an observation post used on hunting trips. It was a rather large place and also used for open-air parties. My brother played the accordion, the moon was our illumination. The youth of the village all came together and we danced. How long had it been since I had last danced?

The day after my arrival, the farmer's wife fetched me as there were two British soldiers in the kitchen, and she thought they wanted eggs. My mother must have bragged about my non-existent English. One of them was Len. He said he did not really want any eggs, and it was just an excuse to see me again. I told my mother about them, and she said enemy or not, we have to be hospitable. We offered them coffee and tried to talk using a lot of sign language. They soon left, but said they would be back.

The farmer had a couple of farm horses. As I was crazy about horses, Louise – the farmer's daughter – and my brother managed to halter them. No saddle, but it was still lovely to gallop around. One horse was Ivan, a really wild pony, while mine was very tall and slightly off balance, with a limp. What fun! There is a German saying: "*Der Himmel auf Erden ist auf dem Rücken von Pferden*" (something like 'the back of a horse is like heaven on earth').

It was now the middle of August 1945 and as I was getting free accommodation and food, I knew it was too good to be true. One morning, when as usual Norbert and my mother were woken up to get ready for work, they shouted through the door, "And we need Ulla too." We had breakfast and, at eight in the morning, we went to the potato fields. Some of us dug out the potatoes; others gathered them in baskets and carried them to the horse-drawn wagons. This became a daily occurrence for me too.

The next time we walked behind the harvester, not like these days when everything is automatic, and gathered up the stalks. We bundled them, tied them together with string and put them up as stacks. It was not just backbreaking, but when I came home that night, my arms were bleeding from the scratches caused by the straw. Well, it took a few days' backache to get used to it. The worst time was later in winter, when we had to dig turnips out from the frozen earth, in below zero temperatures.

There were lighter moments too. When we broke off for elevenses, the sandwiches and the coffee had never tasted so good. We went home for lunch and came back for another few hours in the afternoon, interrupted by another tea break.

Once, one of the British soldiers asked me why I worked so hard. I told him to get our meals. He took one look at our supper and said, "For that?" After that, they always brought some rations when they visited. Tinned food we had never tasted before, and the like.

Oh yes, they had come back, and my English was improving rapidly. Len went on leave and his friend came back a few days later with "Harold". Now there was a hunk of flesh! He was very attractive, and I heard later he was pretty well off. His father owned a car factory in England. The first time he laid eyes on me, he said, "That is the girl I want to marry!" Naturally, I took it with a pinch of salt. But he was a real daredevil. Full of beans and I was smitten.

There was a dance laid on in Soderstorf about four kilometres away, and my mother and I were invited. Well, this was something I had hardly experienced. Throughout the entire war, I had only taken part in one dance, at the officers' school graduation ceremony, when I went with Peter. There had also been a couple of dances in the village while I was still at school. But I was now twenty years old and boy, did I like dancing! What is a walk of four kilometres?

We had a great time. I played the piano and my mother sang. We had a piano at the farmhouse and had kept it up. Of course, we were not that good, at least I wasn't, but our dates were very proud of us. The village had looked down on us a little because of our relationship with the "enemy", but after that night they somewhat forgave us. We were "artists", and they are a breed of their own.

A week later there was a dance at their headquarters, where I had first made their acquaintance. Harry was an organizer, so no walking on foot for us: he fetched us with a military jeep. It was great, and again we had to show off our musical talents. On the way back home, I was sitting next to Harold, driving through the fields, when he suddenly put the steering wheel in my hands, moved over and said, "Your turn." I had no option but to veer along for a bit until he took over again. That was Harry for you. Sometimes he gave me a ride on his motorbike (not permitted, needless to say, but who cares?).

I had known Harold for only a couple of weeks when he told me he was going to England on leave for a few weeks. He said he would have loved to take me with him – what about climbing into his suitcase?, and all that nonsense. He also told me to stop working, that he would look after me. I did not take much notice. But he said he would be back and write to me in the meantime, care of Len.

We still had our gatherings in the "clubhouse" in the forest. I started to teach the villagers how to dance. We told jokes and drank beer. Food might have been scarce, but someone always got hold of alcohol.

My mother had made contact with one of my father's superiors, a major who was now working for the police in Lüneburg. He had always been fond of my mother, perhaps more than fond. I remembered now the times he came to Brückendorf in East Prussia. Allegedly for inspection tours, but they always ended in parties. He came to visit us in a police car and offered to take me to Wiezendorf, near Celle, which became later quite infamous when we heard there had been a concentration camp there.

My schoolfriend, Irmgard, had been living there since the end of the war, and it was lovely to meet her again. She later married an American and went to live in Mexico. A few years later, her husband died of cancer and she eventually returned to Lübeck. She ran a convalescent home for a while as a matron. She is now retired, still living in Lübeck, and I hope still alive, although she is not well.

Her mother and brother had also made it and they were staying together in Soltau. However, her mother was in hospital and Irmgard and I went to visit her.

Six weeks had passed since Harold left and I had not heard from him, so I wrote him off. One day, he reappeared on the doorstep, but I was really cross and would not let him in. I told him to get lost, we argued, I was stubborn and we parted. What an idiot I was! I found out later that he had written letters via Len, who never delivered them. After Harold left for good, Len told me he had done this because he was in love with me and wanted me for himself. Well, it was too late. Harold had asked for a transfer, and I never saw him again.

I decided to visit Peter's parents in Peine, near Hannover. On the way there, I got into conversation with a woman going in the same direction. When I told her who I was going to visit, she said she knew them and unless I was a good Catholic, I should forget about it.

As mentioned earlier, I was born a Catholic, but never really religious. I saw people going to church when I was at school who I thought were the biggest sinners and were forgiven every time. I had to go to church when we spent the school holidays with my grandparents in Allenstein, together with my two cousins who had joined the Hitler Youth. They didn't have any option and had to join, but I think they enjoyed it – probably proud to wear a uniform. We went to church, but not with my grandparents, who attended an earlier mass. My cousins refused to come in, they said they would be laughed at by other boys. Obviously, Hitler did not think much of religion.

I was delegated to go inside and listen to the priest and tell them about it. I did not listen much either, doing a bid of daydreaming. I was good at that.

When we got home, my grandfather would want to know what the priest had preached. I told him, "Oh, he was talking about sinning."

My grandfather would say, "Yes, but what did he say about it?"

"Oh, he was against it," I said. Well, they were always talking about sin in church, so I felt pretty safe with my little white lie.

When Christmas came in Raven, my mother dragged us to church and said it was time for confession. Reluctantly we followed. After confession, Norbert told me he had timed us. My mother took half a minute, my brother two, but I took ten minutes.

I'd had an argument with the priest, who said I did not show real repentance for my sins. I replied that while I was telling him my sins, I had become doubtful. Where does the good stop and the sin start? What some may think is a sin, to others it is just a way of life. Was stealing the potatoes in Berlin a sin, when it was a necessity? He said he could not give me absolution due to my lack of repentance. He asked me to come and see him in the afternoon and talk things over with him in the privacy of his home. Obviously, I never went!

In the village most people were Protestants and when it came to jumping over the fence and "confiscating" some plums from the local pastor, they sent me. They thought, as I was a Catholic, it would not be a sin.

Anyway, back to Peine and Peter's parents. They did not have much to say, as they did not really know me. Peter's brother Rudolf was quite nice to me, but not his sister Rosemarie. I left a couple of days later not very impressed, nor did I think they were with me. I think my opinion on religion was the main reason. In short, I have nothing against religion, I am just not a very good Catholic.

My mother's sister Eva and her husband, and Tante Lu came to visit. They were all living in the same little town, Lütjenburg, on the Baltic. It was wonderful to see them alive.

The day before New Year's Eve, the local villages had arranged for a gathering in the afternoon in Soderstorf. There was a long programme of events. I still have a copy. I see my mother had quite a few slots, with her singing and me accompanying her on the piano. I also played a couple of accordion solos. Other people recited poems.

We went to visit Hohwacht, and I saw my grandparents for the first time since the war had ended. They looked very old to me, yet they were only in their 60s.

13. Lüneburg (1946–1950)

On 22 March, I received a telegram from Peter saying he was back and asking if we could meet up in Peine at his parents' place. I was numb, as he had become a stranger to me, and I felt empty when I saw him. Too much time had passed and did not have much in common. But we gave it a try, as he was obviously still very much in love with me. After a few days in Peine, I took him back to Raven. The trains were very full as so many soldiers were coming back from prison camps and we had to stand on the platform. Others were riding on the roof or hanging on to railings, which were used by the conductors to get from compartment to compartment on these old-fashioned trains.

On 1 April I started work in Lüneburg. My mother's friend, the police major, had organized me a job with the police as a teleprinter typist. It was a very interesting job, especially at night (we worked in shifts). We had to record all the incoming telexes: fascinating stuff, all about burglary etc., and all first-hand at the moment they were happening.

My boss had also organized accommodation for me in a tiny attic room in the Grapengiesserstrasse. When I say tiny, I mean tiny. It was about 3x2 metres and half of that was taken up by a slanting roof.

There was a bed with a small bedside table, on the other wall a small wardrobe and next to that a washstand with a washbasin and water jug. There was not much accommodation around with all the refugees, and so many houses having been bombed out.

Peter came to visit and we went to my mother in Raven for the weekend. They got on with each other much better than I did with Peter. He used to sit and just stare at me for hours. I left him with my mother while I went to work. A couple of days later, he visited me in my new room in Lüneburg. My landlady refused to let him in until I said he was my fiancé, but at ten o'clock at night she knocked on the door, saying, "The gentleman has to leave now." He went back to Peine and I went on with my life.

I was still very partial to the cinema. There were only two in town, and I think I saw nearly every film. My favourites were Heinz Rühmann in the funnies and Marika Rökk in the variety films – she was a wonderful dancer. I also liked Zarah Leander with her beautiful deep voice. She used to sing *Lili Marleen*, which was apparently popular all over the world.

In the cinema I once met a young chap, very naive I thought, but we had great conversations and used to walk in the park. I saw him on and off for a year. I met him again, much later, and he said he had been in love with me, but had put me on a "high pedestal" and thought I was untouchable. Silly boy!

Peter continued to visit, from time to time, and things were a little better between us, but he started talking about marriage, and I was not ready for that.

On 5 June 1946 my grandmother died of a heart attack. She had been washing the dishes singing happily (as she always did), keeled over and was dead. Not a bad way to go!

My grandfather was inconsolable. He was good at fixing things, but had no clue otherwise. I do not think he could make a cup of coffee. The day of the funeral, he was running around in circles shouting for his wife for his shirt, which she had laid out for him every day together with his other clothes.

I quarrelled with Peter and we did not see each other for a while. My life was fine without him.

I was still friends with Paula, and she had two tickets to go on holiday to a place along the Rhine. I enjoyed my work, but the temptress talked me into it and I requested for a few days' leave. They said I had not been with them long enough (four months), so I simply walked out. How things might have changed if I had stayed there. I might have met a nice policeman and settled down with him.

We took the train to Cologne, a steamer to Bonn and a tram to Bad Godesberg. Paula had arranged to meet her boyfriend (the one she had snatched from me in Berlin) and he brought along Werner, who said he was a former SS officer. I do not know if this was true, but he showed me a picture of himself in uniform. If he really had been an SS officer, how come he was not locked up?

He was a good organizer, though. We had a great time travelling along the Rhine, visiting Bonn and Cologne. It was all so wonderful. Werner started courting me, but Paula's boyfriend said I should be careful, he was not what he seemed to be. Once we could not find our ration cards and suspected him. He spoke about love and marriage, but I just could not take to him and found him rather distasteful. We went back home two weeks later and I lost track of him. (Sometime later I heard that he had been jailed as a marriage swindler.)

Another day, I met a British soldier on horseback in the park. As mentioned before, I was crazy about horses. When I was little, I would stand in the street and if a farmer came by with a horse and cart, ask for a ride to the next corner. Anyway, this soldier on horseback must have seen my admiring glances, and probably thought they were meant for him – whereas I was just seeing his horse. We started talking about horses, and got on so well over this subject that we decided to meet the next day in town. I was over the moon when he told me to bring along something suitable for riding, and the next day he brought another horse for me. I did not even wear trousers in those days but found a training suit and boots and off we went. Galloping in the wind, what ecstasy! We went riding a couple of times.

Riding, c. 1946

On one occasion, there was a crowd of riders galloping on a special galloping strip. Halfway along, the route crossed a road and all the horses turned left sharply, apparently to their riding stable. Just about everyone tumbled off and I landed sitting on the neck of my horse. What fun!

As seemed to happen with most of my acquaintances, who came and went, the soldier was soon transferred.

On 4 September, I took the train to Hamburg, about 50 kilometres away. There was a fête on and I again visited a fortune teller. She told me my "king of hearts" would leave me and I would meet a British soldier. It would be a quick engagement, with the marriage straight after. As it turned out, this happened to come true.

I was living on my savings and it was time to look for a job. The labour exchange informed me that the only job they had on offer was working in a sawmill.

I pictured myself carrying planks around and quickly declined. However, German efficiency was working again and they said I had to take the job, whether I liked it or not. I told them I couldn't do the job for medical reasons. I found a doctor who agreed with me that my talents were wasted in a sawmill and he signed me off for six weeks.

Peter came to see me and I said "goodbye" for good. He was very sad. We had nothing much in common, except our poetic love letters, and that time was over.

Werner from our Rhine tour wrote and said he would be in jail for the next few years, but he had not forgotten me and still loved me. I just laughed.

My mother had made friends with a travelling tour in Raven and they invited us to accompany them on a tour through the mountainous Harz area. They organized us a travel permit as artists, although we did not take part in their performances. I liked seeing places and we just went along for the ride, having a good time. German bureaucracy too was working again, or perhaps it was governed by the occupational forces: if you stayed longer than two days at one place you had to report that to the authorities, so to get about unhindered, an artist had to have a special pass. The Harz was very picturesque and we had an enjoyable trip.

A couple of months later, I had to report to the labour exchange as they had found alternative work for me. I had noted on my resume that I could type, and there was a job going with a British quartering office in Lüneburg. They asked me if I spoke English and I had replied "some".

Luckily, I had the whole weekend to prepare for my interview, and I spent the entire time with a dictionary in hand. My English was pretty frugal and I only managed to put together a few phrases they might ask me and my replies. For example, "How old are you? Where have you worked before and for how long?" My sentences were, of course, completely out of context, when I look back, but somehow I managed to secure the job. They said my English was not very good, but they would give me a trial of fourteen days. This was 9 December 1946.

The next two weeks I spent most of the time at my desk with a dictionary. I had to type letters from my superiors which were handwritten, and even if I had been fluent in English, I found that most of the time the words were indecipherable. I kept asking the British girls for help, but they were not very helpful, and said they could not read them themselves, so it was back to the dictionary. My typing was not too bad, but naturally I made a few mistakes, which my bosses merely corrected and I retyped them. After fourteen days I was on the permanent force!

The heads of the various departments were all officers and very friendly. The head boss, Major Thomas, had his own secretary. At the Christmas party a few days later, he asked me if I had a boyfriend. It looked like the beginning of something, but his secretary became suspicious and did not let me out of her sight. She even accompanied me home.

Major Geoff Thomas

Within a few days, Major Thomas sent his secretary on an errand and called me to his office. He had two tickets for the theatre that weekend, but I had made other plans and declined his offer.

As everyone was so friendly, I approached one of the officers, who was in charge of confiscating and allocating German quarters and told him about my small accommodation. I let him know that it was now winter and I had no means to heat my room as there was nowhere to place a stove. There were no electrical stoves around in those days. He said he could not understand this as his room was very warm (central heating, of course). I said to him, "You should sleep one night in my bed and see how cold it is."

Well, you can imagine the answer. "If I were sleeping in your bed we both would be warm." Blushing all over I fled the office.

However, that conversation must have helped, as they were soon investigating. It turned out that my landlady had given me the wrong room. The one that had been confiscated by the British military government was the one opposite and was more than twice the size. It also had a slanting roof, but was much more comfortable.

I still did not have a stove, and one night when I was cold, after shivering for three hours, I suddenly felt very warm and found myself floating on the ceiling, looking down at my body. I thought that was it, my time was over and started to scream. My landlady came in, and all she could say was that she hoped she would not have any trouble with my corpse – what a dragon she was. Nevertheless, she returned with a hot water bottle and a few days later my stove was installed. However, my landlady was cross because she had been found out for giving me the wrong room, and said to me, "You refugees get all the privileges. In future, you can clean the kitchen floor, passage and stairwell once a week." No problem. I employed a girl to come and do it every Friday, and do my room at the same time. You see, I was always lazy. I kept things tidy, but do not look under the carpet!

Major Thomas came into my office one day to ask me something, and discreetly dropped a note on my desk asking if I would go to the theatre with him. Well, I agreed gladly but for some reason the performance was cancelled and Major Thomas, Geoff, offered to drive me instead to my mother's place in Raven for the weekend. I accepted, but was trembling all the way. Geoff was very formal on the journey, perhaps because of the driver, but it did not look like a good start to me. He did not even come into the house to meet my mother, just dropped me off.

Geoff Thomas looked quite aristocratic, and so was his behaviour. But I was impressed, most likely because of his uniform! He was a feather in my cap, being the big boss, and I had heard that he was not married. We started dating on the quiet, although in the office we were very formal. I once heard one of the other officers saying that German girls were easy. In those days, a mixed relationship between a German and a foreigner was frowned upon – not only by the British but by the German people as well. Today, nobody worries about this.

We went mostly to the theatre, with performances in English. They once had a British comedian on the stage and I could not understand what everyone was laughing about. I do remember, however, one joke. The comedian said, "When someone told a dirty joke on stage, only the men laughed; the women walked out, to the cloakroom, to write down the joke."

Weekends were spent mostly driving to Raven, and Geoff got on well with my mother. Once we got stuck in the snow, about six kilometres from our village, and had to spend the night at an inn. We did not even make it to Raven, and the next day we went back to Lüneburg.

We had been going out for a few weeks when he had to go on a business trip to Denmark. It was then that he told me I must wait for him, that he loved me and would look after me. He also said I was the only girl for him.

A few months later, he told his family he wanted to marry me, but they were disgusted with the idea. From what they had heard, I was not sophisticated enough, did not take anything seriously and giggled too much. Well, I didn't know about that at the time, and we continued dating; although he tried to encourage me to become more serious. We argued over that, but soon made up. I think it was nice to have a blow out from time to time, as the making up was worth it.

But then, after a couple of months, he stated that he did not like my background. I felt humiliated, got really angry, and broke up with him. He soon asked for a transfer and that was that.

By then I had had enough of the Quartering Office and started looking for other employment. The labour exchange offered me a job at the Malcolm Club, at the airport, as an interpreter/supervisor, which ran over two shifts – one from 8 a.m. to 2 p.m. and the other from 2 p.m. to 8 p.m. It was a two-kilometre walk, but that was no problem. It sounded good, so I accepted. Unfortunately, the club was run by women officers and not as easy going as the previous job.

Still, there was never a dull moment with all the airmen walking past my office and fussing over me. I had a disagreement once with one of my female bosses, who forbade me to talk to airmen. The airmen took no notice, of course, and she gave up in the end.

It was an easy job. I had to supervise my shift and make sure all was clean etc. But they were all older than me and more experienced, and one once told me to get the duster and do the work myself. I gave up eventually and told the one female officer that I was too young for the job. She offered me a position as a secretary/interpreter with office hours, but that was much later.

I plodded along as best as I could. I had to close my eyes to the stealing that went on. They all had family at home, and to their way of thinking they felt it was like taking from the enemy. I did not need food, I had my meals with both shifts, and there was a bakery in the basement with delicious cakes. To get the contraband through the gate, they used to tie food in sacks and carry them on a string between their legs after the evening shift. If there was a control at the gate, the next day one would find a lot of goodies spread out amongst the bushes by the gate.

Just to show them that they had nothing to fear from me, I took some butter home. It was a piece as big as a small egg, which I lodged in my brassiere. By the time I got through the gate I was already sweating, and when I arrived home the butter had melted and reached my legs. That was the first and last time, but I had made my point and I was now one of them. After that they invited me to all the gatherings they had from time to time. These almost always resulted in parties and I was becoming popular, especially when I got the accordion out.

The war had been over for two years and everyone was trying to make up for the "lost" years and have a good time. I made a lot of friends in those days. From time to time, dances were arranged by the Air Force and I was never short of partners. The trouble was that every time I saw a new face I thought: *This might be the man for me.* I think one always wants what one cannot have and I always lost interest in the ones that chased me.

By then, I had not seen Geoff for a couple of months, but he showed up again, saying he could not get me out of his mind. I sort of made up with him. After that we became really good friends and I saw more of him than before, although he had a long way to come by train from Hannover. This went on for over a year but did not stop me from going out with other chaps. Once, I arranged with some of them to meet me outside the town hall; there were three of them. My girlfriend and I peeped round the corner and we laughed our heads off. Of course, I got it in the neck the next day (from three sides) but I made some excuses.

During the holidays, I went to visit my relatives at the seaside near Lübeck. My aunt, Tante Eva, who was the most attractive of my mother's sisters, had got divorced and was in the process of marrying again. They ran a guest house at the coast, and there was always something going on.

As we had never heard from my father again, my mother moved on with her life and found herself a boyfriend, becoming engaged. He was of Polish origin and his name was Paul. A nice bloke, he had a sister and my mother got on with her very well. So well, in fact, that later on, when Paul had died, she made my mother beneficiary of a lovely flat in Lüneburg. Paul's sister also passed away, and my mother moved into her flat; but more about that later.

Norbert got a job in Lüneburg and stayed with me for a while. He worked as a sales rep for a porcelain shop, and used to drive around with his glass and porcelain samples, selling to shops only. After a week, he showed me a hole in his socks and asked me to mend it. I looked at it and said it was small and not worth mending. After a couple of weeks, he showed me his socks again and the hole was so big it was past repair. That is typical of me. I am not really lazy, but find that type of work very boring.

I was good at school and in my jobs, and I also loved gardening. Wait a minute, that is wrong... I do not love gardening, I love the garden. I like to plan and organize the plants, shift them around and go into the garden a few times a day to admire them. I do not mind planting them and digging a hole here and there, but not weeding, that is far too dull. When I once told my husband I had worked hard in the garden that day, he replied that it must have been a pleasure, because if it had been work, I would not have done it. True, true.

In later years I was lucky to be in the position to have a servant, but on the few occasions when I was in between servants and tried my luck with doing the laundry, my son enquired why I even bothered to wash his trousers, as they were just as dirty as before. My husband also asked if it might not be better to iron his shirts before putting them on hangers (I did not know how to fold them). When I told him they were already ironed he gave up on me.

14. Will

In March 1947, I met a British sergeant at the clubhouse who played the trumpet in a band at functions. They were practising in the big lounge, which I could see from my office cubbyhole. There was a piano, which I tinkered on from time to time, and someone told him I played, so he asked if I would like to join the band. I said I knew nothing about reading orchestra music, but he brought me a sheet anyway. They tried me out on the piano, but I did not understand the "shortcuts" on the sheet music. It only showed the parts I had to play, and I got completely lost. Needless to say, they gave up on me. Obviously, I was not up to scratch.

A couple of months later, I met this sergeant in town after having been stood up by a date (my turn for a change). We found ourselves looking into the same window of a photographic shop and started talking, and ended up in a restaurant. His name was Johnstone and he was called Johnny for short, although his name was William[24].

Will was different from any person I had met before – they were more casual – and he asked me for a date the next day, the next day and the next day. I had only known him a few days when he asked me to marry him. I thought he was insane, yet I was intrigued. I had lots of friends to fool around with, but nobody would take me seriously, so this was different. I told him that the idea was ridiculous. But he was very insistent.

---

[24] To avoid confusion with Ursula's second husband – also known as Johnny – we have standardized on 'Will' for her first husband, which she also used later on

We were dating nearly every day and decided to take up ballroom dancing. We were a great couple on the dance floor, and I became used to seeing him daily. If I did not see him, naturally I began to miss him. A month later he took leave and we went for a week to Sylt, an island in the North Sea. I really enjoyed it, even if it was illegal, as he was not supposed to take any Germans with him. I think he made out I was his wife. We got away with it for a while but one day we were caught out and had to leave the British canteen. We thought it was rather fun but did not want to tempt fate, and left two days later to go home to Lüneburg.

With Will in Berlin

Once I did not see Will for four days, and imagined that this was the end of it, but he soon showed up, saying he had been sick in hospital. He did not tell me why. Shortly after this, I also fell sick and went to hospital for a few days; some bug he had passed on to me.

After that, we went to Hamburg on a shopping trip. There was a shop for British married people only, we bluffed our way in and I got a beautiful coat and items one could not find in the German shops as yet.

20 June 1948 was the day of *Währungsreform*, the overnight shift from the old *Reichsmark* currency to the new *Deutsche Mark*. We got ten *Deutsche Mark* for every one hundred *Reichsmark*, but everyone also got DM 50 free to start with. My

savings, which I started when I was ten, had accumulated to RM 1000, but now I had to start from scratch again with DM 100.

My grandfather, who had two blocks of flats in East Prussia, was eventually compensated at 10% of the value. Still, it was better than nothing, and he gave all his children a share. My mother later invested the money in a house in Lüneburg together with my brother. But at this time, of course, she was still living on the farm in Raven.

Will, Dec 1949

Back to Lüneburg. Once the money changed, our lifestyle also changed. It was amazing what had happened overnight to the shops on this day. There had been nothing before only the bare essentials, now we could get anything, especially in the food sections. Before that, the black market had been thriving. Will got cigarettes at the NAAFI shop. We did not smoke, so we flogged them on the black market for food or other items. We also swapped liqueur, and the names of Curaçao and Benedictine spring to my mind.

In November 1948 Will bought an enlarger, and we started to develop our own films in my little attic room. We became quite good at it. After that there followed a procession of other apparatus, daytime developing boxes, copiers etc. – items many in the 21st century will have never heard of.

I got a bit tired of the long trek to work and looked for a new job, which I found with the 21st Quartering Office not too far from my room. It was as a clerk/typist and I thoroughly enjoyed it.

At that time Will started taking frequent trips to Hamburg. "On duty," he said. We were supposed to go to my mother in Raven for Christmas. He was again in Hamburg that day and I waited for him at the station. He was late and pitched up very dishevelled, saying he had been in an accident. As it was late, we could only leave to visit my mother the next day.

However, Will kept on staying away for long periods at a time and it was really getting too much when he pitched up late for my birthday on 27 February. He brought a bottle of liqueur and said he was on duty, and would try to come by later. Norbert, my mother and her boyfriend were visiting so we carried on without him, but he never arrived. When it got to the evening, I decided to phone the Sergeants' Mess and ask for him, explaining he was on duty. The chap on the phone laughed and said that the kind of "duty" Will was on, he would not mind doing himself. Ha! Something smelt fishy.

I knew he had been friendly with one of my female friends and decided to check at her place. I called Norbert for support and we got to this "friend's" place. There was nobody at home. It started raining and we stopped at a cinema that was showing *"When Johnny Comes Marching Home"*. I decided to hang around as the performance was just about to end.

Lo and behold, there comes my "Johnny" with a woman on his arm, a woman I did not know. I was so upset, Norbert lit a cigarette for me. I did not smoke but I puffed it anyhow. We followed them at a distance and the two of them vanished into a hotel.

I went home in tears, and now things became clear to me. The frequent visits to Hamburg… I also remembered once when he was away on "duty" he had asked me to develop a film for him. I got the pictures out and found a couple of a woman in bed with his pyjamas on. The next morning I was cried out and just furious.

When he showed up in the afternoon, I greeted him as in my usual way and then said to him, "If you have to be unfaithful, why did you not go to Hamburg instead of doing it in the same city?"

He said, "You do not love me, otherwise you would have boxed my ears." So I did!

He was wonderful at excuses. This was a woman from his past who had come all the way from Berlin to look him up.

I do not know why I always forgave him. Perhaps with my past, the Russians for instance, I considered myself as damaged goods that nobody would ever take seriously. Times were bad and I was probably looking for a loophole to get out of my current situation. He assured me that he fully intended to marry me and had applied to the British military government for permission.

A couple of months later, he started making trips to Hamburg again, telling me about his duties in the Sergeants' Mess. When I phoned the mess, the chap on the phone asked if I was the girl from Berlin. Oh no, not again! As usual, he was full of excuses and I just did not want to face the truth. So it went on, but I must say that for him, looking back, when he bought cake, he gave me first choice before taking the rest for those on "duty".

It went on for a few months until he was transferred to Wunstorf, a small town near Hannover. After that he visited me nearly every weekend, but otherwise I could not check up on his activities.

In the meantime, I carried on in the office. I still liked my job and got a promotion. In January 1950, Will turned up with a terrier on a leash. He said it was a puppy, eight months old, and a male. When we took him to the park this dog was always squatting and only later did I find out it was a bitch. I did not know much about these things in those days.

We called her Terry. My landlady complained, the dog must go, but we said it was only for a few days. Well, the few days went into weeks, then months and eventually she gave up asking.

I took Terry to work every day and hid her in the side door of my desk. Lunchtimes I took her to a park opposite our offices. I sat on the bench, munching my sandwiches, and we had a great time. I had her well-trained in no time. Whenever I took her to the shop, I told her to sit outside the door and she never left, except once when I took a bit longer, long enough for someone to pick her up and take her to the RSPCA, where I soon found her. She used to follow me on two legs in the street, sniffing at my groceries, and people just stared.

Over the weekends, I often took her home to my mother on the bus. However, bus drivers were not always keen on dogs and I let her sneak in and hide under my seat. It was about a twenty-kilometre ride and about six bus stops. On one occasion, when I went to get off and called for Terry, she was gone; she must have got off somehow before. There was no bus going back till Monday, and I could do nothing about it. Naturally, I was very upset and could not wait for Monday.

On the way back, I stepped out of the bus and asked people if they had seen a black and white fox terrier. Nothing, until the last stop before town, when, would you believe it, she was waiting by the bus stop trying to get on. I heard from people nearby that they had found her by the bus stop waiting all weekend. They took her home but she ran straight back, so they fed her at the bus stop.

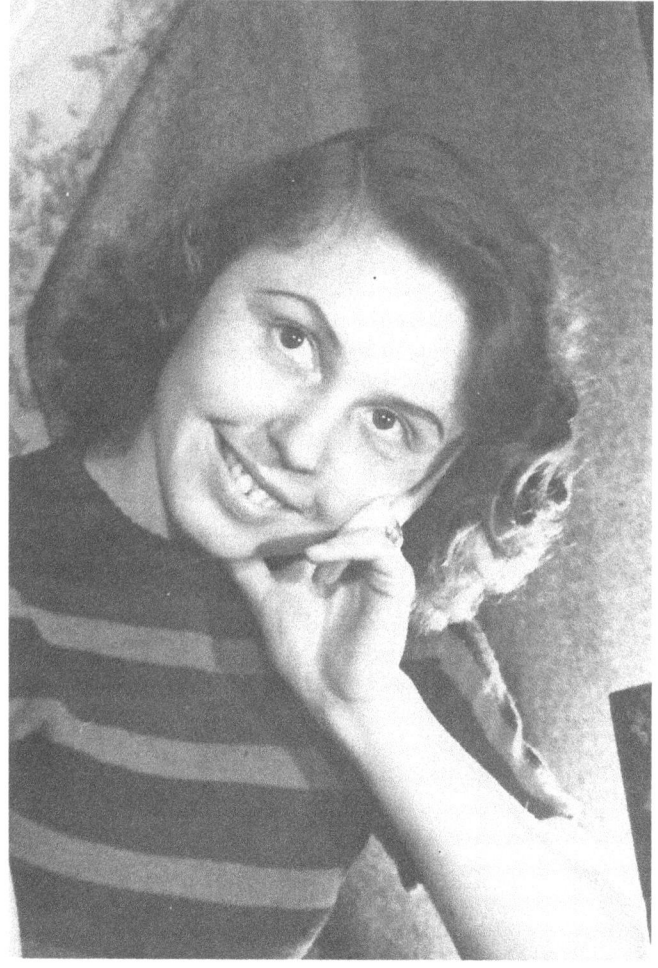

Portrait by Will

What a wonderful reunion that was. I made sure she was on a tight leash at all times from then on. I sometimes might refer to her as a "he" instead of a "her". This is because in Germany all dogs or bitches are called "he", but he was definitely a she. One day I came home and found her on the bed with three pups. You should have seen the mess. After that, I gave her to my mother on the farm and she was very spoilt there.

Since the day that I had discovered Will, a.k.a. Johnny coming out of a cinema showing *"When Johnny Comes Marching Home"*, I had refused to call him by that name. As his full name was William, I called him Will from that time onwards.

I found out that he had been in Berlin again. I had my suspicions when I took him to the station in Lüneburg. He said he had a military pass to do a job on an aeroplane in Cologne. When I wanted to see the pass, he waved something in front of my nose and said he had to go. When he presented his ticket at the control entrance, I tried to look at it, but he kept it slightly folded, and the controller got a bit impatient with him. Well, the strange thing was that the train he got on went in the opposite direction to where he was supposed to go, and Will said he was taking a local train to a bigger station and then a fast train to Cologne.

Something was off, and I phoned his superiors to find out that he was not on a duty trip but had taken leave for a few days. When he came back, we had a big row and I did not see him for a while.

My ex-fiancé Peter turned up, saying he could not forget me, but I was not interested. What is it about me? As I mentioned before, what I can get I do not want and instead go after the ones that play hard to get. It must be the challenge.

Maybe that is why I did not give up on Will. I somehow thought I could change him; after all he was very good at assuring me of his love and we were engaged.

15. Hamburg (1950–1953)

Our quartering office had dissolved and I lost my job. It was not long, however, before I was contacted by the 30th Quartering Office in Hamburg and they offered me a position there. Later, they would also provide me with accommodation. In the meantime, it meant travelling 50 kilometres by train from Lüneburg. But I accepted and on 1 April 1950 I started my new job.

Hamburg could have been a lovely town, but the war damage was still in evidence. Nevertheless, it was great for shopping. Walking along the River Alster and sitting down by the water was also a nice experience.

Will was transferred to England, but the letters kept rolling in. Pages and pages of them, full of love.

On 2 June I received a ticket from Will to travel to London, but obtaining a visa was another matter. I kept going to the Visa Office and they asked a thousand questions, then I had to bide my time. I kept trying to chase them, but was always told to wait. On 1 July, the day came for my departure, but I had to forget about it. A week later, Will came on three weeks' leave and we had a great time.

With Will, 1951

In fact, we had had too much of a good time... as two months later I missed my monthly period. I thought of doing something about it, but Will was so pleased. He said by October he would have all the papers together to marry me.

I decided to go through with the pregnancy. I must say, my mother was very supportive and even said I did not have to get married: she would still give me all her assistance and support. Shortly afterwards, I was told that the Visa Office had finally refused my visa as Will was still married. Oh, my God! What next?

Will returned to Lüneburg on short leave straightaway and assured me he had had no contact with his wife for years and the divorce should go through in October.

Ah well, in for a penny, in for a pound. Next thing I heard, the divorce would only become finalized the following year. But Will was really concerned about the coming baby and I only hoped that I would make it before getting married.

At the beginning of December, my grandfather died from pneumonia. My mother went to the funeral near Lübeck and met his fiancée, with whom he had been staying. He was then 72, and his fiancée revealed that she had been married twice before, but never had such an ardent lover as my grandfather.

My grandfather had always been good-looking, especially as he had such lovely thick hair and it was hardly grey even at his age. After my grandmother died, he was lonely and had answered adverts to find a companion. He told us once that he was on his way to meet his blind date at the station, with a carnation in his buttonhole. He said, to be on the safe side, he kept his carnation hidden in order to get a good look first before agreeing to meet her. She seemed OK, but as he was very outspoken, he circled and then said to her, "You looked much better on the photo you sent me and I bet you've got false teeth too." He was such a character.

Once, when my grandfather visited us, a woman of about 40 came past and we told him she was single. He glanced over his glasses and said he did not like her legs – and him being nearly 70!

Christmas came and Will arrived on a short visit, but there was still no sign of divorce. In January the divorce came through, but it took another six weeks to become final.

He reapplied for permission to marry me, and then the fun really started. His side was now OK but on my side the questions never stopped. They asked for my birth certificate, but I had lost mine, or rather it had been left behind in East Prussia, and there was no connection with the region any more. Eventually they accepted the German pass from my Duty Year, along with a photo and an important looking stamp from the German authorities. But I still had to get a health certificate and a certificate from the police to say I had no previous criminal record.

All this took time and wait, wait, wait. But on 13 April 1951, we got married in front of the registrar. It was when they asked, "Are you so-and-so, born on such a date," that Will looked at me sheepishly. I pricked up my ears – what was this? He was ten years older than he had always told me, which made it a twenty-year age difference altogether. After the ceremony, he asked if I was now sorry I had married him. I gave up. I had other worries – it was only a few weeks to go until the next event.

We were still living in the small room of mine in Lüneburg, when I felt the first pains. Will was hopping around and eventually called in the army doctor. They came straightaway with an ambulance and ferried me to the military hospital in Hamburg. After all, I was now British.

The pains came and went, nothing serious, and I thought it would be a piece of cake. Is that all? But at 10 o'clock at night it got serious. I felt like screaming and the nurse said there was no problem as I was the only one on the entire floor, so I really let go. Later, when they moved me upstairs, the other patients told me they had not got much sleep that night due to the screeching of some annoying woman downstairs.

By 10 o'clock the next morning, they decided to give me an anaesthetic and get the baby out with forceps. It was wonderful to fall asleep and wake up when it was all over. Thus my son Ronald was born. I felt them laying something soft against my cheeks, and the sister said, "Mrs Johnstone, you have got a son."

I could not see him for a couple of days as my face was swollen, keeping my lids shut. They gave my baby to me to breastfeed him, but he tried and kept on crying. It was a few hours later when a nurse came and got him to suckle. Now I felt the difference in his suction; before he had only been licking. I would have thought babies should be able to find that out by themselves, but there was a knack to it. He was always hungry, and when we left the hospital twelve days later, the nurses said they were glad to get rid of this cry-baby. To keep him quiet they had continued to feed him just about every hour, and he gave me a lot of trouble at night as he was then so spoilt.

I suppose it is not unusual to have sleepless nights for the first weeks after a baby is born. It was four weeks until I got him to sleep at least through half the night. After two months I thought he was smiling, but someone said it was only indigestion, however, two months later he was genuinely laughing.

I had put on twenty pounds and my breasts would have given any cow competition. I stopped breastfeeding soon thereafter and weaned Ronnie onto a bottle. I thought that we deserved a holiday, and as my mother was quite capable, we left Ronnie in her care.

We went to the Alps. It was wonderful. The mountains, the lakes and the castles, like Schloss Neuschwanstein and Schloss Linderhof. I had never seen such opulence before. We went to the Italian border, where I placed a foot across it to say I had been in Italy. There were Tirolean evenings with yodelling etc. All very *gemütlich*.

Thereafter, we must have developed an appetite for travelling and kept on going on numerous trips. They were very inexpensive. One trip was along the Rhine from Heidelberg to Paris for the weekend, but the one I remember most was to Italy. (By the way, I stopped keeping a diary when I got married and have to rely on my memories from this point on, so might not always get things in the right order.)

Before we went to Italy, I had learnt a few phrases like "*quanto costa*" (how much does it cost?). However, we soon found out that everyone we met in Italy spoke German or English.

We were on an organized trip and when we arrived by train in Milan, we were split up into three groups to occupy various hotels – ours was a nunnery. We had pasta for lunch and supper. The first time it was served, I thought it was full of dirt and tried to navigate all the black bits to the outside of the plate. However, the people at the table told me they were herbs and spices. As far as I was concerned, pepper and salt were the only spices for me. To this day, I do not understand why people always have to put so many spices in food. I like to taste what I am eating, not just the spices. Every meal was accompanied by Chianti wine, and I think the afternoons in Italy were always a bit hazy for me.

The next morning, we just had a roll with butter and jam for breakfast, and assumed this was because it was a nunnery. But when our groups came together, one group complained they'd had a dry roll and jam, whereas the other group only had a dry roll. And they were in proper hotels, so we were still lucky with our fare.

We went to Venice and then to Rome. We did a bus tour around the city and the driver said, "See this old Italian building? It has been standing here for years, and do you notice that block of flats over there? It was built five years ago and already falling to pieces." Never was a truer word spoken.

Will did not join the tour in Naples as he had some trouble with his visa and had to visit the consulate in Rome. I did the tour and was appalled by the conditions in some of the Italian quarters we passed by on the bus through Naples. There was one-roomed accommodation that one could look right into. It was hot and all the doors were open. We saw people sitting on boxes. The flies had a busy time.

I really fancied Capri and the boat trip into the Blue Grotto, where we had to wait for the waves to recede and duck to get through the entrance hole of the grotto, which was as blue as we'd hoped.

At the quayside in Naples, we were inundated with poor students selling watches cheap, 'real gold inherited from their grandfather'. We were not that dumb. However, when we got back to Rome and sat down for super with our fellow travellers, Will turned up proudly showing one of these watches he had just purchased, I told him to hide it quickly to save embarrassment.

We bought a lot of Chianti to take home, but shortly before the border they came round and told us only two bottles each were allowed. Well, I tell you, everyone was sloshed by the time we crossed the border. It was a pity to throw the wine away, so everyone drank as much as possible.

Back in Lüneburg, Norbert had now his own place, and my mother had moved in with us, so it was a relief when Will was transferred to Wunstorf and we got a two-bedroom flat from the Air Force. Even Terry our dog joined us, and it was great to have a room for Ronnie. I straightaway got a German maid; you will recall my opinion of housework.

Christel and Norbert, 1952

Ronnie was only a few months old when I found myself pregnant again. I was not too happy with the timing, still having one in nappies, but *c'est la vie*.

The new baby was due in May and we were getting ready. A couple of months before that, Will was up to his tricks again, duty trips etc. When I told one of my new friends, another Air Force wife, about his trip, she suggested that I should go and pick up his mail at the Sergeants' Mess, as everyone had been talking about his numerous letters. I would not dare, so she went and brought back six letters. Well, I had no aversion to opening them. Two were junk mail, one was from a woman who thanked him for answering her marriage advert, but she was already fixed up. Another one was from a woman in Frankfurt who was looking forward to meeting him there at the end of the month, around the time I was due to give birth, and one was from a woman in the UK who was worried about her monthly after his last visit. The best one was from a woman in Lüneburg who said she had to shower every morning as she was so hot for him, and how she was looking forward to having his blond, blue-eyed children.

Something died inside me. There was no address on the Lüneburg one and when I told my mother about these letters, she suggested not to say anything but to find out more about this woman.

So I kept quiet, and the next week he suggested it might be a good idea to fetch the crib for the new baby from Lüneburg and offered to go. He went by train and I phoned Norbert, who followed him from the station at a good distance right to a block of flats in town, which he entered. I jumped onto the next train and, together with Ronnie, made for the flats.

We did not know her address, but knew her name: Helen. Norbert stayed outside and I went to the first flat on the ground floor. When I rang the bell, an elderly woman opened the door on the chain and asked if she could help me. I asked if Helen lived here and she enquired what I wanted with her daughter who had, she said, gone for a walk with her fiancé. She would not let me in until I told her my name was Mrs Johnstone. That opened not only her eyes but also the door.

She started crying and told me that she had treated Will like a son-in-law. Well, a short time later my "beloved" Will came in, whereupon his future "bride" was yanked into the kitchen by her mother. I could not say he was shocked to see me. Astounded rather, and annoyed perhaps, asking me what I was doing there.

Before I could say anything, his "fiancée" came in, full of tears. Will went to her, put his arms around her and told her he only loved her. He said, "Look at that woman over there!" (referring to me, of course,) "How could anybody love that! She has no figure and I am sick and tired of the same old dress she has been wearing for the last few weeks."

He was talking about me, a woman nine-months pregnant with his child. That seemed to put a new slant on the conversation as Helen soon got stuck into him, saying, "You wanted to marry me and produce your children, and then one day when I look like her, you would throw me away? If you do not shut up and leave immediately, I shall report you to your superiors for breach of promise." Good for her, she certainly had more spirit than me.

So he left and meekly I followed, as if it had been me who was the guilty one. We went home by train, not talking to each other. But on the train, he turned to me and said, "I am glad you came; she was getting too insistent with her demands to marry her." When we got home, he said something to the effect that he still loved me, and I became hysterical. I started screaming, loud enough for the neighbours to hear me. I heard later they had said that it was no wonder the poor man went astray with a hysterical woman like that. Obviously, the odds are always stacked up against us females.

Sometimes I wonder if anybody can believe all these stories, but believe it or not they are true, and there is more to come.

On the last day of April 1952, during a shopping trip to Hannover, my waters broke while I was in the cloakroom. I was immediately loaded into an ambulance and taken to an army hospital in Rinteln, about twenty kilometres from Wunstorf.

This time it was easier. I had learnt all about how to cope with labour. Breathe in, breathe out, when the labour pain starts. I kept counting and told myself I shall endure it until the count of ten and then I was allowed to give in. When ten came I gave myself just one more number and so on. As a result, this birth was easier. We had arrived late in the evening and the sister had told me it would be a long night yet for me. But it was only a few hours after that when, shortly after midnight, "Evylyne" was born. I must say here she was stuck all her life with her name being misspelled. I think it was Will's fault, as he was the one who registered her and wrote the name as it was pronounced in Germany. We generally called her Eve.

Whereas Ronnie had been an eight pounder at birth, Eve just made it to seven. Well, she was a girl, after all.

This time I did not stay long in hospital and my mother kindly came to look after me. A while back, she had moved into another attic room, which at least had a separate kitchen, although both rooms were really small. There was no way I could leave Will and stay with her. Well, I thought, I had sworn to stick it out for better or for worse!

Maybe I was getting used to it, or better at it, but coping with the babies got a little easier. Oh yes, and there was still my maid. One day, however, when I was enjoying a longer rest due to what seemed to be an extended lunchtime nap, I went to investigate what was happening to find the wall and cot "decorated". I leave it to your imagination with what. My maid was off, and when I tried to clean up the mess I felt sick, so Will took over. I suppose he was good for something after all. When I told my mother, she said I had been no better, and had done the same thing to her when I was a baby, except that I had been more creative – as I was left in the kitchen, I had made a lovely mix with the ashes from the oven.

At Norbert's with Mother & her boyfriend Paul, and sister; Xmas 1952

My mother also told me that I was placid as a baby and very obedient as a norm. She used to go shopping and leave me sitting on the table with some paper and scissors in my hand and I would sit for nearly an hour patiently cutting out "pictures" from the paper. I suppose sitting on the table kept me from crawling around. Still, looking back on it, I do not think it was such a good idea. (Health and Safety these days would not be happy about this.) But in those days, there were different rules. It was not a crime to get your backside tanned from time to time and I was already sixteen or seventeen when I got my last hiding.

We stayed in Wunstorf for a couple of years. Once, when my mother was on another visit and Will was on another of his "duty tours", I checked with the Sergeants' Mess and a sergeant major told me Sergeant Johnstone was "on leave". But he knew very well what was going on, everyone knew, and he suggested I should return the favour to Will and have a party. I thought it was long overdue and my mother, who was always up for some fun, readily agreed. The sergeant major brought along a friend and some wine and we partied.

Will was supposed to come back the next day, and so there was plenty of time to clean up in the morning. Our guests left late and my mother and I went to bed. At about four in the morning, Will came home. He saw four empty glasses and the wine bottle, but he had so much trust in me (or my stupidity) he believed that we had staged the setting in order to pay him back and did not believe a party had really taken place.

I decided to try something else. The next day, I went to stay the night with a friend of mine across the street, who knew all about Will's affairs. I hoped Will would suffer. He came home from work and I peeked at him through the curtains. I noticed him coming out of the house and looking up and down the road, seeming very worried. He was extremely happy to see me back the next day. Served him right!

16. England (1953–1955)

A couple of years later, Will was transferred back to England to an RAF camp in Henlow, near Hitchen in Bedfordshire. We packed up for the big move. Luckily, I still have an old cancelled British passport and can see from the stamps that we crossed the border on 26 August 1953.

We had to stay in a transit camp, some distance away, until family accommodation became available at RAF Henlow. It was very primitive with wooden huts and when October came, it started getting really cold. Ronnie and Eve had a cot each, but Ronnie was in the habit of tossing off his blankets. Several times at night I got up to cover him again, but eventually I gave up. Obviously, he generated enough heat for himself.

Will came every weekend from Henlow. I do not remember the name of the transit camp, but it was not far from Carlisle, where Will's family lived. One weekend we went to visit them. Will warned me that his mother was very strict, and nobody was allowed to smoke. She must have liked me, as after a day she told me it was OK for me to smoke in the bathroom, not that I smoked in those days – that came later. We stayed a few days and I was well received by all. I do not remember how many there were, but there must have been quite a few siblings. They were in the habit of going to the pub every night for a couple of hours (TV was rare in those days), and it was fun. I lost track of them in later life. Will was not attached to his family.

A month before Christmas, Will organized accommodation in a caravan at his camp, and my first Christmas in the UK was spent there. A bit like gypsy life. We suffered the cold weather in the caravan for four months and then, at last, we got proper accommodation in the form of a flat in a terraced house surrounded by Air Force families. It was a typically British two up and two down flat with a sitting room and kitchen downstairs and two bedrooms upstairs. There was also a small garden at the back and a patch of ground at the front. I was not that crazy about gardening at that stage, and only a remember planting some tulips and irises.

Taking care of my family was keeping me busy – there were no maids here. But at least Will got his uniform and shirts done at the mess. There was still enough left to wash as there were no washing machines in those days only boilers and one had to make a fire to get that going.

Shopping was a bit of an ordeal too, just a café nearby selling odds and bits, but otherwise we had to take the bus to Bedford. Imagine getting on the bus with two tiny children. No conveniences for prams as yet. Ronnie was about two and Eve one year old. I had to lift one into the bus and then the other one. By that time, the first one would have fallen over and when I got myself onto the bus with the second, the bus did not wait for us to be seated, so we often landed somewhere along the passage. I could not understand why people did not come to our assistance. Did I smell like a German?

Even later, when we used to visit my mother with the children in Lüneburg, nobody helped. We had to change platforms in Hannover. The only way I could manage was to leave one child standing next to a suitcase while I walked with the other, then leaving that child hanging on to another suitcase while I returned to collect the first one along with the rest of the luggage. One day, I was dropping the luggage and turned back to fetch Ronnie, and he was already halfway there, dragging the heavy suitcase all by himself. Once in a while a soldier in uniform would help us get on the train, but the German people were just as bad.

Initially, I thought that British people were unfriendly because I was German, but in time they started thawing and things improved. We met up with another couple, where the wife was also German. My English was not perfect, but hers was worse. We had a good laugh when we walked through a park and she was saying, "There is a fresh wind coming from the backside!" She meant behind, of course, although "behind" had the same meaning.

I was really popular on the day of the coronation of Queen Elizabeth II as we had a small black and white TV. It must have been the only one around as we ended up with probably a dozen people watching. I missed a lot of the event as I was too busy serving tea.

Every long holiday I travelled to my mother with just my two kids, by train to Dover, then by ferry to Calais and train to Lüneburg via Hannover.

My mother was still living in two tiny rooms, but she found space for us somehow. My children never had many toys, as Will thought they were untidy. I gave them some building blocks, but one day when Will came home, these were lying on the floor, which he could not bear as it was too messy – so he threw them all into the fireplace. They also had a small toy dog, and when Will fell over it, both children got a hiding.

Will was terribly neat. In his wardrobe, one could take a ruler to the way he had piled up his clothes. It was seldom that I got a glimpse of his wardrobe as it was locked and he took the key with him.

The RAF laid on special transportation for outings to visit London, usually to the theatre. We went along a couple of times. We took in the shops along Oxford Street and did the usual rounds.

Originally, when we arrived in England for the first time, we took a taxi from one station to the next one. I was really scared as they were driving on the wrong side of the road – not the side I was used to riding in Germany – and I was just waiting for an accident to happen.

However, the best times I had was visiting Lüneburg. Will hardly ever came. It was lovely getting away from the constant nagging. It was on one of these visits that, out of the blue, Peter (remember my ex-fiancé?), turned up at the door. I had not had any contact with him since I got married and it was a big surprise. I never did find out how he found me, but I have a suspicion my mother contacted him. She was not happy about my marriage and was probably hoping that Peter and I would get together again.

He had not changed much, but I noticed his face was always red and he sprouted a sort of drinker's nose. He still loved me, of course, and had kept all my letters. Nevertheless, it was a change for me to be found desirable again and as he had come all the way from Hamburg, where he now lived, we had to offer hospitality. He stayed until the next day, but started drinking early in the morning. I saw him once more on my next visit, when he told me he was still single and wanted to marry me. I did not pay much attention to that; after all, I was married – for better or for worse.

Then something happened. I had noticed that Will was absent quite often again and when he was away, I managed to open his wardrobe and found a whole pile of women's panties. I did not want to know where they had come from. I just sent my mother a telegram to come and fetch me. I told Will I had enough and was going to get a divorce.

My mother came, and I packed my things. I shall never forget sitting by the fireplace waiting for the taxi to the station. Will was sitting on the floor, his back to the fireplace, and my mother and I in front of him in an armchair. The two kids were standing behind our chairs.

My mother said, "Will, you have never shown your children any affection, never picked them up or cuddled them. You've never tucked them into bed or kissed them goodnight. It is probably the last time you will see them. Can you not give them a last hug?"

He looked at Eve and said to her, "Come here." Hesitantly she edged closer to him. Then he said, "Put your arms around my neck."

Eve put her hands behind her back and said, "I haven't got any arms." But, gradually, he got her to come closer and awkwardly she put her arms around his neck.

Now Ronnie – of whom Will had never taken any notice at all except to reprimand him – was more affectionate and edged closer to his father to touch him. Will just pushed Ronnie away with his feet.

Ronnie stood behind my mother and said, "Omi, today we are going to make a big fire in the boiler, and when it is really hot, we will throw Pappy in and boil him for supper." This sums up Will's relationship with his children.

We left England, having lived there for a couple of years, and moved in with my mother. The children still did not have any toys as now we were really struggling, but my mother gave them our cutlery and they played trains with it.

I had a hard time coping in these cramped quarters. I tried to find a job, but without success. I had an English passport and the German attitude was: Germany was not good enough for you to stay, so you are not good enough to take back. They would not give me a permit and without that I was now, so to say, an illegal immigrant.

One day there was a knock at the door and a woman standing there. She asked my name, and said hers was Frau Petersen – Peter's wife. Apparently, the b*****d had been married for a long time. We decided to make for the nearest café and talk about it. She admitted that he kept my letters in a box under the bed and said if I wanted him, I could have him, together with his drinking problem. They did not have any children. I told her, "No, thank you. You can keep him." After that, we had a good chinwag and parted big pals. That was the end of Peter.

In the meantime, Will kept sending me long letters. He had requested a transfer to Rhodesia[25] and, when he got there, he kept on begging me to join him. He continuously sent me newspapers and I looked through the adverts and noticed there were plenty of jobs going there. The one that intrigued me most was as a typist with a tobacco firm in Salisbury[26]. The pay was really good, with plenty of leave and every two years a free trip to Europe, all expenses paid, and even £10 for tipping or spending money. Now that was a job I was after.

When I had worked at the quartering office in Hamburg, I had met two chaps who used to live in South West Africa and were full of nostalgia. Africa sounded really great and I thought, let me get a job first and become independent in Rhodesia. Divorce was on hold for the time being.

As there was no hope of a future in Germany for us, we got tickets to travel on the *Durban Castle* from Rotterdam to Cape Town. From there we would take a

---

[25] Now Zimbabwe
[26] Now Harare

train to Salisbury. My passport indicates the stamp mark in Rotterdam as 23 December 1955. Travelling on the ship was great. The first few days Eve and I were seasick. Ronnie walked like a sailor without weaving or waving and looked after us, holding the bucket when required. Of course, Eve and I were not in the mood for eating, but Ronnie had a great time at the dining table in the hall. Some sailors took him under their wings and he came back with glowing reports about sailing boats and the captain's deck.

MV *Durban Castle*

Once we got better and ventured to the dining room, Ronnie introduced us to the captain and we even got a seat at the captain's table. The captain and I become good friends, although at times he really bored me with talking either about his wife or about his stomach troubles. But I was a good listener.

There were a number of Germans on board and I become popular as an interpreter, having to go to the ship's shops with them and translating what they wanted etc. There was a German family I talked to a lot; they were getting off at Walvis Bay to make for the former German colony. There was a student on board, sitting at our table, who started talking to me. He had big glasses and looked like a professor and he talked like one too. When we got to Cape Town he took us to the beach for the day.

There was an Italian who really pestered me, but when he saw he could not get anywhere, I became his great confidant. In the morning, he used to point to the woman he had slept with the night before; they were never the same ones. He said the German and French girls were a bit cool and that the British women were the hottest. They ignored you during the day, but were hot at night.

I had such a good time travelling, I decided to pay a couple of pounds extra and continue on by ship to Beira. I shall never forget my first sighting of Table

Mountain in Cape Town. Ever since then, Cape Town has been the place of my dreams. Often in later years I wished to live there, and believe that if I had, I would probably have stayed in Africa – but such is fate.

En route to South Africa, Dec 1955

We stopped for half a day in East London and went to the beach, but the wind was blowing so much sand into our mouths that we had to leave. That night, we could taste the sand at dinner.

Port Elizabeth was our next stop and was nicer, but better still was Durban, where we stopped for a couple of days. The captain took me out. We went dancing – it was great. The next stop was Lourenco Marques on the east coast, not a bad place, and our final stop was Beira, which was not a pretty town. We took the train from there and crossed the border. It had taken two weeks longer, but the experience was worth it and I was not in a hurry to meet my husband again.

Part 3: RHODESIA

17. Salisbury (1956–1959)

Will had organized a flat in temporary accommodation, from where he commuted to the airport. He had left the RAF and was working for Rhodesia Airlines as a fitter and turner. We stayed there for six months.

One day, when he was working late, there was a knock on the door and a woman stood outside with a baby in her arms. She asked for Mr Johnstone and I told her I was Mrs Johnstone and asked her to come in and wait for him. She said she did not want to break up my marriage and I assured her there was nothing to break up. She told me they had been corresponding in answer to a marriage advert and she thought it would be nice to surprise him. She had a taxi waiting and left. When I told Will she had been, all he said was, "Damn these women, they always let you down."

He suggested buying a house in Park Meadowlands, not exactly the best area in town but only two kilometres away from the airport. I do not know how it came about, but he put the house in my name, probably on a guilt trip, which was just as well. He had some army money paid out to him and just enough for a deposit on the house. We paid £500 down and took a loan for £2,000. We were offered a few houses in Park Meadowlands, Salisbury. They all looked the same as, at one stage during the war, they had been built especially for army wives. However, I picked one opposite an open field with a great view.

Park Meadowlands

A new life started. I already had a job with Central African Airlines which was located in an old army camp on the other side of town; still there were buses. Everyone had an African nanny, who worked for next to nothing, so there was no problem with childcare. The children had one acre of ground to roam around in, and had a good time digging it up. As everyone knows, it is the land of sunshine. Things did not look as green as the continent, but it had a certain appeal. In those days there were many white expats and it was easy to make friends. Away from home, we were all the same and all in the same situation.

I did not really like my job, which consisted of stamping envelopes and stuffing them with timetables and adverts. I kept looking in the newspaper and, what luck, there was a job advertised at Imperial Tobacco, who were looking for a schedule typist. I did not know anything about schedules, but typing is typing, and I applied.

A staff bus was laid on from Salisbury town to Msasa about six kilometres away. There were quite a few girls on the bus and they were very friendly. As a test, I had to type a schedule, and I tried my best to spread the columns over the paper. It did not look much like the schedule I typed on, but I still got the job. There were three other applicants and they must have been really bad. Later they told me that we were equally skilled, but when the girls were asked who they would choose, they chose me because they liked my smile.

When I started work, they showed me my typewriter that, to me, looked miles wide. When they gave me my first schedule to type, I asked the girl I was replacing to show me how to do it, as the typewriter was kind of strange to me. Luckily, she agreed and I watched.

She counted the letters of the longest required space for every column, plus a couple of spaces to draw lines down in between, then the total, and fitted the whole lot in. This involved a lot of figure work, even the heading was counted. I watched and learnt. The next ones I did perfectly and that was that – I was in.

It was interesting work, from schedules working out the calories provided for the workers' luncheon to sales of tobaccos – split into various grades and quantities. Somehow I coped and, when I left two years later, my boss said to me, "I have worked twenty years for this company, but you were the best schedule typist ever."

I replied, "When I started here, I did not even know what a schedule was."

All my life, I found that you can achieve a lot if you try hard. However, working in a tobacco factory and getting cigarettes so cheaply, sometimes for nothing, I started smoking, only two a day, which over the years increased to 60 a day. Every time I stopped smoking for a short while to give it up, something drastic happened and then I smoked more than before. I only stopped when I retired, probably because I could not afford it.

I was not inhaling much, but it was great to have a cigarette in your hand, and to come off it, I would walk around holding an unlit cigarette. Many people stopped to give me a light!

Will purchased a second-hand car; I forget the make – it was from the Morris Oxford series, I think, and started teaching me how to drive. He was a very impatient instructor and once when I was practising round some quiet lanes, he got so cross when I stalled the car that he boxed my ears. A couple of chaps saw this and came over to my assistance. I said, "Thank you, it is only my husband."

Before I went for my licence, I had a couple of lessons with a driving school and it was then I learnt how to stop on a steep incline up a hill on the outskirts of the city and the testing point of the inspectors.

I nearly didn't pass my oral exam, as they gave me trick questions to trap me. When I gave the right answer the first time, the inspector just laughed and said, "Are you sure?"

I wavered. "Maybe not."

"Make up your mind," he said.

I stuck with my first answer. All this made me so angry I went through the test with ice in my veins, even the reversing through the drums, which I had I never succeeded at first time before, was a piece of cake. When we came back, the inspector said, "I must give you a pass, but I am sure I will see your car in the scrapyard at the end of the month." He was wrong.

I was quite happy in my house and garden – it was all mine. I planted roses and in the next couple of years I accumulated over 100 of them and nearly all different varieties. Even in the later years, my garden was not beautiful, but interesting, more like a collector's piece. You name it and I have to have it, or rather try it out, if it did not work, for some reason or other, there was always the compost heap.

Then, my nanny gave notice suddenly. Will said he already knew about another one and we went by car to pick her up from the "location". Locations in Rhodesia were compounds, a certain area of the town where the African population lived. It was still in the times of apartheid, and black and white just did not mix. I think 99% of them were very poor, mainly due to lack of education, I thought.

When I first arrived in Rhodesia, I did not like the attitude of the white people towards blacks, who were treated like slaves and considered as a different species. I had had no contact with black people before that, but I had seen them in Germany in the streets and they looked very presentable to me. As far as I was concerned, they were people like us only of a different colour. I was not so sure about that in the later years, but whether or not they burgled my house and stole from me, the ones I met were more or less treated as equals by me.

So, we picked up this nanny, who I detected was very pretty and unusually well-dressed. It was raining. In Rhodesia, it did not rain often, but when it did, it poured. When we got home, Will stopped the car, opened the door for the new nanny, opened an umbrella over her and led her to the house, only a few metres away. Never mind me without any umbrella. When I got to the house, I said to him, "Why didn't you carry her over the threshold?" He just laughed.

It was not long after that the nanny informed me that my husband was circling her *kia*[27] late at night in a dressing gown. So, I got rid of her pronto and the children went to the crèche. I got a male domestic instead for the house, I also had another one for the garden. Labour was cheap. There was no minimum wage in those days. Later, when that was introduced, lots of them were out of work, and begged to come back and work for just about nothing.

Park Meadowlands 'swing-bed'

In the crèche, the kids picked up any illness they could lay their body on. In one way it was good: they picked up immunity for later years. At the time it was a nuisance.

I was waiting for my husband's next escapade – looking forward to it, really! I had my house, my car, a good job and I could easily stand on my own feet. It was only a matter of time before I got divorced. Callous, you may think, but he did

---

[27] Adapted from the isiXhosa and isiZulu words for 'home', *kia* was used in the vernacular of white settlers to mean traditional huts or workers' living quarters

deserve it and probably would not mind – not that he treated me badly otherwise. He gave me all of his earnings except for a few pounds, which he held back – probably to buy stamps.

We had been in the house for only a few months when Will asked me if I could help him out with accommodating a woman from England for a few days. He had met her on the station in England when he left and had told her about the lovely country of Rhodesia. He'd said if she ever decided to come to this country, he would give her assistance. I said that it was OK with me and she arrived the next day; not much of a warning.

As I mentioned before, I was not the best of cooks. I could have easily got my domestic help to cook, but did not trust his cooking. He just prepared the vegetables. I could work in the garden for hours. Well, what I call work; I did not do the heavy digging and weeding; that was done by the gardener. I loved organizing the garden and planting or shifting the plants around if they did not do well in one place or did not look good there.

When this woman arrived, I put her up – it was only for the weekend, after all. She did not look like someone Will would be serious about. Not much to look at, and at least ten years older than me. She started complaining straightaway about my chicken lunch, she reckoned that was for poor people, where was the roast? Monday came, Will said he was looking for accommodation for her, but she did not get off her backside. When it was nearly the next weekend, I told Will if she did not move, I would have her moved, and he found her accommodation, temporarily, with the Salvation Army. In the meantime, she was nagging from morning to night about something or other. I'd really had enough.

She was supposed to leave on Saturday and on Friday, when Will was at work, she came to me and started giving me the works. She said, "Your husband said you forced him to move me out, but before I go, let me tell you the whole story." What a story it was. One of those "believe it or not" stories again.

Apparently, she and Will had met in a nudist camp in the United Kingdom. This was some time ago, and when he went to Rhodesia he continued writing to her. He eventually asked her to come out, as he was busy divorcing me and he would marry her afterwards. So, she came. She was disappointed that the house and car were in my name, although he had written to her stating otherwise. I did not say much, nothing surprised me any more.

When Will came home, I asked him for a divorce and then he could marry her. What did he say? "You think I would marry her? Since she has arrived, she has done nothing but nag. I would not think of marrying her." So she left, crying bitterly.

18. Divorce

I had enough of crying and a month later I said to Will, "It looks as if you cannot find anybody to marry you."

"Well," he said, "as a matter of fact there is someone in Berlin."

He told me he had corresponded with the woman through answering a marriage advert. She was well off, had two boys about sixteen and seventeen years old, who could get work straightaway and she herself was a qualified chemist so would have no problem getting a job either. She also spoke English well, according to her letters.

What an opportunity! I readily agreed to a divorce and, before he could change his mind, contacted a solicitor. It was plain sailing after that. When I got into court, I had written down a lot of my husband's escapades. The judge gave up after the first page. He asked if my husband had ever hit me; conveniently, I was able to say he had done so, the time I "misbehaved" while driving the car. It was the only time I could think of. And what about swearing? Oh yes, he sometimes swore in "Arabic" which I could not understand, but someone had told me that was swearing. (And he was not really swearing at me, but luckily the judge did not ask me that.) Divorce granted! I got the children. He would pay £10 every month towards the children and £5 to me until I remarried. It was good money in those days, as Will earned about £90 and me about half of that. So that was that.

Will had nowhere to stay and wanted to wait for his new family to arrive to look for a place. Well, I had lived with this bloke for seven years, what is a few months extra to put up with him? We carried on more or less as usual, and a month or so later, the divorce became final.

In the meantime, he wrote to Eva-Maria (I am not good at remembering names, but I know this one, as she brought me a music album for my piano with her name on it and it is the only sheet I still have from those days). She had told him that it would take a bit of time to get her money together from her investments, and could he send her the air tickets in the meantime. He bought three tickets, payable over six months, but I must say that Will never stopped paying me maintenance before looking after his new family.

She arrived shortly before Christmas, with nowhere to go, but wanting to be kind, I offered to put them up for a few days (or was it to be weeks… or months?). I was only too pleased to get rid of him. She was very disappointed when she arrived, and so was Will. She had no money but was expecting £200 to be paid out from a pension fund soon. She was not a qualified chemist, had just worked for one, and did not speak much English. The letters had been written by her sons, and the sons wanted to go to university. Well, well, well. Will had met his match. But she was nice looking, her sons too, and pleasant to live with.

They got married shortly afterwards, although she told me later that if he had given her a chance to get to know him, she would have thought better of it. Well, the deed was done. Of course, they stayed until her money was due to arrive. In the meantime, she attended to Will and her family, and I tended to mine. She did her own cooking and I did mine. I knew they were short of money and her meals consisted of pasta every day, which Will did not like at all. Neither did he like sardines, which seemed to be their staple diet. I was aware of that and felt sorry for the poor man, and sometimes I would hand him a plate of food behind the kitchen door.

After a month or so her money arrived, which she straightaway put down to buy a house (in her name), never mind paying for the air tickets. Still, it was a good thing for me as they moved out into their own house.

I even went to visit them. She found a job at a chemist, and her boys were also looking for work. Two months after they got married, she asked me if Will was answering marriage adverts when I was married to him. She, of course, would not put up with any such nonsense and Will and Eva-Maria got divorced. She made sure she kept everything, so poor Will was left with nothing.

Will got married again to a woman he had corresponded with and left for South Africa. This time, again, I think he found his match, as she had the same attitude as him, and for the rest of his life they were both so busy keeping an eye on each other, they had no chance to stray. It appears there is a lid for every kettle.

I enjoyed my freedom. I forgot to mention that while Will was staying with me, awaiting his future bride, he said that he had answered a marriage advert for me on my behalf in *Farmers Weekly* and had made an arrangement for me to meet this tobacco farmer. Will probably thought he could get out of paying maintenance if it worked out.

I did not want to go, but the girls at work insisted that I give it a go just for the fun of it. So, I arranged for the farmer to pick me up at the doorstep and we went to Le Coq d'Or – a well-known bar in Salisbury at that time.

We met up with another couple, and my farmer – I forget his name – asked what I would like to drink. I was not very experienced in the drinks department, but a couple of times I had had a drink with my friends, where I learnt to drink brandy and ginger ale. The farmer asked what type of brandy I wanted? The first name that came to mind was Limousine Brandy, which I had heard somewhere. He was not impressed and said that no one in his company would ever drink Limousine Brandy, and if I liked brandy then he would order something more appropriate.

The waiter came with a huge balloon glass and a tot of brandy in it. I started to move towards taking a sip when he told me that first I had to wait for the brandy to warm up. So there I was, sitting holding the brandy in both hands as I was taught, whereas everyone else was enjoying their drink. I asked him a couple of times if I could start and he kept me waiting a bit longer. After a while I got tired of waiting and asked him to get me a brandy and ginger ale in the meantime.

I think he was pretty disgusted with me. To crown it all, when he took me home there was my ex-husband in pyjamas opening the door for me. A week later, the farmer wrote to say that he had gone back to his wife. I think after meeting me, his wife looked good to him. At least I had brought them together again.

For fun, I went on a date with the next person Will had lined up for me. He took one look at me and said I was too old for him and boy, did he look ugly. His face was red like a beetroot with blue veins mottled in between. On top of it, he was over 60. I would not have gone out with him a second time either.

I was surprised Will was not jealous, as he had always been very jealous when we were married. If we went out, I had to sit facing the wall in case I had any idea of flirting, and I was never allowed to dance with anyone else.

I sold the car, as it was too expensive to run, and got a Lambretta scooter. I drove around on a learner's licence for a year, never getting round to passing the exam.

I was too short to straddle the scooter when starting it, so I had to jump on it after I started it. Once I must have pushed the accelerator, and it started running off without me, luckily landing in a shrub close by the house.

I had a lot of fun with it. One day, I went to town and as I was crossing the robot[28] on green, an old man was still walking on the other side of the road, crossing against the light. I tried to avoid him and get round behind him when he jumped back, so I turned to the front the same time that he jumped forward. It was quite a dance and he kept shouting at me that I was doing this on purpose.

Another time we had a party at the office and were allowed to leave early to get ready. I thought I had plenty of time, and went along a side road where there were new buildings going up, to see what they looked like. Unfortunately, they had dug up a trench across the road for some power lines. It was not deep, but deep enough for the front tyre to get stuck.

The bike bucked up like a bronco and I fell over the head of my "horse". Just a few scratches here and there, but the steering was now off. The handlebars, instead of going from east to west, went from southeast to northwest. No problem, just keep going. I even went to the party like that, although they would not let me ride home afterwards. I got a lift home, and the next day someone had already fixed the handlebars.

I must say, people in Rhodesia were very friendly. It was a great country, and I liked the cosmopolitan feel. When I still had the car, I went to a sale at a garden

---

[28] Local colloquial term for traffic lights

centre. When I arrived, I noticed my tyre was flat (the car's, that is!). I thought I might as well get on with my shopping, and the owner said he would give me a hand after they closed. I decided to wait in the car later. However, when I got to the car, the spare tyre was already in place. A chap parked next to me said he was getting rather bored waiting for his wife to finish her shopping and had fixed my tyre to pass the time.

Back to my scooter. I had a windscreen installed, but it had no wipers, and one time when it was raining hard and I came home at night, I was in trouble. I could only see the lights shining from the oncoming cars. This was very dangerous, as some of the poorer people would drive a car with one headlight and you did not know if it was a motorbike or a car. Furthermore, the tarmac roads were so narrow that cars had to go off the tarmac for oncoming traffic.

I tried to keep as near as I could to the edge of the tarmac, but it was unavoidable that I would fall off, and the drop was a couple of inches off the tarmac. I was lying on the side of the road and a car stopped with a couple of chaps, asking me if I was alright. "Thank you very much," I said. "I am more experienced falling off the damn thing than riding it."

I took the kids to primary school on my bike. One stood in front of me and the other at the back. It was only around the corner and a quiet road, but they enjoyed it.

I made friends with one of the other mothers, Sheila. I visited her on my bike or her boyfriend came by to pick us all up, including the children, in his car. It was shortly after Will had moved out and we all went to a restaurant. Sitting in the garden, her friend brought us a cool drink. While Sheila's kids were running all over the place, Ronnie and Eve sat on their chairs, not moving, and nursing their drinks. (I think it was their first iced drink.) Will did not believe in that stuff, and when he was around the kids had to sit still. So they too were beginning to enjoy their newly found freedom, and gradually thawed – becoming naughty like normal children.

One day, I visited Sheila and we were busy sewing dresses. She had a sewing machine and had taught me how to sew. I had a pattern, very simple but nice and easy, I liked it so much I made three of them in different materials. I then found another pattern and made another three dresses. A couple of years later when we got burgled in Johannesburg, they pinched all our clothes except the six dresses. Maybe they had a better eye than I had!

19. Johnny

On one occasion, Sheila's boyfriend brought a friend – both of them were working for the airways, and boy did they look smart. He caught my eye and he was only a year older than I was, which made a change from having been married to a man twenty years my senior.

Anyhow, I fell for him. Luckily, he was also interested in me and we started dating. He had a car and did not mind children. As a matter of fact, he was kinder to my children than Will had ever been. I shall never forget the day when Johnny (whose full name was Johannes[29]) bought Ronnie a wristwatch and Ronnie ran to me shouting, "It's real, it's real, not just a pretend watch."

Picnic, 1957

---

[29] See note above about potential confusion with Ursula's first husband Will "Johnny" Johnstone. Ursula, Ronnie and Eve's secret nickname for Johannes was Frankie (short for Frankenstein, due to his sporadic monstrous behaviour).

So for the first time I got to see places outside of Salisbury. There were quite a few picnic spots. Some beautiful open gardens where they had built *braai* (Afrikaans for 'barbeque') places and there was even chopped wood lying around. The parks, at that time, could have rivalled parks in England. Nowadays one sees only mealie[30] growing in any public or open space. But that is now and this was then.

Johnny with his sister Baps, and Eve & Ronnie

It was a very well-organized country, although some natives understandably bore a grudge against the settlers for invading their country at the end of the last century. Yet some also argue that had it not been for the settlers, locals would still be living in mud huts and having donkeys pull their carts – and the way things are going in Zimbabwe now, even though they might not have been better off, they could still have been happier than they ended up after independence. Anyway, it is

---

[30] maize: staple diet of the native population

only the older generation who might in any way miss the "good" old times of working for white bosses.

Johnny was really a character, full of fun and a bit daring when driving. He loved to show off. He drank, perhaps a little too much, but I thought that would change once he settled down. And settle down he did. A few months later he asked me to marry him and, naturally, I could not refuse.

He was also divorced and had a son and a daughter who lived with his ex-wife in South Africa. We went to the Registrar Office and were married there and then. Being me, nothing ever went without a hitch. We were waiting in the hall for the magistrate to arrive. Johnny got thirsty and went for a quick beer at the pub next door. The registrar arrived and we all went into another hall, waiting for Johnny. After a while the registrar said, "Don't tell me this will be another stood-up wedding procedure." How embarrassing! A policeman went next door and got my intended out of the bar and the wedding ceremony proceeded.

Driving from Rhodesia to Johannesburg

We had a party at home. He had lots of friends and they parked all over the place. When the guests left, they took shortcuts through my flowerbeds, some roses broke, but who cares?

Johnny wanted to go back to South Africa and he got a transfer to the airline in Johannesburg. I was really sorry to leave my house behind. To be on the safe side, I let it out to a couple who asked me to reduce the rent as they had just got married. They said if there was anything to be fixed, he would fix it. Six months later, a letter arrived asking me to repaint the house or else. I did not have the money, so I ignored them.

In any case, Johnny tended to be contrary: if I wanted a wall painted green, he said it should be blue. I would just bide my time; soon, he would shift to white, and eventually when he reached green, I would quickly have it painted, before he could change his mind again. My mother had a similar habit of saying no to whatever I wanted. So, if I wanted to go out, in order to get my way I would first say that I did not feel like going out, then she would insist that I went.

Part 4: SOUTH AFRICA

20. Johannesburg (1959–1964)

We rented a house in Bezuidenhout Valley, Johannesburg, bordering on Kensington – a posh area. It was big enough but had only a backyard and a garage, under the house as it was built on a slope.

Eve and Ronnie outside the house in Bezuidenhout Valley

I got a job with the travel company Miller Weedon & Carruthers, with offices in the middle of Johannesburg, and commuted by bus. Johnny used the scooter for work most of the time. There was no way that I would drive through Johannesburg on my scooter. One evening, Johnny took me for a ride and I fell off when he veered, but he did not notice until about 100 metres later. Not only was I a bad driver, but also a bad back-seat passenger.

As before, when I went for the job, I had to do a typing test, and I was shaking so much I made three mistakes on two lines. Still, I got the job.

Johannesburg was then a town with a lot of crime. We had not been there long when, one Sunday coming home from a picnic, we found the front door wide open and all our clothes gone (except my six home-made dresses). Maybe we'd interrupted them (the back door was also open), but nothing else was missing. We suspected it was a young chap Johnny had once hired, who had stolen all his clothes before. He'd been caught (thanks to a distinctive Fair Isle pullover I had knitted), sentenced to six months but released after four, and had then had the cheek to ask for his job back. Of course, Johnny had told him where to get off.

Shortly after that, my Lambretta was stolen right from under our noses. Johnny had just polished it, before going on the afternoon shift, and was having a quick lunch, leaving the bike in our open garage. When he went out, there was no sign of it. It was so easy for them, just freewheeling it down the hill.

We got it back one month later. The police had found it lying in a ditch outside Johannesburg. It was still OK, but we decided to sell it as we had the car.

Every weekend there was a crowd of Johnny's pals at our place and Johnny would be dishing out drinks. Once, Johnny was bragging how many friends he had, and I told him they only came for the free drinks. He would not believe me. So I told him next time they come, tell them you've run out of drink and serve them coffee. They did not come back again.

Johnny was one for teasing, and one time he returned from work in a jovial mood. I had bought Eve a small toy tea set, and when he came home, he teased her by putting the cups in his cap and rattling them, pretending he was trying to break them. Eve was very upset and said to him, "I wish you were twelve years old and we could send you to boarding school."

Once when he was working on his car and came in for a quick lunch, he washed his hands, but his face… The children asked me to tell them about the end of the world. When I told them there was no end, Ronnie said, "But I think I saw the end of the world when I saw Pappy's dirty face at the table." Children can say the funniest things.

21. Linmeyer

On New Year's Eve we went for a drive. Johnny wanted to show me a lovely area on a *kopje*[31]. It was high up and one could see the whole of Johannesburg laid out. On the other side one could see open places for miles. I really loved that place.

Sometime later, we found out that the plot was for sale and we bought it with a £200 deposit, money I had got from Salisbury when they paid out my pension. Actually, they required £400 deposit, but they just upped the mortgage and this also included having a house built – in my name, of course. It was an exciting time seeing the house going up. We could not afford a villa, but it was lovely with large windows, which I always favoured.

House on the *kopje* in Linmeyer

I had the bathroom decorated in black and pink and even had a black ceiling. Johnny thought I was mad. But later on, it was the best feature of the house and the first thing he always proudly showed his friends when they visited.

---

[31] Afrikaans: small hill

As I mentioned, the house was on a *kopje*. We could not afford to have a road laid right to the top, so the garage was at the front part and we had stone steps built in the grounds up to the house. It curved halfway and, one day, one of Johnny's friends forgot about the curve and tumbled right down against the garage wall. He must have been anaesthetized by alcohol as he felt no pain and did not get a scratch. Another pal fell through my large plate glass window in the lounge and we had a job getting his head out without cutting his throat.

The area was called Linmeyer and the whole township was elevated on a hill and we had a lovely view down onto the city of Johannesburg on one side and on the opposite side we had the view of various valleys and other townships.

But what am I talking about, we had not even moved in. The plan was to finish the house in six months and we had given notice at our house in Bezuidenhout Valley accordingly. However, the builders had not calculated the delay that would be caused by digging through rocks for the cables. However, as they had committed themselves to that specific time schedule, and we had to vacate our previous house, the builders booked us into a hotel in town for one month at their expense.

Now, living in a hotel should have been like a holiday and, in a way, it was at first. However, it was not long before the other guests complained about kids pressing all the buttons in the lift and throwing things out of the window at the people in the street.

Johnny and I had to go to work, and the children were booked into the school in Linmeyer, our new residence. They managed very well finding their way through the city to the bus – and they were only around six or seven years old. But there was still the afternoon to carry on with their mischief. After three weeks we had had enough, and moved to the new home unfurnished, save some mattresses and blankets. We lived by candlelight, cooked outside (you can do that in South Africa as there is always a lot of sunshine and not much rain). Luckily, the water supply was already running.

It was a great feeling, having a new home, and we could start on the garden. This was not easy as the ground mainly consisted of rocks, and every time we wanted to plant something we had to dig out some rocks and carry soil up the steps from the bottom of the garden. There were some wild proteas growing and we planted more varieties. They became the talking point of visitors, as normally they only grow in the Cape Province of South Africa.

Johnny was an ardent Boer, the name for the Afrikaners who had their own language – half Dutch and half English. He was proud of his heritage and spoke mostly Afrikaans with his friends when they visited, ignoring the fact that I could not understand their language, although everyone could also speak English. When I started to get to know a few words and wanted to say something, by the time I got the words sorted out in my head they had changed the subject. He taught me the Afrikaans word for a certain succulent in the garden and when someone asked me the name of it, I proudly let them know the name I had been taught. When they all burst out laughing, I found out it was a rude word in Afrikaans. His obsession with his country was so great, I had to stand up with him when they sounded the Afrikaans national anthem[32] on the radio.

Johnny digging on the *kopje*

Johnny's surname (and naturally my name now) was "la Cock". His forefathers came from France about 100 years ago and had their name changed straightaway from le Coque to la Cock. My children were not happy about this, as Johnny had changed their names as well when he adopted them. Johnny would not accept any maintenance payments from my ex-husband, not even my alimony. I bet old Will was happy.

A few days after moving in, we got the cables fixed so we could move our furniture in and get on with daily life. I employed an African nanny, who could not understand a word of English, as they all spoke Afrikaans, which I had yet to master. After doing something wrong every day – usually the opposite of what I told her –

---

[32] South Africa had joint English and Afrikaner national anthems until 1957, when *Die Stem* became the sole official version

I had to get rid of her. This suited us at the time, as it turned out we were having financial troubles.

Johnny had given up his job at the airport. We now lived miles away from the airport, on the opposite side of the city, and he had decided to make it on his own as a travelling sales representative. He took in a few lines that barely covered his expenses and one line, clothing, that promised to bring in a lot of money. Unfortunately, commissions were only to be paid after six months – at the end of the season.

This meant I had to visit the bank and explain the situation. Luckily, they were very understanding and did not pressure us if we were a little short of funds that month or late with our repayment on the house. I got a better paid job at a company that imported mainly spices from all over the world. I was a shipping and costing clerk, and although it took a little time to get into it, it was the best job I ever had. Especially the costing side, when one had to jiggle the figures, pricing the cost of one item of spice, taking into consideration the cost, transport, duty etc. If there was damage, I had to go along with the inspectors to assess it and put in a claim. Very challenging. Fortunately, after Johnny had worked for this clothing firm for six months and the company then went bankrupt and did not pay him, we managed on my income.

Johnny came home one day with a black dog (at least I think it was a dog underneath all that hair). He had noticed it in a pet shop in a window and felt sorry for it, so there he was. He was very lively and cheeky and about the size of a fox terrier.

Sputnik, as he was subsequently called, was obsessed with cars and would not stop chasing them. While we were all out during the day, he refused to budge from the garage downstairs, which was always open, and stayed in it waiting for the next car to pass. Luckily, it was a very quiet road. On one occasion, builders were working in our street, and they later told me it had started raining heavily so they looked for a place to shelter. They spotted our garage with the door wide open and, as there was no fence in the front yard, decided to head there to sit it out until the rain stopped. However, Sputnik was having none of this and barked and snarled at them, not letting them enter. They ended up huddling together in the front seat of a small truck, waiting for the rain to cease.

Whenever we returned from work and parked our car in the garage, Sputnik would sit in the car or beneath it until we took off again. His favourite activity was to chase any car that passed, barking madly and nipping the tyres of the moving vehicle. A couple of years later, he chased one too many and was run over, so we lost him.

Sputnik

I had always wanted a Collie; doesn't everyone? They looked so majestic standing on the rocks, with their beautiful manes blowing in the wind. We saw some puppies advertised in *Farmers Weekly* and had one shipped out by train from the countryside. He was beautiful, we loved him to bits, but he got sick after six months and died. After that we noticed that the same place where we had bought this Collie was advertising a new litter, and I decided to get two puppies to be on the safe side. Chummy and Cheeky lived to the ripe old age of twelve and thirteen and were greatly loved.

Early in 1964 Johnny was offered a good job in a town called Welkom in the Orange Free State, so we sold our house and moved there. As things turned out, after six months, Johnny's job did not work out. On top of that, the people who had bought our house in Linmeyer failed to keep up the payments, so we decided to buy the house back from them and return. In my whole life through to retirement, these were the only six months where I did not work (apart from the first four years when the kids were little).

We had to give the owners one month's notice to vacate, and therefore rented a house in another area of Johannesburg called Norwood. While there, on 11 June 1964 we woke up to a landscape covered in snow, up to eight inches deep in places. My kids had never seen snow before, but even for grown-ups, this was something that only happened once in a lifetime. Everyone went crazy, running out into the street and snowballing each other.

Snow! June 1964

After that month, it was time to move back to Linmeyer. There was not much packing as we had been living out of boxes anyway. The van set off, and I was waiting for Johnny to come back by car and collect us, when after a couple of hours, the van returned – with all our goods still in tow. The people in our Linmeyer home had locked themselves in and refused to move! Luckily, we had a few days left on our lease, so the boxes were offloaded back into the Norwood home.

The next day our solicitor managed to get a messenger from court to present to the reluctant occupants with an eviction order, and we were able to move. It was good to be home again.

Johnny was still struggling to obtain work and after two years he decided to get a job in Windhoek, South West Africa[33]. Of course, wherever he went, so must I, and we sold the house. Johnny travelled to Windhoek and after a while wrote to us letting us know he had bought a house.

I gave my notice, whereupon my boss, sad to see me go, asked if I could not stay a bit longer. When I said we had sold our house, he replied (in jest) he would get me a new one – and when said that my husband was already in Windhoek, he

---

[33] Now Namibia

responded, "Not to worry, I can get you another one of those too!". In retrospect maybe I should have taken him up on that.

The day of our departure arrived. The furniture had left with my husband, so Eve, Ronnie and I headed off to the station with Chummy and Cheeky, who were booked to go into the goods van. However, we had to wait a couple of hours for the train and it was raining heavily outside. When we brought the dogs into the waiting hall, we were quickly turfed out. No dogs were permitted, so we spent the time standing outside under the eaves, but we found time to stock up on supplies for the three-day journey.

Eve and Ronnie with Chummy and Cheeky

When the train finally arrived, we said goodbye to our beloved dogs, whom we had to leave in the goods van, and headed to our compartment. This usually slept six people, but we were lucky enough to have one all to ourselves. At that time, trains in South Africa were luxurious by Rhodesian standards, and it was an exciting experience. The compartments were upholstered in green leather and there was a washbasin that, when the lid was placed over it, doubled up as a table. We enjoyed our meals in the dining saloon at tables that were beautifully set with white linen and shiny cutlery. The menu was substantial and consisted of many courses. We were served by smart waiters wearing white uniforms with a burgundy red sash and a fez on their heads. It was wonderful watching the beautiful *veldt* go by while we enjoyed our meals.

We were worried about the dogs travelling in the van, and at every station we visited them to give them water, which they had accidentally knocked over in the meantime. Chummy had just about bitten through the door of his cage, so they had to give him another kennel. On longer stops we were able to take them for a walk, but it was not easy heaving them back onto the train – especially as the luggage vans were usually at the very end of the train, outside of the platform.

Six kilometres before we reached our destination of Windhoek, the train stopped at a small station and there was my Johnny, picking us up by car. I was worried leaving all the luggage on the train, but Johnny assured me it was quite safe and we would pick it up at Windhoek. This was typical of Johnny. He often behaved like a schoolboy, but I loved him for it.

Part 5: SOUTH WEST AFRICA

22. Windhoek (1964–1968)

We made it to Windhoek in one piece, but there was another surprise in store. What was Johnny thinking? He had bought a house that was pretty dilapidated and, stupid me, I had signed the papers. We were in shock and stood there for quite some time with our mouths open. True, it was about 100 years old and the walls half a metre thick, but the roof was leaking and, as we could not afford to have it fixed, we had to use buckets to catch the water when it rained. Fortunately, in South West Africa, it only rained for about two months in a year. At least there was ample space and quite a large plot of land with some garden, but the 'soil' was what one expected to find on the seaside. Water was very expensive as South West Africa had no wells or lakes, due to the rain shortages, and relied on desalinated salt water from the ocean, not far away.

The children were enrolled at the Windhoek English school (Centaurus High) and as they had bicycles, they cycled to school. Later on, a new bus system was started and they then took the bus to school. I had to catch the same bus. There were only a couple of buses a day and the return route was even longer, as the bus took the scenic route on the way back, going through the suburbs.

I was lucky to find a new job in town with an import/export company called S. Cohen. It was in the shipping department and that was my forte. They principally dealt with tractors, but I was only a small cog in the wheel. There were about eight people in the department and I mainly handled customs documentation. Our chief clerk gave me the costing of the tractors eventually as well.

The hours were terrible. I had to work from nine to one and then three to six. The climate in South West Africa was extremely hot, and most firms closed for lunch at the hottest time of the day for a two-hour siesta. Unfortunately, as I did not have a car to drive home, I was not able to use this time effectively and spent two hours whiling away the time, waiting for 3 p.m. to arrive. In the evening, as the bus took the longer route going home, my usual ten-minute journey ended up taking an hour, so I only reached home at seven in the evening.

After a year I was no longer interested in this job, and certainly not the hours, so I looked for another position. There was one going at the local newspaper office as a proofreader, but as my spelling has never been very good, I had to pass on that. Eventually, I found a job that interested me at Nedbank: the Netherlands Bank.

When I handed in my notice to S. Cohen, I was called in by the big boss, whom I had never met before, and asked to stay. Apparently, he had only just found out that I existed and learnt that I was the person who was doing the costing, not the chief clerk. They even offered me more money, but it was too late.

My new career at Nedbank started as a clerk and I especially liked the hours: 9 a.m. until 4.30 p.m. with half an hour lunch break – perfect! On top of it, as it was with all banks at that time, we had every Wednesday afternoon off and Saturday was only a half day. Well, I had told my father a bank would be the last job I would ever go for, and it turned out to be just that.

I worked in the Bills Department for a while and was soon promoted to the Foreign Department. It was not exciting but not bad either. In 1968 there was a plane crash at Windhoek Airport and it was pretty gruesome to be presented with banknotes for exchange which were either half burnt or covered in blood. One of the victims happened to be someone I knew well. He had been a client at the bank.

At home, I started work on the garden, planting cacti, the only plant species that would do well in such a climate, with that sandy soil. Once I found a new interest, I gave it my all and subscribed to all sorts of cacti and succulent societies. I imported seedlings and seeds from all over the world and was thrilled when the parcels arrived with these cute little balls covered in cotton wool. Have you ever looked closely at cacti, how many different spine formations you can find?

23. Mick-Mick the meerkat

One day the kids came home with a meerkat, an animal that featured greatly in the documentary *Meerkat Manor*. It was really cute and quite tame. He followed me everywhere around the place with his funny purr, purr sound, which changed to a frantic "mick, mick" when he lost sight of me, so we called him Mick-Mick. He crept under my blouse at times and insisted on sleeping in bed with us all the time. This was very awkward with such a tiny fellow – we tried placing him in a basket and shutting him into the wardrobe, but he protested all night, so we gave in. In the morning, he would place himself in front of the bed where there was a small shaft of light coming through the curtains, and stand upright, sunbathing. As the sun rays moved, he moved with them.

We left him with the servants to take care of during working hours, but one day when I came home, he was gone. I looked everywhere. We still had the Collies with us and Mick-Mick had no problem getting on with them. I noticed that Cheeky kept sniffing at an old well in the garden. It had long since run dry and had been used for dumping rubbish in. I took the lid off and listened and behold deep down I could hear his frantic calling. How to get him out? You could not even see him – it was quite a distance down to the bottom. I phoned the Fire Department and they told me not to bother them with a stupid meerkat.

Mick-Mick the meerkat

I had an idea. Mick-Mick was in the habit of sleeping in a little basket at times and we looked for a string long enough to let the basket down. We had to use about twenty metres of string, but it hit the bottom. We pulled it up several times hoping he would jump in, but gave up after a while. I thought that perhaps he would eventually enter the basket in order to sleep in it, and after an hour we went back and pulled up the basket, but there was nothing. While the basket was down again, someone moved the lid, and it fell and clattered like an explosion. "Quick, pull up the basket! If he did not jump in out of fright now, we will never see him again." Slowly we eased the basket into sight and there was Mick-Mick standing up on his hind legs, no worse for wear. We were worried he might jump out before we lifted him to safety, and fall back in again, but he made it. Thanks be to Cheeky, our Collie sniffer dog.

Mick-Mick was with us for some while, until one day we came home and found him drowned in a bucket that was left half full of water for the big dogs to drink. We were inconsolable.

24. Valerie the baboon

Next my husband came home with a baboon! Someone had not wanted her anymore because she was now grown up and becoming vicious. I can't imagine what he was thinking to bring this baboon home. What was peculiar was that she seemed to love wrapping an old sack around her when she went to sleep. We called her Valerie. We soon found out that she loved men and hated women. Johnny and Ronnie were fine but not us girls. She had a "collar" placed around her waistline and attached to this was a long leash which was tied to a large tree. This meant she was able to circle the tree freely but within a certain distance only. Whenever I fed her, I ensured that I placed the food in a bowl only as far as I could go without risking the baboon reaching me. Every time I came out with a dish and placed it carefully just within her reach, she shrieked, pulled faces and threw rocks at me – sometimes even the plate of food.

Ronnie would take Valerie for rides on the back of his bicycle, much to the enjoyment of all the neighbours' children. He managed to seat her on the back carrier and secure her leash firmly around the seat so she did not fall off, however, while they were setting off, her tail would sometimes get caught in the spokes. This caused great mirth among the children as Valerie would grab hold of her tail and pull it up to her chest, making faces at us as if she did not appreciate our laughter.

Once I noticed through the window that she had managed to get loose and there were no men around to help: I was alone. I quickly rushed from room to room shutting all the doors and windows, and only just in time. She managed to perch herself on a windowsill, flashing her teeth at me. I was a prisoner. Eventually, I saw an African man walking past and beckoned to him to come and help. Being a male, he had no trouble tying her up again.

Another time we were sitting at the kitchen table enjoying our Sunday breakfast with the window wide open and the sun shining in. Suddenly, Valerie appeared and leapt on the table. We all shouted "Sh*t!" and scattered in different directions away from her… and she did just that: pooped right there on the table.

At last, my husband got the message and took her to a sanctuary. We visited her couple of months later but when she saw me, she still remembered and threw rocks at me again.

We also had an awkward situation with a female Collie we had been given by someone who left the country. A colleague had called to say he was coming to the area, and could he and his wife drop in for a cup of coffee. I was thrilled at this news, as to me he was the big boss, so I was keen to impress him. No sooner were they seated, enjoying a cup of coffee, than in came our newly acquired female Collie. As she was in season, we tried to keep her separate from our male dogs. Chummy followed her and got hold of her straightaway and next thing the two dogs were stuck right there in the middle of the living room. It was not something one could ignore and my face had gone bright red. But luckily, my guests saw the funny side of it.

We also had unwelcome visitors, especially scorpions which loved to hide under rocks, but sometimes took a detour through our house on their way to the next rock.

Eve's bedroom was next to the sitting room, and one day, Ronnie came in from the porch and said that he had seen a snake on the porch and it had spat at him and looked like it had moved into the house. Nobody believed that, but Eve decided to keep her bedroom door shut – just in case.

A little while later she went to get a glass of water and noticed, when she returned, that Cheeky was sniffing at her bedroom door, so she immediately ran to us to ask us to investigate. As soon as Johnny entered the room there was a cobra, rearing its ugly head next to Eve's bed – it had probably been under the bed when she locked herself in the room before. Johnny grabbed a hammer, the nearest thing that he could find, and crazy as that he was, he went after it. The snake came out into the lounge slithering around the walls and I can still see Johnny chasing it. He succeeded in the end.

The children became teenagers and my husband's attitude seemed to change at the same time. He had lost control over them and I think it bothered him. When they came home late, he let them have it, especially Ronnie as he was the older one and should have known better. Maybe I should have stood up more for them. But I knew Johnny's temper and there was no stopping him. Ronnie had by then moved into an attic bedroom so it was easy for him to sneak out over the rooftop of the porch. One day, Johnny caught Ronnie and went for him. Ronnie ran away and hid in an old deserted pump house in the grounds. We didn't find him until the next day and Johnny coaxed him to come back to the house saying he would not punish him – but when Ronnie was sleeping that night, he pulled him out of bed and gave him a whacking. Now that was unfair.

I had my own battles with Johnny drinking early in the day. He was very agreeable when he was sober, but when he came home drunk, he always chose to attack me accusing me of being unfaithful to him. Later he said attack was the best form of defence, obviously feeling guilty about his drinking. Once he picked me up from work and we took a journey around Windhoek just to look at any new houses that had been built. I spotted a colleague of mine's home and when I said "look there is Hase's house" I was immediately accused of having an affair with this chap. The only reason I knew where he lived was because I had once borrowed a letter punch from him. He had offered me a lift home and we stopped at his house to pick it up on the way.

Things started to unravel from there. Johnny said he knew about the things that went on in the strong room. He ranted on and on and, when we got home, having had more than one too many drinks, he kept saying, "Admit it, you had an affair!" and slapping me when I said no.

He asked me a few more times and hit me every time I said no. Eventually, I said, "Yes, I did." Then he hit me again and told me I was now a liar. Sometimes you just can't win.

It got so bad at times that I had to hide when he came home, outside in the unused pump house which was by now secretly furnished with essentials, like blankets, cigarettes, matches, and a water bottle – until the children told me all was clear, when he was fast asleep. Once, in despair and worried for my safety, Eve came to my aid and hit him with her high-heeled shoe. Another time he threw a glass at me, which hit me around the eye. When the blood started dripping from my eyes, I thought I would be blinded for good. Eve has always been the brave one, whereas, as a child, Ronnie was the responsible one.

Eve phoned the police from a neighbour's house, and they came to investigate but said it was a domestic matter and they could not get involved. I replied that I supposed he would have to kill me first, and the policeman agreed that that was unfortunately the case. As it was, they were all his pals as they were Afrikaners who were connected with him.

After that we could not even talk to each other properly without a fight erupting and if we had something serious to discuss I found it safer to do so in a café in town. The problem was not other women – I don't think this was the case, as there was no time for that between drinking, but it was time to talk about divorce.

Johnny liked to tease and flirt. Occasionally when dancing, but once when we went to a dance in Windhoek, he so busy drinking that I ended up dancing with other guys. One danced with me a few times and found out I was German. He only spoke English so he asked another chap that spoke German to tell him something nice in German to say to me. When we danced again, he whispered into my ear, "*Du bist ein kleiner Schweinehund.*" You can guess what he said: "You are a little swine". I knew what had happened and was amused, but told him that it was not a nice thing to say. He must have found out afterwards what he had said as he vanished.

There were a few good moments when we travelled to Bloemfontein to visit Johnny's father. It was a long way but very romantic, travelling all through the night, sleeping a few hours in the car and carrying on the next morning before sunrise. I always liked to set off early before the sun rose and enjoy the dawn. There were springbok on the road and we had to be careful.

We also visited his brother called Bull, who had just started a farm near Warmbaths[34] towards the border. The first time we went they were still living in *rondavels* – round huts usually put up with clay soil, by and for Africans. There were three *rondavels* together so it was more spacious. It was a bit embarrassing though, as the walls did not go quite up to the ceiling, and we could hear what was going on. In particular, his brother kept pestering his wife for you know what, but she was not interested. We had a good laugh the next day. Later they had a proper farmhouse built.

We visited one of Johnny's sisters in Hillbrow, Johannesburg, and another one in Pretoria. I was impressed her husband was a professor. She had since adopted Johnny's son, Jasper.

Johnny was very proud of his son and older daughter Yvonne. Once, when he was complaining about my kids coming home late at night, I told him I had heard from his sister that his daughter had also snuck out of the window at night. I got my ears boxed for saying anything bad about her. I never met his children, but saw pictures of them, both very good-looking, obviously taking after their father.

25. Another divorce

We agreed to a divorce and it was again very easy. I did not even go to court; the solicitor did all the talking and for the second time I got divorced on the grounds of "mental cruelty".

I had made about £4000 on the sale of the property and generously I gave Johnny half. A month later he came and said he was cheated as I did not give him half of the furniture, so I gave him another £500. After a month I came home from work one day to find the place devoid of any furniture save the beds and the stove. Luckily, by that time I had already decided to leave Windhoek and head back to my old house in Salisbury.

He lived on the other side of the town, but kept on pitching up all the time – usually drunk. Once he just got into bed and refused to budge. Eve had to phone the police to remove him.

When they came, he was still in bed. He told them in Afrikaans that he was not doing any harm, just lying there. They eventually coaxed him outside and were laughing their head off. Probably they thought I was mad to complain, having such a handsome chap in my bed.

Johnny also came by from time to time to check up on the tyre tracks as he wanted to know who was visiting me. He said they were definitely not his car's tracks as he could see there was a scratch mark on the left front tyre. I told him to

---

[34] Now Bela-Bela

go round town and look at all the cars for a mark on the tyres. It really got too much when once he came with a gun and threatened to shoot us all. Again, the police came. It was not loaded but they took him outside. They never charged him, as he was their mate.

Eve gave a big party after we got divorced. They darkened the lights so much that one could not see a thing – well, they were teenagers then and I suppose they liked it that way. At the end of the party there was a commotion at the gate, a couple of chaps fighting. I was worried about the neighbours and went up to these strangers. I thanked them nicely for coming to the party. "I am sure you enjoyed yourselves but I think it is time to go home." They were nonplussed and left quietly. I found out afterwards that they had never been to Eve's party, they were just standing by the gate. They must have thought they were drunker than they'd thought, as they could not even remember being at the party, hence they left.

I was in two minds whether I should invest in a place in Cape Town. I always fancied living there and I could have got a transfer from the bank, but decided the funds were not enough to get me started and, after all, I still had my house in Salisbury. Or did I? I was not even sure about that; it had been so long. Over the years, and after getting so many bills, I had given up on it and never heard from them, so was uncertain whether I still had the house. I made some discrete enquiries and found out that although I was far behind with my payments, it was still my house. At that time things were getting a bit dicey in Rhodesia. With UDI[35] looming, there was no market for property. I gave the present tenants notice to leave and we prepared to travel back to Rhodesia.

Ronnie did not want to come with us. Unfortunately, I could not give my children any further education and he had found a job on the Railways in Keetmanshoop, in South West Africa. He liked trains, and got on better with Johnny once he left me. Johnny said he would keep an eye on him. I can still see Ronnie packing his small suitcase, but he had found room for his big teddy bear, which by then only had one arm and one leg.

Johnny offered to take us to the station and he was fairly sober. When we got onto the train he cried and wanted me to stay. No way! About one kilometre out of the station the train stopped and I looked out the window to see Johnny being put off the train. Apparently, he had parked his car on the side of the track and climbed onto the slowly moving train in order to be with us. In his own way, I suppose he loved me. I like to think that had he not drunk so much, it could have been much better. After all, this marriage had lasted ten years, the first one only seven.

---

[35] Unilateral Declaration of Independence

Part 6: RETURN TO RHODESIA

26. Park Meadowlands (1968–2008)

We celebrated New Year's Eve on the train, seeing in 1968 as we crossed the border to Rhodesia. We had the two Collies with us and took a taxi from the station to our house in Park Meadowlands. The house was rather run down, not a bulb left, not even lights – everything had been removed. We decided to make do with only the essentials while we waited for the house to be repainted. In the garden there were only about three roses left. I heard later from the neighbours that the night I left, my garden had been raided and most of the plants taken out.

I also found out why the mortgage repayments had fallen behind, although I had left it in the hands of an agent. I thought at first that the house had been standing empty for long periods but this happened only once, and for four months only. Otherwise, my money was taken up with repairs etc. A plumber had apparently been renting the house for the last year, and instead of paying the rent he merely presented his bills every month.

I had been away for twelve years and, in all this time, only about £200 of the capital had been paid off. Not to worry. I managed to get a transfer through my bank and started work straightaway in Salisbury. Eve was also looking for a job and I got her a position at the bank, but she only stuck it out for a month as she said it was too boring.

In the meantime, we had acquired the most essential items for the house: a bed, a stove and a stretcher[36]. The Dutch church in South Africa had not believed in TV, as they considered it sinful, and had banned television. As a result we had not seen TV in ten years. In Rhodesia it was different, although only black and white television was available and it only started at 5 p.m. and ended at 11 p.m. after the news. So when I mentioned essentials, having a television was a priority. You could hire televisions in those days, and that's what we did. I remember the television arriving encased in a wooden frame (like a commode) with doors on the front that could be closed when not viewing. The next evening Eve and I sat on the stretcher, eating our dinner off our laps, watching *The Flintstones* and *I Dream of Jeannie*.

The neighbours on the other side came over with a tray of tea and cakes to welcome us. That is how it was in Rhodesia. They looked at our meagre surroundings, felt pity on us, and brought over a camp bed and some mattresses.

When the painting was finally finished we went furniture hunting. We had thought of buying second-hand pieces, but what the heck, this was a new life and I

---

[36] Local term for a reclining deckchair

was earning a good salary. I also had some money from the house sale; so we made ourselves comfortable. I felt we deserved this.

My six wooden crates arrived, one with books, three with cacti and succulents and two with household items. I always got my priorities right, ha! Unfortunately, we arrived in the rainy season, and I had placed the crates in the workshop out of the rain to do the planting later. However, the painters were busy with the outside and thought it was more important to keep their paint dry, so they put my plants outside. They even "kindly" covered the boxes with plastic! When the rain stopped and the hot summer sun came out in full force, most of my plants were "cooked". As it turned out, Rhodesia did not have good conditions for growing succulents – there were plenty of other plants to be found which were more suitable.

Eve had seen an announcement on TV stating that they were auditioning one night that week for "Go-Go Girls" on Salisbury TV. She phoned them straightaway for a job which she ended up getting – not having any experience in dancing other than loving to dance. Proudly, I told people, "My daughter is the one with the long hair in the middle. Oh sorry, I mean the one in the middle with the long hair." She did very well – no wonder, as she was much prettier than her mother had ever been (I don't know where she got it from). And she was very popular. When the mini skirt came in, I used to sing, "Evi has the miniest skirt in town." Eve was very independent. Somehow, she managed to be photographed for local papers and magazines. I took dozens of photos of her at home as well. I thought of my father, who used to run after my mother and me with the camera.

I still did not enjoy chores and I got a "houseboy[37]" straightaway. I can tell a lot of stories about houseboys, but maybe I'll get round to that some other time. They just could not help "helping" themselves. In short, they all pinched, so it was no use changing them for another one, unless you wanted to do without them. And I had the garden! In a way I was glad that my garden was now bare, as I had changed my opinion about a formal garden and went for the natural look, all curves.

The garden looked at its best the first year as I only shaped the beds with the help of a hose pipe and otherwise filled it up with petunias. I found that boring, and in the coming years I went for a variety of plants. I had this mania to have everything (I still do as far as plants are concerned). I have to try anything and everything. I started with a dozen roses, every one different. I soon gave up on them. Between the mildew, the black spot and the beetles it was a losing battle. Every October when it was springtime, (actually, there was no spring or autumn in Rhodesia, the winter jumped into summer and the summer into the winter season), the beetles devoured my roses. I used to go out with a torch at night and strip them off the plants and place them into a bucket of water. This was during the time of

---

[37] A young male servant

terrorist attacks and the first time I was in the garden, removing beetles, Eve came home after dark and found the doors wide open. There was no sign of me but someone was sneaking around the garden with a torch. She feared the worst and called the neighbours, who locked all the doors and hid under a bed. But it was only me.

I let the roses go to ruin and concentrated on my next mania – dahlias, but I found out they were not well suited to the climate. They looked nice the first year, but did not perform much after that. On to the next… so I went from Barberton daisies to Hawaiian hibiscus. Later I grew irises, then daylilies and eventually orchids, which was my last fancy. More of that later.

27. Death of a husband

Six months after I left Windhoek, someone sent me a cutting from a South West Africa newspaper stating that Johnny had had an accident and was dead. He had got himself a job as an agricultural inspector and travelled a lot. He overturned his car somewhere between Windhoek and Walvis Bay. Apparently, he had then walked to a nearby brook for water, where a car had stopped and found him, still moaning about his head and asking for water. Ambulances were miles away so they took him to the nearest hospital, but he was dead on arrival.

They were looking for his next of kin and someone mentioned that he was divorced, but I only found out a month later. They had buried him near the hospital. Eventually his daughter, who was now married, contacted me and asked if I would pay for his body to be brought back to Windhoek. However, I heard in the meantime that he had left her a life insurance of £10,000, so I thought it was up to her to do something about it. I am sure if he had lived, he would have come back to Salisbury looking for me.

It was tragic. He had survived quite a few accidents in our time together. Once the car went flying over a fence and landed upside down on the other side, sliding along and cutting the roof in half. It missed him and he just had a couple of scratches. In humour, the policeman asked him where his pilot's licence was. I had to look after him on a couple of occasions. Afrikaner men do not do housework, and he could hardly do anything. He used to sit by the kitchen door and shout at me to come and make him coffee.

The Afrikaner custom was to pamper their men. Once when we went to visit relatives of his in Umtali, the wife refused to wake her husband up from a nap. We had travelled about 60 kilometres but we had to wait until he woke up! On the whole I was much better off on my own.

28. Nedbank

A week or so after we arrived in Salisbury I started my job as a clerk in the Ledger Department at Nedbank. I was lucky to have got a transfer, although the work was dreary. Those big ledger machines! It did not take long, however, for them to find out I was a better typist, and I did the department's typing, in something like a typing pool. I really got fed up when my typist stool broke and I had to straddle across it, feet on the ground so I would not fall off. I complained profusely and after a few days I threw the chair out and got hold of a wooden crate which I used as a stool. They seemed to get the message as my brand-new stool arrived in the afternoon.

Still, I was not too keen on the job and started looking round for another one. I was offered a position with another company in town as a shipping clerk.

I gave in my notice at Nedbank and once again was called in by the big boss. Maybe they had since discovered that I was good at my job, so he asked me to stay. I told him I had been offered £20 a month more at my new job (my salary was then about £60 a month). He said they could only give me £10 more. I said I would stay on condition that the bank took over my housing loan from the building society, where I paid about 5%, whereas I had heard that the bank was giving loans to their staff at the rate of 2%. In later years it was even reduced to 1%. This would have been worth quite a few pounds extra every month. He said this was impossible as it was the bank's policy only to give loans to men! But somehow he wangled it to arrange the loan for me, and I stayed on.

Shortly after that, the typist in the Letter of Credit (L/C) Department went on leave for three weeks and I was asked to replace her. This was a vast improvement. The clerks filled in the application forms from customers and transcribed these into draft letters of credit for me to copy. Soon I discovered some discrepancies and pointed it out for them to be corrected. They got so fed up with me telling them their job that they left me with the application forms to type out the letters of credit as I saw fit.

When the girl came back from leave, I am not sorry to say, she was transferred to another department and I remained there. This was an important milestone in my life as I worked in the Foreign Department for the next fifteen years. Due to the rapid growth of our department, we were shifted around to offices all over the town to other branches until I was transferred to the head office in First Street.

There were two clerks, one check clerk and two typists in our section situated in one corner of a huge hall split up in sections for Bills Department, Foreign Transfer Department and telex room. I was one of the typists.

After a couple of years, the check clerk left and I asked for the job. My boss said that he had offered me the job of a clerk before and I declined. I said, "Yes, but check clerk is a different story."

I got the job, doing my work and sometimes helping out the sub-accountant. After a couple of years, when he left, our accountant asked me if I would be interested in this job. He applied to head office on my behalf, but they refused.

Years later, when I reached a managerial role and had access to the staff files, which were locked in my office and in my charge, I found the whole story. Head Office had declined as it was not bank policy to promote women beyond a check clerk. It was simply unheard of.

My accountant did not give up, and he tried again a year later, in October 1979. I saw the glowing report he gave about me taking on a sub-accountant job when he was on leave. They gave up in the end, and I think I was the first female in the bank to get that far. Normally, I should now have had my own little glassed off corner in the bank, but for that I had to wait till I was promoted to sub-manager.

This was a job more to my liking and far more interesting. I had to compile the month-end reports and was forever interrupted by some member of staff asking stupid questions or telling me their sob stories. After a few months, I closed the door at month-end and put up a "Do not disturb" sign outside. After a couple of hours, I found I could not get used to the stillness around me, and opened the door again.

My career blossomed, and after a short spell as an assistant accountant, I was promoted to accountant, getting my own office. I got on well with the customers, mainly big firms or companies. At Christmas I received many presents from them (I assure you they were not bribes). One customer once said to me, he would love to give me a job but I was too honest for his type of business! I was also invited to their Christmas parties.

One of our customers ran a posh nightclub in Salisbury and he made me an honorary member. Later, I took my boyfriend there sometimes. It was a grand place with a stream going through the restaurant stocked up with live carp: you could pick one for supper. I have my doubts they were the same ones. Who could tell?

I was popular with the staff, always joking with them, whereas they seemed to be in awe of me. I felt like a teacher at school being presented with some apples. One brought me an avocado sandwich nearly every day after I had tasted one at his desk. They were delicious, one third bread and two thirds avocado. Thanks to his mother. That reminds me of the times at school when I had only jam sandwiches and other girls, who were bored with their ham and salami sandwiches, gladly swapped mine with theirs.

Eventually, in April 1983 I was promoted to sub-manager, and in October 1984 to assistant manager, but I retired before becoming a manager – more about that later.

I had acquired a second-hand VW Beetle car, which I parked three blocks away from work. I did not like driving through heavy traffic in town so I got in at 7 a.m. and started work at 8 a.m. I liked to read the newspaper in the morning, as there was plenty of time. However, after a while I gave up trying to read in the office as the staff who had also arrived early were soon in and out of my office letting me know of their latest escapades. I ended up going for a cup of coffee every morning at "Le Paris", a tearoom opposite the bank, where I could read my newspaper in peace.

Nedbank company car, 1983

A couple of times I went for a piece of cake to go with my coffee, and found an Italian guy eyeing me up. After the smiling and "good morning" stage we ended up sitting at the same table. He said he was single and had no girlfriend. But straightaway he asked me how much I was earning, did I have my own house, and was my house paid for. So I skipped "Le Paris" from then on.

We had staff parties too, and one Christmas, shortly after I started in the L/C Department, I found my boss eyeing me up. We danced beautifully together as I floated around the dance floor. I knew he was married but made a date with him anyhow. I was probably honoured that someone in his position would pay attention to me. After that we went out a few times over the next three years – secretly, of course. And nobody found out about us, although my friend at work, Marina, was full of stories about other "affairs" going on the offices.

After a while, I noticed he was cooling off, and saw a woman visiting him in his office every few days. She did not come out for an hour and I think I also noticed the key being turned.

One Christmas, I received a present from him, and he told me it was over: he had found someone else. It is no fun being jilted, so I spent a great deal of time crying that Christmas, listening to nostalgic records by Engelbert Humperdinck, Ge Korsten and my favourite, Gert Potgieter. Never heard of them, I bet?

Eve was then working at a bar at the Le Coq d'Or and told me to stop feeling sorry for myself, and to come and join them on New Year's Eve. That is when I met Neville, but I shall come back to that after I have told a little of Ronnie's and Eve's stories.

29. Ronnie

As I said before, Ronnie had stayed behind in Windhoek when we moved back to Rhodesia. While living in Keetmanshoop, Ronnie married Agnes, whom I never met. Sadly, his firstborn son Anton drowned when only a couple of years old. Ronnie had been digging holes in the garden to plant trees, when it started raining. It was a deluge and the garden flooded making the holes invisible. Somehow, Anton managed to get outside, fell into one of the holes, and drowned as a result.

Ronnie had another son Calvin and a daughter Charmaine, both of whom I didn't meet until they were over twenty. Ronnie was not sentimental, so I did not hear from him for a long time, and meanwhile he had divorced Agnes and married Driekie, moving to Ermelo, in Transvaal[38]. I met Driekie a few times and I thought she was very nice. Ronnie had two more sons with her: Kevin, who was always close to his mother, and Richie.

I was somewhat surprised to see Kevin sitting on his mother's lap, even as a teenager – this was before his wilder days. Richie spent most of his time in his room, the walls of which were plastered with rugby pictures and one wall made up of empty beer cans, which he collected. He was always very conscientious, never unemployed, and eventually went to work in England.

When they bought their own house through the Railways, Ronnie got a keyboard. I think he thought I was deaf, the way he made it sound. Between that and the two boys keeping the TV on until three in the morning, it was a trying time.

---

[38] Now Mpumalanga

But we had nice moments when we had *braais* outside or went to Bedlams[39], a caravan park, for a couple of days. Or was this place called Warmbaths? That is more appropriate, because of the warm water wells filling a large swimming pool.

When I told Ronnie I was coming to visit, he proudly announced he had bought a whole sheep; however, on our return, the fridge had packed up and, in the African heat, everything was spoiled. I still can't eat mutton to this day.

Ronnie was quite restless in those days. When I visited him in Ermelo while he was living with Driekie in a small place in town, he was very much into videos. I usually travelled by night by plane from Salisbury to Jan Smuts Airport in Johannesburg because it was cheaper. There Ronnie picked me up by car. The flight was only an hour or so and the car ride took another two hours. As soon as I got to his house, he wanted me to watch some videos he had specially rented for me and had to return by a certain time or pay extra. They were mostly Leon Schuster videos. Hilarious comedies, which I liked then and still do. Ronnie said he enjoyed hearing me laugh. After that he wanted to take me to town. It was always pretty hectic.

Ronnie on his motorbike

While Ronnie was living in the Railways' house, he had a blackout for about ten minutes. The Railways took a dim view of this and asked him to go for tests. When they did a head scan, they found out that he had no sense of smell. He had

---

[39] Bedlam was a brand of storage heater popular in resorts

lost it in an accident in South West Africa, when he smashed into another bike and landed with his head against a wall. In short, the Railways said he could not drive a locomotive under those conditions, in case there was a fire and he could not smell the smoke. This was after about twenty years of driving a train.

Ronnie was very proud of his job and on visits showed me the long trains he drove. They consisted of about 200 wagons (with a few locomotives in between) which were very difficult to manoeuvre. He found the job very rewarding. If he drove overnight, he was paid overtime and if he had to do overnight waiting to take back the empty or full train, he got paid double even when he was sleeping. So, when the Railways said they had to remove him as a driver, and perhaps he could have a job as a stationmaster, he declined; it wouldn't be worthwhile as there was no overtime. So they pensioned him off.

I think it was around that time that he and Driekie got divorced. When I asked him, he acknowledged that the reason was 'fooling around', as it had been with his previous wife. "Like his father," I thought, "the apple does not fall far from the tree".

In the settlement, he gave the house to Driekie and had a part of his pension commuted, which he also gave her as a one-off payment. He got a room in town and found work in a hardware and electrical goods store, where he liked to show off the keyboards.

After that I did not see him so much; he did not like going on long journeys and did not write letters either. He phoned from time to time, had another job in a guesthouse, which he liked and after that lived on his pension.

Richie remained with his mother, as he was very attached to her. Kevin stayed for a while and then returned to Ermelo to live with Ronnie. Ronnie could have come to Salisbury, but he had become a true Afrikaner Boer by then. He hardly ever spoke English. At one stage, Ronnie had a heart attack. I only heard about it when it was all over. He had trouble speaking as one side of his tongue was partially numb. I could hardly understand him on the phone and it took years for him to recover.

However, let's leave Ronnie for a while and return to Eve.

30. Eve

Eve had got a job at Art Printers, but was bored and looking for more excitement, so she decided to go to South Africa. Eve was, and still is, very independent, and in 1971, she left. I remember it was Easter; I was in hospital having my appendix out. She did not want to leave until she was reassured that I was OK, but I told her not to worry, I would be fine. I went in on Good Friday, had the op the same day and Eve came that afternoon to say goodbye. I was still under the influence of the anaesthetic and saw her only dimly. She cried a lot but the operation had been a success so she left.

Saturday and Sunday nobody came to visit me. But on Monday they must have sent a priest round to give me company. He was not of my religion, but I was never fussy. In later years I had quite a few friends of different religions. They all said their prayers at my table, and it sounded all the same to me. They all said "Amen" at the end.

As previously mentioned, I had a good friend at work called Marina, the only one I had in those days. She started typing about the same time I did. I often visited her and her husband at their house. Unfortunately, she had applied for leave over Easter as she wanted to visit her parents in Mauritius, but she had to cancel as I had to go into hospital and could not cover for her. She was cross and did not speak to me for three weeks. As if I had planned it! Nobody from the office visited till Tuesday when they came with a big bunch of flowers from the bank, and a get well card signed by the staff. I was already sitting there waiting for the taxi to take me home. Well, better late than never.

Eve joined a dancing troupe in Johannesburg, and travelled all over the place, including Mozambique. It did not last long, and she decided to go to Durban, where she found a job with *Scope* magazine, which was very popular in Africa. I subscribed to them for years later on, after they changed their name to *You* magazine. I still miss the crossword puzzles. It was here that she met a number of Australian youngsters, her age, who later on visited her in Salisbury. They stayed with me Bohemian style, e.g. sharing one big bowl of fruit salad with eight spoons. I was not really prepared to cater for them but they enjoyed themselves. They all slept on the carpet in the lounge, and I had to step over them in the morning on the way to the kitchen.

Eve had a lot of success getting her picture in various publications. She was very pretty and had her pictures in *Illustrated Life* magazine, a sports magazine, Christmas cards, dressed in a mini Santa Claus outfit, etc.

Once when we visited my mother in Lüneburg, Eve went to the local swimming stadium and the next day there was a picture of her standing in the swimming pool licking an ice cream, with a short article about her in the *Lüneburger Locale*.

31. Neville

Eve returned to Salisbury and got one job during the day, while at night she helped out at the Le Coq d'Or bar, running a disco. That is where I met Neville.

Apparently, Neville was a regular customer and a good tipper. He was about twelve years younger than me and told me later he really had his eye on Eve, only to be landed with the mother. Eve asked him to keep me company while she was working, and he was fun to talk to. Full of nonsense he was. He was not unattractive although a bit overweight. He also drank quite a bit, but not as much as Johnny. He took us home that night, but we did not want him to drive home in his drunken state so he stayed the night, which become a regular occurrence. After a couple of months, he moved in with me.

Ursula, Neville and Eve at the Coq d'Or

When he drank, he got quite morose, saying things like, "I suppose you don't love me anymore, so I might as well go home." We would beg him to stay, and he seemed to enjoy that. After a couple of times, I got fed up and told him, "Just go." But he did not get further than halfway to the gate before coming back. He never threatened again.

Eve got a flat in town, sharing with another girl, then moved to another place, but kept on working at the Coq d'Or. Once when she was still living with me, she met a band called "The Sands of Time" from England. They brought Eve home one night but would not come in, as they were tired and wanted to get back to their hotel. The next morning, when I got up early. I noticed a van across the road in the ditch. I called Eve and it was her friends. Our bridge across the ditch on our side was very narrow and they had misjudged the turn. I asked why they did not come inside. They said it was dark and they had heard about the snakes in Rhodesia.

It was also at the Coq d'Or where Eve met Doug playing in a band that came from Canada. They became very friendly, and one day when Eve had to go into hospital for a few days, he tried to sneak through the window during the night and visit her. They chucked him out, so over the next couple of days he came at night-time and serenaded her under the window with his guitar.

It was around this time that she went out of town with Doug, and they hit a Land Rover that had turned into their road without warning. Eve suffered a knee injury, which was not treated properly. By the time she went to see Doug in Canada, the leg had shrunk to half its size. In Canada, the hospital discovered that the sinews in her knee had been severed, and they had to tie them together one by one. It grew back normally after that. She stayed in Canada for a while, writing rosy letters which gradually did not sound so bright any more. Next thing I got a telegram: "Please send return ticket". No problem.

So back she came and stayed with me, but by then she was disillusioned with Neville and his drinking, and after a couple of arguments, she left. Fortunately, she had met Karl and he asked me very formally if he could live with my daughter. Well, it was up to Eve, and they moved into a block of flats where the ceiling was the roof. I called it the bat house. One day, Eve phoned frantically saying that there were bats flying all over the place and she had locked herself in the kitchen. Karl was not home yet. Neville and I went to the rescue. We chased away the bats and calmed Eve down. Karl had come home and straightaway gone upstairs to the bathroom. I can still see him coming down the steps in a bathrobe – when he turned round there was a big bat on his back.

Karl came from Austria and he founded a clothing partnership with Manfred, who was from Germany. As far as I understand it, Manfred had provided the funds and Karl added his expertise in the clothing line. They started two men's clothing shops in Salisbury. Manfred stayed in Durban with his girlfriend Geraldine. He ran a transport business and only came occasionally to Salisbury. Apparently, Manfred was doing very well and so did Karl. They even expanded later on to another two shops.

There was no shortage of money as far as Karl was concerned. He gave Eve anything she wanted and took her everywhere, even to visit his uncle in the USA. His generosity also extended to Eve's family, which meant he took us to the best places in town. When Ronnie came to visit with Driekie, Karl paid for all of us to go on a trip to the famous Victoria Falls for a couple of days, from there to the Wankie Game Reserve[40] and on to the Kariba Dam, which had not long been built. I had been in Rhodesia for many years but not been able to afford to see these places. Naturally, it was awe inspiring to visit the falls, and I even went to a casino for the

---

[40] Now Hwange National Park

first time in my life. Karl gave me a few bucks to gamble with and I won Z$50, which I didn't gamble away but spent the next day in the shops.

At Victoria Falls with Eve and Karl

We travelled by plane to the game reserve and then by car through the park. I had never seen wildlife so close up. Wild animals did not come near the towns and would have landed up in a cooking pot anyhow.

Eve and Karl stayed in the bat house only a few months more and then moved into a house Manfred had bought for the company in Ballantyne Park, a smarter area on the opposite side of town from Park Meadowlands. It was very grand with four bedrooms, two sitting rooms, a big kitchen and a dining room which they revamped into an impressive Bavarian style breakfast room. There was also a swimming pool, tennis court, two garages and an outbuilding for servants' quarters; not a *kia* like my servant had.

When I think of the small room my servants had, which we had split into two as there were two of them. They only had an outdoor toilet with a hole in the ground, with a water cistern. They gathered wood and built their fire under the stars in order to cook their staple diet of *sadza* (a kind of maize porridge) and rape, a cross between cabbage and spinach. In the early days when it was still Rhodesia, they even had meat most days. After it became Zimbabwe, they could not afford it any more. If I did not give them leftovers from time to time, they would have forgotten what meat looked like. They grew mealies and rape in the corner of my garden. After all I had one acre.

Eve and Karl lived happily, but unfortunately not for ever after. In the meantime, I enjoyed visiting them over the weekend in my little Volkswagen. They also gave great parties. Their relationship lasted six years, although they had their tiffs. Karl could be very nasty at times and often Eve came rushing to me in tears. Once they quarrelled, but the next day a garden shop came to deliver flowers, and when I visited, I could hardly walk through the lounge because it was so packed with bouquets. In the end, Eve had enough and decided to return to South Africa. They parted amiably and always remained friends.

Karl organized for a dress shop to be opened in Cape Town for Eve to run. It was very elegant and modern in Adderley Street, the main street, and had great potential. Eve found a flat nearby and later moved to a beautiful apartment in Clifton, high up in the hills, overlooking the ocean and mountains, situated across the road from the beach. I loved Cape Town. It was the only place in the world where I wanted to be. I hated leaving my house and garden even for a short time, but once I was in Cape Town I could forget all about it.

The garages were at the bottom of the street and one had to walk up steep steps to the flat, which had another flat above it owned by two gay men. Cape Town was known as a paradise for the gay communities and I met quite a few there. I found them to be so much more friendly and polite than other men. Probably because one knows they are not just after one thing.

There was a bus into town and apart from all the lovely second-hand bookshops which I had a passion for, there were bus tours to take you to wine tastings at famous vineyards of the Cape, flower exhibitions in Paarl or one just took a bus to Kirstenbosch, famous for its gardens. There was Table Mountain with a cable car to take you up the mountain and sky huts, for the winter sports. The winds could get very strong at times (usually around October) and you would have to hold onto the railings, which had been specially installed on some street corners, to avoid being blown over. I did experience it once, it was impossible to go forward, the wind just blew you back, but one got there eventually.

In comparison to Salisbury, the shops were modern with shopping centres, of which Salisbury had not even one. If Eve had stayed in Cape Town, I am sure I would have ended up there. It was a long flight from Salisbury to Cape Town, but I still visited at least once a year, sometimes stopping in Ermelo on the way back to see Ronnie.

It was in Cape Town where Eve met Juan, the father of their daughter Alexa. I thought he was a real windbag. He sounded utterly irresponsible. I do not know what he did for a living, but he was handsome and very athletic. Blond, blue-eyed and young – Eve was smitten. He was more than ten years younger than her. They told me they had married on the quiet. Well, the deed was done.

The next moment, he went off to run a crocodile farm on Lake Tanganyika. I don't remember the details, but after Eve had visited him a few times there, they separated. Not long after that, Eve left the shop in the hands of her friend Annelise, who worked with her, and went to the USA. Annelise subsequently contacted Eve to say that business was not so good. Eve wanted to send Karl to Cape Town to review the situation, but he said just to let the shop go, as he didn't have the time or energy to sort it out.

Juan too moved to Los Angeles, and eventually he and Eve met up again and made up. She had a good job and, as far as I was concerned, was not stingy with her money, organizing to have irises sent to me from Oregon. I only realized in later years how expensive this must have been. But I had this new fad and browsing through catalogues, I saw irises of unbelievable beauty in the USA. I never saw any like that even in England in later years.

Eve and Juan were together just for a short while until she left him again, this time pregnant, and returned to Salisbury. She was not keen on staying with Neville and me, so moved in with Karl, who had by now permanently moved into a suite in the top floor of the Holiday Inn. There was not much room for Eve and Alexa, but Eve did not mind, and neither did Karl. As I mentioned, they remained friends all their lives. Manfred had previously returned from Durban and he and his girlfriend also moved into the house in Ballantyne Park. There were a lot of arguments between Karl and Manfred, one accusing the other, mostly over money and the distribution of it. In the end Karl did not get much out of it.

Close to her due date, Eve came to stay with me for a few days. The first evening about 11 p.m., she came rushing into my bedroom to say her waters had broken. I immediately rushed about getting the kettle on and collecting towels. When she asked me what I was doing I replied that I was doing what they always did in the movies! She said no, we needed to call Karl to come and collect her with her packed overnight bag.

Sure enough, Karl was there ready to take Eve to the hospital. Nothing happened, so the doctors suggested she spend the night on the hospital ward and they would induce her the next day. On 13 September 1990, at about 11 a.m., Alexa was born.

When Alexa was three months old Eve decided to return to Los Angeles with her daughter. For a moment, Alexa was stateless and had no right of abode anywhere, as the Zimbabwean government had written "no right of abode" on Alexa's birth certificate. She was also not permitted a UK passport as she was regarded as a third generation Brit. Luckily, I remembered that although born in Germany, Eve had been born in a British military hospital, which was technically classed as UK so that made her a first-generation Brit. This gave Alexa the right to get a passport, which she received within a few days.

I do not remember much of what Eve was up to in the USA during this time, but she eventually decided to go to the UK. She got a lovely flat in Oxted, in Surrey, found a crèche for Alexa and started working. She managed without the support of her ex-husband, who never made any contact with them for fifteen years. Somehow they muddled through.

In the meantime, Neville and I had settled into unmarried bliss. He wanted to marry me but I had enough from the previous two failed marriages. I felt better that way. I felt I was still free to walk away if it did not work out. Neville curtailed his drinking sprees to Friday nights. I do not know how he ever made it home; he merely said his car knew the way. "What about the narrow bridge?" I asked. He replied that it was no problem, as he always closed his eyes when crossing that bridge.

Quite often he left the car at the gate and only made it halfway up the drive to the house. There was no way I could have got him into the house as he was rather heavily built. But it was always warm in Rhodesia, so I just threw a blanket over him. A few hours later, when he had sobered up, he snuck into the house.

Well, Neville's drunken escapades could not go unpunished and, one day, he smashed into a tree on the way home. I went to the hospital in the middle of the night, but there was not too much wrong with him and he was full of his usual nonsense.

When he went to the toilet, he usually fell asleep on the seat, pants down. I wish I had taken a picture of him. Eventually, I thought maybe I should go with him on Friday nights. The "Rose Bowl", a pub not far away, held dances every Friday, so for a year we went and I danced. Neville drank instead as he was no dancer. There was a Scottish chap, a little fellow but a good dancer. I assure you we only danced. However, there was a commotion outside on one occasion and I was told Neville had just bashed this little chap, who had to flee in his car.

I asked Neville why he had attacked the poor man and he said, "He did not ask me if he could dance with you." I pointed out that he had been dancing with me for a year already without his 'permission', so why now? He had no answer and just sulked, as he usually did when he had nothing to say.

That was the end of the Rose Bowl so we tried Hatfield Sports Club, where they only had dances on certain occasions. Still, there was good company. One day two policemen came to ask if anybody had seen a certain car they were looking for. Things in Rhodesia were more laid back, and the policemen used the opportunity to enjoy a couple of beers. Later, one guest was leaving and returned to enquire whether the policemen had come by car. When they confirmed that they had, they were informed that their vehicle had been stolen. This, in a nutshell, was Rhodesia at that time.

Neville had hundreds of friends, and going through town with him he knew just about everyone. Yet it was difficult to like him at first. He had the habit of making derogatory remarks. He thought it was amusing to insult people, and they took objection to this, until they got to know him and got used to him. I was often asked how I put up with it, to which I replied, "That is why God gave me two ears – one to listen in and the other for it to go out."

He often showed off in front of people by trying to be the macho man, with me the nitwit. He only did this when I was present, though; otherwise people told me he used to sing my praises. In the 30 years we lived together, we did not have one fight, nor did he ever raise his hand against me.

He was very helpful around the house, putting up fencing, laying slasto[41] paving and even building orchid houses for me, one after the other, when I ran out of space. I hardly ever had to give him instructions, he just noticed what was required. Shortly after I met him, I was sitting in the lounge under the standing lamp doing needlework, when he got up and put a brighter bulb in for me. Things like that have always got me – not the big presents, although once in a while, he would bring home a huge bunch of flowers (I would have rather have had a small one in a tiny vase, but who's complaining).

I was very fond of him. Love? I think by then I was incapable of it. I had one great love in my life, my first one, Gerhard, and I still haven't forgotten him. But Neville was easy to live with, did not make any demands on me or moan about what I was doing. Although he did complain a lot about other people.

He was forever helping people with their problems, and he was good at fixing things. One day, when my car broke down and someone looked helpfully under the hood, he said, "Your husband must be a mechanic, I always recognize the signs." Neville was eventually put in charge of the garages at Securitas, the firm where he worked.

Being overweight, Neville suffered back problems and had a few operations. On one occasion, he said to the doctor who was going to operate on him, "Will I be able to play the piano after the op?"

The doctor said, "Of course, I don't see why not."

Neville replied, "Good, because I couldn't play it before."

The nurses adored him and told me if I did not want him, they would have him. I bet they said that to all the men!

---

[41] A kind of shale similar to slate

However, one person who did not take to him was my friend Marina. I visited her regularly and I would take Neville along at weekends. She did not like his common jokes, and he was only a mechanic after all!

Gradually, Marina came up with excuses about visits, and eventually our friendship petered out. Her two sons got married and she was now involved with the in-laws. Her grandchildren were born and we visited them when they were all together.

As I said, Marina did not like Neville, but she just about hated her husband. Although he was an accountant, he was otherwise hopeless around the house. Once she said, "If I ask him to put a nail in the wall, he would ask me to bring the ladder, bring the hammer, hold the ladder, hold the nail and he would just hammer it in. Then all week he would stand near the nail, admiring 'his' handiwork." This was said tongue in cheek, naturally.

Marina and I shared a love of gardening and were forever swapping plants and gardening books. However, she discovered she had breast cancer and her breasts were removed. After that she lost interest in the garden. Five years later, she was tested for cancer again and got the all clear. She and her husband returned to England, but I never got her address. Her sons stayed behind in Salisbury, and when I contacted them, I found out that Marina had moved to Derbyshire. After two years she died of cancer. Her husband suffered from dementia and we lost all contact after that.

Marina had been my only friend, but through Neville I would make friends that lasted for ever, and it started with the dogs.

32. Dogs

Our two Collies were getting on in age, and Chummy had rheumatism in his hind legs. There was a stray cat in the yard, that would hide unless it was flushed out unintentionally by the hosepipe. I noticed this cat licking out the dogs' dishes and eventually sharing them, especially with Chummy. She would not let people get near her, although she later came to the house as far as Chummy, who always used to lie in the doorway. The cat was always leaning up to Chummy who would then try to mate with her. However, with the rheumatism in his leg he always collapsed on the cat; it was hilarious. One morning, we found Chummy dead in the garden. We buried him by the fence.

Cheeky had trouble with his one ear blowing up and we took him to the vet, where he had an operation. When he came home, he straightaway made for the fishpond to drink some water, then he fell over and died. He had made it to twelve years, which for a big dog is a long life.

A couple of months later we got another Collie that we named Lassie. But I thought she was lonely, and when Neville was in South Africa picking up motorcar parts for his company, I saw an advert in the paper for Chow Chow puppies for sale in Bulawayo, some 400 kilometres away. I had always wanted a teddy bear and this was the closest to it, so I ordered one and then told Neville when he came home. He had no idea what a Chow looked like, but took my word for it. Off we went to pick up Charlie (the founder of a dynasty).

Neville and Lassie

It took over five hours by car, but even Neville was smitten when we saw six of these little teddy bears running around in a playpen. The cutest dogs you can ever imagine. The owners asked if we would "show" the dog. I did not know what they were talking about and said, "Of course, we will show him to all our friends." Only later did I find out there were such things as dog shows. She said she would keep the one she thought had show potential for some other people.

On the way home, Charlie was lying between Neville and me on the front seat. For half an hour he lay facing me, then he turned to stare at Neville for another half hour. Eventually he gave a big sigh as if to say, "I think they will do", and went to sleep. Neville was not even cross when we stopped halfway for a break and Charlie peed all over him while being lifted out of the car.

With Neville

A short time later, a couple came past our house, saw our Collie and asked if we showed her. They then introduced us to dog clubs. There were about ten in the country for various breeds and main shows. It was an exciting occasion, benching the dogs, seeing them win and their "Challenge Certificates" (CCs) displayed after the show. It took three wins for your dog to become a champion, and there were plenty of trophies to be had and displayed on the benches. Charlie was competing with a few other Chows. The first time he was beaten but after that he was well away.

Neville mainly did the showing but I had trouble getting him to the ring, Neville that is. When his turn came, he was usually in the bar. Therefore, I began to show Charlie more, especially when Neville was elected Chairman of the Chow Chow Club, a position he held for 22 years.

By that time, Rhodesia had become Zimbabwe. Many people had left the country, times were becoming uncertain and the interest in showing dogs waned. The new generation were not interested. To them a dog meant either protection or hunting wild animals for food. I once had an enquiry from one of them about a Chow Chow puppy. As they were called lion dogs by some people, they thought they must be good for hunting. Really! Of course, I would not sell them a puppy. Mind you, an African once said to me he would rather face a lion than our dogs.

Cheeky, Bobby, Lassie and Charlie

Let me tell you a brief history of the Chow Chow. The Chow was first bred in Mongolia by monks in cloisters. Some say the species was a cross between a bear and a wolf which would not surprise me due to their aloof nature, similar to cats. They seldom jump all over you and are very gentle on their feet. They have a stilted walk but are unique for their black tongue, something the judge always looks for. Apparently, the only other animal to share this trait is a bear somewhere in the north.

The monks used them as guard dogs. In later years the Chinese used to breed them for eating, as they had a different type of flesh to other dogs and also could be fed on very little. I, too, noticed that it did not take much food to keep them going. A horrible thought, although I could understand shaving them for their hair, as they have such beautiful long coats.

The children that met us were always overwhelmed by the black tongue and wanted to know how they got that, usually we said they had eaten too many mulberries. They are perhaps not the best companion dogs for small children and people always said one could not teach them anything. Charlie soon learnt how to sit up, give paw and dance around. He was also taught not to touch food given to him unless I said OK. But he did not do it for nothing: if you did not show him the reward in your hand, he just sniffed the hand and walked away. They said they were stupid; I do not think so. Would you work if you did not get paid?

Anyway, Charlie soon got his championship certificate and went on to accumulate over 40 CCs. He also accumulated a great many annual trophies, which were Neville's pride and joy, but one had to give them back. However, a number of trophies still show the name "Cinchar Kennels", which we registered our dogs under. This was made up from Cindy, our first bitch imported from South Africa, and Charlie. Every litter had to be registered in order to show the puppies.

With Charlie the Chow Chow

Charlie went from glory to glory. We went to dog shows all over the country, even distances where we had to stay in a hotel. Dogs were not very popular in hotels, but ours were well behaved and they always told us we could bring them back. They liked to keep their bed clean and were soon trained. We even travelled all the way by car to Johannesburg in South Africa where the competition was much greater.

Bathing Cindy

Charlie beat 22 Chows and got a double CC because of the big entry. However, the next day he had a Rhodesian judge and he came second. Judges do not like Chows. They usually handle the dogs to get their mouth open not only for their black tongue, but also to count their teeth. With Chows they always asked the owner to open their mouth; the dog's, of course! As a result they did not do so well against other breeds and seldom was Charlie in the line-up, but came second one year when they had a judge from England who knew more about Chows. His name was Arthur Westlake, who was very well known in the dog world. In the early days, there were a lot of visitors at the dog shows, I even managed to catch Ian Douglas Smith[42] on camera.

---

[42] Prime Minister of Rhodesia 1964–79

Ian Smith at a dog show

It was here I met my friend Sue. Her father had been breeding Chows for a long time, but Sue was then only a youngster. Her father later left for Australia and it was years later, when Sue returned with her husband Josh, they took up Chows and bred a few. It was then that our friendship grew and has been kept up to this day, although distance-wise we are now miles apart. I also met another Sue (Bews) who showed Schnauzers at one stage, and we later became friendly. But it was always Neville who made the first move and started the connections.

We started breeding Chows and, at one stage, three litters were born on the same day, distributed all over the house.

We had imported Lindy Lu from South Africa. She was not a good show dog, but a fantastic mother and bred good stock. We had another bitch, Jenny, bought when young, who was hopeless, as when puppies were born, she kept them in her mouth and would not let go.

Lindy Lu gave birth to seven huge pups. She was not supposed to have any puppies that season, but somehow Bobby, our Old English Sheepdog, had managed to get hold of her, and the pups inside her had already felt as though they were chasing sheep. Bobby was left with us by Eve when she moved in with Karl, who was not keen on keeping the dog as she insisted on Bobby sleeping in bed with them, preferably in the middle. Bobby was much better off with me and all the other dogs. My dogs always slept outside. They would not go into the kennels we bought for them, but slept on the *stoep*[43].

Bobby in hat and scarf

Lindy Lu wanted all the other pups as well and tried to get at them when she heard them crying. So, every time a pup was born in the next room, we swapped it with one of Lindy Lu's big mongrels. There was plenty of milk for all the pups and some to spare. I never had any problem with her births, they just popped out and she did all the work.

---

[43] Afrikaans: veranda

A couple of hours later the third bitch gave birth. She was given to us at the age of two as the owner said she was a cat killer and killed all the cats in the neighbourhood. We had no cats and the place was fenced, but every day she used to spend hours staring at the cat next door. She had little interest in her pups either and stopped getting milk after a couple of days. As Lindy Lu always wanted to get to her pups, we gave all of them to her. Their birth mother did not complain.

Marina with The Hulk

The vet came and took six of the mongrels with him, but Lindy Lu was still looking after seven pups, including the ones she fostered. We kept one huge mongrel and called him "The Hulk". Old English Sheepdogs are beautiful and we could never get far through town with Bobby without being stopped every few metres. You would have thought the combination of two beautiful dogs would have produced something special, but The Hulk was really ugly with long grey hairs sticking out all over his body. However, the children liked him and so did my Portuguese accountant, who wanted him. We could not keep all the dogs, otherwise we would have ended up with fifty over the years.

It was always hard to let the puppies go, especially when they looked their cutest. We usually kept one, always hoping for a really special winner. But it was so much fun getting them to that stage.

Chow puppies are very clean from an early age. I just put a piece of newspaper in a corner and they obliged. They did not like to soil their bed. When they reached the age of four weeks, I quickly took them outside first thing in the morning, listening to their stirring next door, which was usually at five in the morning. Once they got the message I got up, opened all the doors and ran outside making funny noises to attract them to follow through the kitchen and outside onto the lawn. I took a video of them once. There were six of them, neatly lined up in a straight line, and the stream facing the ground.

Dogs in the garden

We lost some pups at the age of just under a year, when they seemed to be most vulnerable to diseases. They were always been injected against everything, but one could not do this against the ticks, and some of them got biliary. This could kill within a few hours. We would call the vet on duty for the night, and were told the usual story, "Give them an aspirin and see me at the clinic in the morning."

We lost one that died in my arms on the way to the vet. Another one died right in front of the vet. We lost two more that way and I cried every time. We dipped the dogs, but it did not help.

Cheeky developed white growths around his gums and the vet took a test and told me he had cancer. When I walked out of the clinic a black attendant came after me. He had been doing this job for twenty years, and told me he thought they were warts and I must not worry. They fell off after ten days. I insisted on seeing another vet after this. I heard the first vet did not like any animal smaller than a sheep, just cows and horses. He had also been the one to recommend "aspirin".

One dog was nearly in an advert for the cinemas. They asked would he come along, and they even paid Z$10 a day. There were dozens of dogs of all kinds and sizes milling all over the place. They endeavoured to do a shot of five dogs sitting in a row, moving their mouths as if speaking. Well, the other dogs all had special training and stood there with their handlers. They got them to sit eventually, and my Chow just sat anyway. When they were ready to take a picture a couple of dogs moved off. Every time they got them lined up another one walked off. My Chow just sat.

They succeeded in the end, and started to shout at them "speak". By that time my Chow had enough, he gave a big yawn and walked off the set. I also gave up and retired him.

A big Dalmatian was supposed to do the talking. He had been trained, but would not open his mouth to get the food in. Someone suggested liver and fetched it, but it was frozen and the owner did not want to wait half an hour for it to defrost. Apparently they succeeded in the end, and the video also showed a dog I had watched roller skating.

Eventually, however, we gave up on breeding. The atmosphere in the country was changing. People had other worries than dogs and there was no demand for them. The Africans would have loved to buy them and I had many offers, but they only wanted them for guard dogs which, admittedly, they are good at with a bark that means business!

33. Karl

After Eve left with Alexa, we continued to visit Karl on the farm, where his best friend, a rich farmer, had built him a house. The house was very picturesque, like something out of a fairytale, with a thatched roof, balconies, porches and stairs leading from one side of the house to the other across mezzanine floors. Alexa made an authentic model replica of it when she was in junior school. She recreated the roof using grass, and used wood for the walls. We called it the "Hans and Gretel" house.

He had become involved with the film-making industry – he had an artistic temperament and was a very good writer of scripts, both for films and a sixteen-part TV series called *Moses*. It had mainly African actors, but Karl also appeared in a couple of episodes himself. He ended up falling for the African lead actress, another Ursula, and after going out with her for ten years, she insisted on marrying him. The marriage lasted only a year, however, before they got divorced. I am not sure why – perhaps she was just after his money. In a way I could understand: when we visited Karl, we noticed that he treated her like a servant. But we were of course on Karl's side, and when he kept getting ill, we worried she might have put the "voodoo" on him. I had a friend that ran a garden nursery and once Ursula asked us to bring her some herbs on our next visit to the farm. My friend was also into voodoo. She brought a voodoo plant along, guaranteed to ward off all evil spirits, and we placed it in between the herbs. It must have helped, as Karl got better.

Once, before Karl split from Manfred, he asked Neville to take part in a video advert for men's clothing, to be shown in the adverts at the cinema. They were all shown changing from cheap looking clothes into "Karl's Fashion" clothes, with Neville being the awkward one struggling to get his pants on.

After that, Neville was even shown in a full-page advert for a restaurant in the Salisbury newspaper. It shows him sitting at the table, smartly dressed, shoving food in his mouth. He also modelled for an advert for a sports shop and a brochure. He sat there trying to handle a dozen pieces of sports equipment at the same time.

I was never included in the pictures. Once they came and used my lounge for a couple of pictures in a catalogue for the newspaper. It was supposed to present a Christmas party with decorations hanging from the ceiling, paper hats and a beautiful spread of food. I thought they would at least let me have some of the food, but it was all packed up and taken away. I got Z$25, which was more than I got for playing the accordion.

One of my clients at the bank had a big tobacco farm, and on a couple of occasions I was asked play the accordion at her Christmas parties. There were about 100 guests and in spite of all her wealth the menu consisted of *sadza* (mealie pap, i.e. maize porridge) and *boerewors* (spiced sausage). They were mostly white Boers and I knew quite a few Afrikaans party songs.

They would drive around the farm first, spread over a few wagons drawn by four oxen. This always took place in the moonlight and was very romantic. At first, they asked me to sit in the front of the wagon and I got out my accordion. They were still getting the oxen together from the meadows and busy tying them to the wagon, but when I started playing all the oxen ran away again. So I had to sit in the back.

I played on repeat occasions and once they decided to give a party for their German-born friends at a restaurant. I was asked to play German songs, but there was not much response from the guests. Then I played Afrikaans music and everyone got up and started dancing and having fun. They might have been German-born, but they had all become Afrikaners. I even got paid Z$10 a night.

Playing the accordion

Another Christmas, the Salisbury Kennel Club decided to stage a pantomime. No, they did not ask me to play, it was Neville's turn to shine. They staged *Snow White and the Seven Dwarfs*. All actors played opposite roles, i.e. the tallest men were picked for dwarfs, and vice versa. Neville played "Snow White". He was well suited to the role, playing the fool all the time, and it was a great success. A video was made of it, which was excellent.

One gentleman (he really acted like one), showing Dachshunds, who was also chairman of the club often invited several members from the club to parties at his house. His son was killed on a motorbike. I was coming home on the bus and saw the bike lying in the street, but not knowing who it was, we did not stop – only to learn later that his son had hit a lorry and been beheaded. His head had rolled down the street, still inside the helmet. Gruesome.

Six or so people from the dog societies died. Something nearer home; the neighbours who had once welcomed us with a tray of tea when we moved into Meadow Crescent decided to leave the country before Rhodesia became independent. They were worried about violence and moved to Durban in South

Africa for safety. A few months later we heard that their daughter Angie, who was friends with Eve, had died in a bomb explosion in Durban – she just happened to be passing when the bomb went off.

The next experience with death was even closer to home. I had a good friend, Shirley. She was Asian and the most beautiful woman in Rhodesia, in my view. She reminded me of Sophia Loren, an actress I always liked. She was running a garden nursery about a mile from us. When I heard that there was a nursery so close by, I simply had to visit it. She was charitable to a fault. People used to leave with wheelbarrows full of plants having only being charged for one. She was always giving me plants and, as a result, the nursery did not make any profit and her partner Slav (from Slovenia) had to pay the wages from his own income. He was fairly well off running a motor and tractor spares factory. Every visitor was offered a cup of tea and cake, sometimes even a samosa – nobody could make them as well as she did.

We did not become really close until Neville accompanied me to the nursery and she invited us to sit in the middle of the garden, where chairs and tables were laid out for tea and cake. Her husband was mowing the lawn, sitting on a lawn mower and shouted to her to bring out the samosas and he came and sat with us. Neville and Slav were soon talking animatedly about motorcars and engines. Slav said they had a *braai* laid on for that night and would we come and join them. That was the beginning of a great friendship. It lasted for years.

Shirley suffered from bad circulation. Her veins started swelling and gradually her stomach as well. She never had any hesitation to parade in front of me *à la nature*, as she was never ready when I picked her up. Still busy in the shower and washing her hair, she was always late. But on those occasions, I saw how parts of her body had turned blue-black. I always thought Slav had hit her.

She had married Slav in her garden, which was like a park with rocks, waterfalls and bridges over ponds. They made a lot of money later by renting the place out for wedding parties and photos. She had shut the nursery by then.

They also had a guesthouse near Kariba Dam, close to a river and it was a beautiful place. The elephants came right up to the house. One Christmas, Slav went there with friends to go boating and fishing. Slav was scuba diving and as there was an empty boat floating in the middle of the river he went to investigate. He found it was anchored down and he dove to investigate. Somehow he got entangled with the chain, came up a couple of times and shouted for help. His friends stood helplessly by the river and watched him drown. I often wonder why they did not swim out to help. Perhaps they were scared about crocodiles, which sometimes turned up.

Eventually, Shirley's condition became so bad she had to go to hospital. We visited her nearly daily. They were worried about blood clots and treating her with warfarin. She improved at home but then suddenly got worse.

Shirley was very much into voodoo and other mystic matters. She had started getting entangled with a guru who ran charity buses for children who could not afford to go to school. Sheila provided the funds – she was really a Mother Theresa type. The guru told her she would only get better if she stopped taking warfarin. Unfortunately, she trusted the guru and did as he suggested, then deteriorated by the hour. I visited her every day in her bedroom.

I asked an Indian doctor to look at her who booked Shirley into hospital straightaway. They told me she was feeling much better, but a day later she died. The patient across the passage said they heard her crying out (she was in a single ward) but nobody had taken any notice. Like Slav before her, she had an Indian style funeral, and looked beautiful in the coffin, as if she was only asleep like Snow White.

34. Flower clubs

I joined Hatfield Flower Club shortly after I arrived in Rhodesia. I also joined the City Garden Club Society and a few others. I put a few of my flowers on show and became especially known for my irises, which Eve had kindly sent me from America. I gave speeches about them and did well at the shows; more trophies to engrave. However, one year all the trophies were stolen.

Once in a while, Neville came along and was so popular that they made him chairman (they must have been desperate). He did very well and was great at organizing meetings and flower shows. He had a lot of experience from having been chairman of the Utility Club for 21 years, at which stage they gave him a big party and the "key" to the kennel club: a golden replica of "21". When he made speeches at the openings of the Hatfield Flower Shows, he surprised me. I did not know he had it in him.

I was by now becoming bored with irises that only performed for a few years and then succumbed to the hot climate. They simply refused to flower, missing the cold nights to get them going. I then started growing daylilies. They did well and I began cross pollinating them and produced some really beautiful varieties. I did the same with amaryllis and was very proud of my achievements.

But there was still room for orchids. We joined the Orchid Society and Neville straightaway made friends with a Dutch couple. They were both honeys and we became best friends: Dieuwe and Piet, a little bit younger than I, more Neville's age. (Remember, Neville was about twelve years younger than me.) We exchanged many visits although they lived on the opposite side of town.

The journey was twelve kilometres through town and out again. But the roads were not as congested with traffic as in Europe and the streets were wide so it did not take long. Apparently, when the settlers founded the town years ago, they made sure the roads were wide enough to turn an ox wagon around. Even out of the middle of the town the roads were still wide and the houses all had big grounds, mostly an acre.

Winning a cup at the Hatfield Flower Show

In the past Neville and I had often gone for a ride around the suburbs to admire the gardens and houses which were clearly visible behind the low fences. Later, crime started getting so bad that everyone built huge walls around them and installed security gates. Not that that stopped the burglars from entering as they climbed over the walls and, when people decided to electrify the top of the walls, they just dug under them.

The Orchid Society was still in existence when I left Zimbabwe. I was told that in the early days, membership was restricted, the entrance fee was high and one's background scrutinized before one could join. When Rhodesia changed to

Zimbabwe, we had some black visitors at last but only a couple of them became members. Some told me they did not like the atmosphere. Amongst the ones that were enthusiastic enough to join was Bertha.

Bertha was married to a German engineer, who had done very well in Africa. They had a beautiful house in the better part of town, and her garden was really something. She had a real open nature and had no problem getting on with anybody. She was one of us.

Her husband, Kurt, was not liked very much and he did not like anyone either. Strangely enough, he and Neville became great pals. Bertha became my friend and we visited each other frequently. She gave really elaborate parties, but never had much time, and was always busy, busy, busy. Also, she had a big family in the area so we did not see too much of her.

I think Kurt had mental health problems. Nobody could understand what he was talking about, except Neville. One day, when Neville was in hospital (I will come back to that later), Kurt had some kind of fit and Bertha took him to the same hospital. I was visiting Neville, when Kurt came in and just plonked himself on the bed. Bertha had left Kurt at reception while she booked him in, but he somehow wandered off and, having visited Neville before, knew his way. It was really funny.

Later, on one of their visits to Kurt's relatives in Germany, she just booked him into a home there. He was not too happy when he realized this, but it was for his own good, and at least he had all his family (children) nearby. Bertha later inherited a portion of a farm in Zambia and moved there, with her boyfriend and all her orchids.

We were still showing our orchids but it was difficult to obtain new ones. We "brought" some in from outside the country, mainly when visiting the UK where we'd heard they threw orchids into the dustbin when they stopped flowering. We often wished we could have those.

Although the Orchid Society had their own clubhouse and grounds, usually used for exhibitions, over the summer months the club also visited other orchid growers. They came to my place at least once a year. One time, a new chairman was elected while at my house, a doctor specializing in spine surgery. I had met him once when he did a lumbar puncture on my back, and I asked him if he remembered me.

He said he did not. I said to him, "Of course, you would not remember me with my clothes on." I was his pal after that! I was always clowning around. To me, life is not only full of fun, but also funny.

35. Birth of Zimbabwe

Things changed drastically when Rhodesia became Zimbabwe; it was the end of an era.

The British settlers had taken over the country during the 1880s and Southern Rhodesia (now Zimbabwe), Northern Rhodesia (Zambia) and Malawi were all under British control. It was split up and the other two provinces got their independence. In 1965, British government in Southern Rhodesia broke down, but Ian Smith would not give up or give in, and took over. He declared UDI, and this lasted until 1979, when British rule was asserted once more for a brief period before the country's independence was internationally recognized.

Following UDI, sanctions were introduced and trade with Rhodesia was forbidden. However, some countries ignored this, mainly South Africa and Portugal, and the ports via Mozambique and South Africa were still accessible.

Goods were snuck into the country, even weapons. This was relevant for my job, as they were mainly paid via letters of credit: any direct transfer of funds was impossible. Tobacco, meat, grain and even flowers were exported the same way, and also covered by my department.

Some of my customers gave fantastic Christmas parties, to which Neville and I were invited. Neville being a meat eater especially appreciated their buffets. One of the import and export firms that I dealt with gave parties in some of the hotels. I was invited and the food tables were simply bulging with the huge array of canapés. I once was invited to a Greek party where I saw food I didn't recognize. I was especially impressed with a stuffed turkey, which had a duck inside, the duck had a chicken inside and so on with other meats.

Yet, although things appeared to be normal on the outside, the pinch of no investments was felt and there were shortages, for instance, luxury items.

The bush war started. The original owners of the land rebelled and took up arms. The rebels at first only had a panga which was an axe-shaped weapon they made themselves, but eventually they received military aid, mainly from Russia.

The police tried to deal with it, but the attacks against white farmers increased and the Rhodesian military was called in. They stated that 70% of the Rhodesian Army were non-Europeans.

Personally, I do not think they had anything against Ian Smith, the same would have ultimately happened under British rule. The difference would have been that the UK would have handed the country over long before that, and the white farmers would have had to leave earlier too. Ian Smith declared "independence" to try to keep the whites in the country.

A lot of people were killed on both sides, including civilians, even by their own people if they did not toe the line. People in the country were more vulnerable and there were many stories of farmers being killed. They built fences around their homes and cut down trees to improve visibility, but bravery does not help when one is outnumbered.

In town things looked almost normal. Everyone was a little apprehensive, but people had their jobs to get on with. Urban Africans were better educated, not so easily swayed, but in the country the population was wider spread. They never knew much about what was going on in the world, they just wanted a full belly and if they refused to fight or give assistance to the guerrillas (the "freedom fighters"), they would suffer, sometimes even with their life. One can understand that they wanted their land back. Did not every country in the world?

On the other side, the Rhodesian government could not hang on forever. There were less and less weapons being supplied by South Africa and more weapons were smuggled in for the guerrillas, who perfected their bush war tactics. Although I feel it would have been better to focus on education first, in 1976 Ian Smith gave in to the pressure and accepted majority rule, which threw many people into a cauldron.

It must have taken a long time for the news to spread, as fighting continued. In 1978 a plane was shot down by Nkomo's[44] soldiers between Salisbury and Kariba, killing 59 people. A great many farmers had been murdered during the year, cars were attacked in the open roads and the passengers killed. On longer journeys, whites organized convoys escorted by one armed car in the front and one in the rear. Once when I attended a dog show in South Africa with Neville, we had to wait outside town until there were enough to form a convoy. Sometimes even convoys were attacked.

The elections were held in 1979 and Bishop Muzorewa, United African National Council (UANC), became the first black prime minister. He left the whites one third of the seats in Parliament, which was of course very much out of proportion as the total population of Zimbabwe Rhodesia – as it became called – was over 7 million and the white minority a mere 250,000. However, the new government was not internationally recognized nor did they receive any support from the outside.

The majority of the population resided in the part of country that supported Robert Mugabe, who represented the Zimbabwe African National Union (ZANU). They had been eyeing the farms, but unfortunately did not have a clue how to run them. Another election was held and Mugabe naturally won. He was generous enough to let Ian Smith stay on his country farm. We all thought he would not turn out to be so bad after all. To err is human!

In April 1980, Rhodesia became Zimbabwe, and in 1982 Salisbury changed to Harare and streets were renamed. It was at first very confusing to remember all the

---

[44] Joshua Nkomo, Mugabe's rival and Vice-President of Zimbabwe, 1990-99

new street names in the town, but besides this for a while everything went on as before.

However, there were rumours that Mugabe planned to throw out all whites that were not Zimbabweans and confiscate their houses, so a number of white people applied for Zimbabwe passports, myself included. I still had British nationality, but through my second husband, who had insisted I also carry a South African passport. As the rules were coming out to forbid dual nationality, I kept quiet about my South African one.

In 1982, I applied for Zimbabwean citizenship, which was no easy task, as the requirements were numerous. We heard that it took a long time, as the demand was high and the queues long. Two years later, when I made enquiries as to the progress of my application they stated they had lost all my documents although they still had my file number, so I had to start all over again. Seven years later, I gave up and applied to have my South African passport extended. Before I had filled in the form, I received a letter saying my Zimbabwe passport was ready. It was the easier option and I picked up my new passport.

36. Visit to Germany

While Eve was still living in Rhodesia, she persuaded me to visit Germany. I had not been back for twenty years. When I originally left Germany, I was in constant contact with my family there. My mother sent parcels for Christmas mainly with marzipan, my favourite, and her home-baked biscuits. However, when we moved from Johannesburg for a few months, the parcels were not forwarded and were returned to my mother two months later – everything ruined, of course. To this day I never found out why, but from that time on my mother never wrote to me, and there was no reply to my letters. My brother never wrote letters anyhow but at least he would phone me at Christmas time. Whenever I phoned, they were very abrupt. So, I gave up.

Eve has been, and still is, a great one for getting family together and insisted I should visit them. I was not keen on flying so she came with me. We told my mother we were coming and off we went.

My brother picked us up at the airport and, on the way from Hamburg to Lüneburg, he said to me in the car, "What made you come back after all these years? Do you think Omi is getting old and there is something to inherit?" I'd never even thought of it. It was like meeting strangers and I just could not warm to the German attitude.

I had bought a new outfit for the journey and my mother said, "I hope you have better things in the suitcase." That hurt; she eventually relented and said, "At least your glasses look expensive."

They were keen to show off and bragging all the time. Perhaps my mother had something to brag about. She had received a small inheritance of 4000 *Deutschmarks* and had bought a house in the suburbs of Lüneburg. I visited the new place and it was rather pleasant with a lovely big garden. My mother lived with Norbert for a while, until she met her new partner, Paul.

Anyway, no expense was spared. If she had seen how we drunk out of mugs in Rhodesia she would have had a *cadenza*. Only porcelain here and not just one set but three, all matching. Three sets of cutlery, one was silver, one was gold, crystal glasses etc. I got the message.

I had warned her that I was smoking 60 cigarettes a day, so she put up old curtains. I tried hard to cut down to twenty during my stay, and thought I could make up on the way to town, but no smoking was permitted on the bus, or in the shops either. Once when I lit a cigarette, an old woman came up to me in the street and mumbled something about polluting the air. It was not only our family that had become impossible.

One day, the handle of my handbag tore and I went into a shop to have it fixed. The saleswoman said to me, "You realize your bag is only an imitation and we would have to fix it with leather, which would make it rather expensive." I had it fixed anyhow.

My mother had two different tones of voice. With strangers she spoke in a nasal tone. She spoke to me in that tone for two weeks, but changed in the last week. Things got a little better after that but it was upsetting as she had always been such a good sport in the past. We were often treated as sisters when we were younger, as she was only nineteen years older than me. In later years it became even more apparent that my mother looked ten years younger than her age, while I looked ten years older. It does not bother me. The climate of Rhodesia was to blame. When I worked in the garden in the hot sunshine, I never thought of wearing a hat.

I visited my mother a second time later on and things went much better, and with Norbert also. He took me to Hamburg, and it was lovely walking along the Elbe. He showed me the famous street in Hamburg, the Reeperbahn, where at night the women sat in the window inviting men.

My mother and I went to Berlin to visit Tante Lene, the one that had looked after me when the Russians came. My uncle had since died, but her daughter Gerda was now married with a family. Tante Lene lived in a beautiful, most spacious flat with lots of rooms.

It was exciting to see Berlin again, which had been quickly rebuilt. However, they had left the ruins of the *Gedächtniskirche*, a church in the middle of the famous Kurfürstendamm, the entertainment area of Berlin. They just put a small building in front. I remembered the night during the war when I had been in town at my dancing lessons. We had waited out the alarm in a bunker. The town was in flames, the ruins of the church reaching up to the sky like a silhouette against the burning skies.

With Mother, Tante Lene and Gerda in Berlin

The Berlin Wall was still up and I could not go to the eastern zone to check up on my old abode. We could just look over it. We hardly saw any British or American soldiers but plenty of Russians on the other side. Stories were told about people trying to escape over the wall or tunnelling under it and a few being killed in the effort. I noticed the presence of Russians on the train on the way from

Lüneburg to Berlin. We had to keep all windows closed, but saw on every station a policeman with sniffer dogs running under the train in case of illegal passengers.

On the American and British side of the border there was no sign of Germany being occupied, yet in the Russian occupied Zone there were high watch towers every kilometre along the border, manned with Russian soldiers. They really seemed like a different race, as expressed in a joke I remember from those days:

An officer at a Russian interrogation centre is questioning detainees: "How much is two plus two?" "Five" replies the first one. "Good, Good" says the interrogator. The same question is asked of the next one: "How much is two plus two?" This one answers "Three". "Excellent" says the interrogator. However, when faced with the same question, the third prisoner replies "Four". The interrogator calls in the guards, saying, "Shoot this fellow, he knows too much!".

37. Banking

On the whole, I was glad to return to Rhodesia, or let us call it Zimbabwe from now on. Over the last few years, the atmosphere in the country had already changed as a few Africans were employed as clerks, whereas in the past they were only there to run errands and make the tea. One of them was really advanced when he was promoted to be in charge of the mail section. This chap, by the way, became quite involved in the labour movement later. He was one of the few blacks to own his car at that time, which he proudly drove to work. Once I asked him if it had been difficult for him to get a driving licence. He told me in confidence, he drove without one and he got away with it somehow.

From the day Ian Smith stood down, if there was a vacancy we could only employ Africans. By now, quite a few white people were leaving the country. It took, however, two Africans to replace the one white person who had left. In the Letters of Credit Department for instance, there were soon ten employed instead of the six before, even though the work had practically been reduced to a third. Over the next few years, this was not only the case in our department, but in many others too, as money was slowly running out in the country. Eventually it came to a standstill in around 2005.

In the meantime, we got on with our new "comrades". I would not say all were behind – we had one girl, for instance, whose work I admired, and who became the accountant eventually. I was glad as, on the whole, I found African women more dedicated to their work and brighter than their male counterparts.

There was a lot of office crime by then, even in the higher departments and by whites too. Maybe they saw the writing on the wall and wanted to feather their nests before leaving the country. This happened a couple of years before the "takeover".

We had a charming chap in head office who often came by for a chat and was very much liked by everyone. One day he vanished and so did a few hundred thousand dollars, which was only discovered by the auditors months later on their routine inspection. As this chap was one of the chief signatories for drafts and transfers, it had been easy to smuggle the money out of the country. They never found him or the money and the whole matter was hushed up and never made public – not to spoil the image of the bank or scare the investors I suppose. In those days that amount was still a lot of money.

I was introduced to a black sub-manager who had been promoted from another bank. He was very young and always teasing me that he wanted to marry me. One time, he came into my office and asked me for advice. As sub-manager he also had co-signing power on foreign transfers etc. and someone had asked him to sign a bogus transfer, offering him a bribe in return. He needed a second signature which he asked me to provide. I told him not to be stupid, that I would never agree to such a thing and he should keep out of such situations.

When he went on leave, and I had to get something from his desk, I found a couple of syringes in his drawer. I gave him the benefit of the doubt, besides I knew a lot of Africans smoked "dagga" (marijuana), which they grew in their gardens.

I had once found a plant looking like a marigold growing on the compost heap in my garden. When I asked my gardener (it was some time before I employed Fibian who would stay with me for 25 years) what kind of plant it was he said it was just a weed and he would pull it out. I told him it looked interesting and would he put it somewhere else in my garden. The next day the plant was gone; he said he had thrown it away. Only in later years I saw pictures of this plant which turned out to be a dagga plant.

On one occasion, when my gardener was on leave, a youngish European chap came to my door, asking for him. I told him he was away, so this chap asked me if I would sell him some "dagga" as that was where he used to get his supply. I told him to get lost, but spoke to the neighbour on the side of the yard where my gardener's *kia* was situated. They told me they had noticed a lot of activity going on near that *kia* late at night, people coming to the fence and talking to my servant. I realized he was dealing in dagga.

I was very scared as I was living alone in the house at that time. I thought if I went to the police this chap would take revenge on me and come back and kill me. One never knew what they would do when under the influence of drugs. I had noticed the shiny eyes of my servants from time to time, but did not look too closely, so obviously he was also a user. Now I was wondering how to get rid of him. When my gardener returned, I told him the police had been looking for him while he was away. Had he done anything? Anyhow, the next morning he was gone and I heard later he had moved to another town far away from the scene of the crime.

By the way, after I retired from the bank, my sub-accountant took over my job and a year later got killed in a car accident. Apparently he crashed into another car, but was fine. However, when he got out of the car on the street side, he got run over by another passing car and died.

They put graduates in managerial positions. They sure had the education and had learned about banking and knew their sums, but the Foreign Department was a bit more specialized. I got fed up with doing their job, while they sat around and chatted. I used to be told off if one of my staff did something wrong, while any praise for doing things well went to the manager. With over 60 on the staff, I could not be everywhere at the same time. It was the job of the people in charge of the different sections, but if they overlooked a mistake, it was my fault. And they did make mistakes.

One day, a new clerk arrived. He started at 8 a.m. and by 9 a.m. he came to my office asking for a loan. He could not understand when I just laughed. He said he thought overdrafts came with the perks of the employment. After one hour? I ask you. Another one proudly told me that he had listed all his brothers, sisters, parents etc. on the income tax return as dependants. I told him he would not pay any income tax anyhow as he was earning very little and would get into trouble for false declarations.

38. Retirement

Coping with their ignorance and my responsibilities was getting too much for me, so I decided it was time to retire. I was than 59 and had been at pensionable age for three years, although I could have continued till 65. Anyhow, I had had enough. They were all very sorry to see me go and gave me a great farewell party, with some presents. Afterwards, I visited them from time to time but eventually there were only one or two familiar faces left.

Ten years later when I went to get a signature on my life existence certificate for pension purposes, I found a manager who had started as a clerk in my office. He looked at my signature and said it had not changed over the years, he could still recognize it from the 100 or so drafts I had signed, sometimes in one go. I was very proud in that moment. I had never thought about my signature having been lodged in all the banks in the world at one stage as authorized.

Fortunately, I had opted to keep my South African pension and not change over to the Zimbabwean one. On the election of the new government, the majority of the shares of the bank had been bought up by the Mugabe government from Nedbank and it was renamed Bank of Rhodesia, then Zimbabwean Banking Corporation when Nedbank pulled out. The Zimbabwean money became worthless in time, but the rand became worth its weight in gold.

Some years before, the staff were allowed to purchase shares in the bank and we received great dividends once a year. Eventually it stopped, as things were going a bit haywire by then and everyone gave them time to sort this out. But it was found some clerk had embezzled the dividends and the whole issue was closed down.

I straightaway enjoyed my retirement. I also found I had less time than before. I stopped doing my tapestries of which I had done about 100 over the last ten years – very exquisite for someone who always got only low marks at school for needlework! I imported the sets from Germany, and did them in my spare time after work.

As I could no longer afford to have two servants, I let my cook/houseboy go and kept the gardener, who could also do washing and ironing, and clean the house daily. I decided to do the cooking myself. Luckily, Neville cooked from time to time.

I also had to give up smoking which was getting too expensive. I had tried to give up before. It lasted three weeks (it was easier to give up if you had a cold and did not feel like smoking for a while). However, the day it was announced that Mugabe had been elected I said to my friend, "Quick, give me a cigarette," and that was it. But now I really had to give up and I managed somehow. For years, I still enjoyed inhaling the smoke of someone else's smoke.

I managed to pay my last instalment on the house and could now proudly consider myself the owner of a house. When in the later years I was alone, I used to get up in the morning, look out of the front door and like Tarzan beat my chest, saying, "It is all mine!"

We had built on another large room a few years previously when I was working and benefitted from cheap housing loans. That was another beautiful era of my time in Rhodesia.

Shortly after Neville moved in with me for good, I got a loan from the bank at 1% and built an extension to the house. I drew up a plan the way I wanted it, the main thing being to have big windows. There was a window facing the front which reached just about from one wall to the other and the room must have been four metres wide. The side to the rear garden also had the same width of glass, but with a sliding door opening the space halfway. I would have liked sliding doors all the way but the builders said it was not possible for some reason. But both glassed sides reached right down to the bottom and nearly to the ceiling. Under the front window I had a flower box from one side to the other, about a metre wide. The floor was slasto paving, which also covered the *stoop* (porch) in front of the sliding door. If necessary, one could close off this portion and make another room out of it. But it was lovely sitting on the *stoop* and handy for parties and garden club meetings, providing cover when it rained.

At the same time, we had a wall-to-wall wardrobe built into the main bedroom, which had previously been the lounge. I wanted mirrors all the way along but the builders said due to the availability of building materials they could only cover the doors. I think they thought I was a bit of a pervert with my mirrors, but agreed later it made all the difference. At least the mirrors were not on the ceiling!

The kitchen was extended using a previously small bedroom, cupboards were built and, in the corner, I created a breakfast nook. As soon as the builders knocked off work, I took my chair into the partially finished room, sat down with a cup of coffee and a cigarette. I had a photograph taken. These were all uninteresting things to an outsider but to me it meant a lot.

39. Alexa

Eve never lost contact with me. She had moved to the UK three years after Alexa was born, found a small flat, a job and settled down there. Alexa must have been a few years old when the two of them came to visit me in Zimbabwe.

I had been used to strong discipline in my youth and could not quite follow the new idea that children never even got their hands smacked, to say nothing of a good hiding. Alexa was a spirited child and full of energy, who sometimes I felt needed a firmer hand. In my view, withdrawing privileges as punishment does not seem to work too well with children, especially when the parents soon relent and give in.

One time, when Eve and I were ready to go to town, we could not tear Alexa away from the TV. We could not leave her and I got a bit impatient. I took the practical approach and switched off the television. Alexa turned it on again. After a couple of times, I waited for her to reach for the television knob and slapped her hand.

Alexa was distraught, and ran to tell her mother. Eve came running in. "You do not hit children!" she said. I explained I had only lightly smacked her fingers. Alexa went into the bedroom and continued to cry, or pretend to cry, which I felt was an overreaction, but I quickly realized my approach to parenting was not in line with modern thinking and at odds with that of my daughter. My view was that although children should not be beaten, a smack now and then would not kill them.

A couple of years later I went to visit Eve in the UK. She then had a tiny flat (tiny especially by my standards at that time). It was situated two floors up with no lift. I called it the doll's house. It was rather cute. If a second person came to the kitchen, the first one had to get out first.

Eve always had a job, but bringing up a child on your own is not cheap. Still, she sent me a flight ticket from time to time. The first time I drove to Oxted, in

Surrey, I could not believe my eyes. Years ago, when I was married to Eve's father, we lived for a couple of years in Hertfordshire. I found the country very dreary as I was used to wide-open spaces. This time I noticed that there was plenty of space. It was not flat and pretty bare, but hilly and full of lush trees and meadows. Everything was green. In Zimbabwe, most of the spaces are sparsely treed. There are some bushes here and there, but the grass is never green. I changed my opinion of England.

The family in Oxted

And the shopping! Zimbabwe had slowly fallen behind with that. I had a bit of a battle getting used to the stairs but after a short time I went up and down as if I was on even ground.

I bought Alexa a teddy bear, but it was hardly looked at and vanished into the attic after a couple of days. I heard she had plenty of stuffed toys. I got her to bring all of them down from the attic and lay them on the bed, there were about 250 of them. I couldn't believe it. After all, I had had to wait half my life for one. How things had changed, and no wonder my present was not appreciated.

I was very good at unintentionally giving the wrong presents. Once, when I visited my mother in Germany, I thought she would like a carved armband from Zimbabwe. I paid Z$100 million for it. My mother looked at it, said very nice, thank you and put it away. When I went to the shops in Lüneburg later on, I saw a much better one, which came from Asia and only cost about $10. She must have thought me a real miser.

In Zimbabwe, giving presents was hardly the done thing. On birthdays or Christmas, one brought a bottle of wine when visiting. There was no giving or receiving of Christmas cards – a phone call was enough. Perhaps Ronnie's children from his first marriage will understand now when I was not generous with my presents. When I met them for the first time – all grown up, it was embarrassing for me when they covered me in presents.

Alexa and a few of her teddy bears

In common with many children, Alexa spent a lot of time in front of the television. When Eve went to work, I would have loved to see some new programmes, as in Zimbabwe we'd only had one local station. Instead, we watched *Children's Hour*, or one of her fairytale tapes. Recalling my previous bad experience in respect of the television, I suffered in silence and waited for Eve to return so I could watch some grown-up programmes with her. The next time I visited Eve, she had two televisions, each with a full range of paid channels – one in the bedroom and one in the lounge. Eve suggested one day to Alexa that it would be more economical to have only free channels on one of the TV sets, whereupon Alexa said, "Fine by me… but what are *you* going to watch?" When I arrived, Eve told me she had specially acquired a number of Disney movies, as Alexa had told her how much I liked them!

One day, early in the morning, we heard a commotion outside in the street, and we looked out to see a car had smashed through the window of a television shop across the street. The thieves had balaclavas covering their faces. They just picked up widescreen sets through the window and went off. However, while they were busy a man working in the post office nearby spotted them and phoned the police.

The police were there in two minutes (not hours later like in Zimbabwe or not turning up at all). They chased after the car and we were told later that they caught one of them while the other got away in a waiting car. When the police came to cordon off the scene of crime, Eve shouted from the window. "We are witnesses, we saw everything." So they came upstairs and asked us questions.

"How many were there?" Eve said five, I said three and Alexa said four. "What kind of car was it?" It was a Peugeot, no, a Renault. Only Alexa was sure. "What colour?" Brown, green, grey. I must say, Alexa's replies were usually the correct ones. Anyhow they took a statement, but we never heard from them. I am not surprised – unreliable witnesses, they must have thought. There, I came from a country full of crime to witness one in the UK.

Another time, at midnight, there was a disturbance in the street. There was a pub down the road and some drunkards were fighting. It was too dark to see and we only heard the slap – like someone hitting another with a plank of wood and shouting, "Hit him, hit him!" Never a dull moment.

I always had a great time visiting Eve. She took me on a trip along the River Thames right up to Greenwich. It was really something unforgettable for me. So was seeing the *Phantom of the Opera*, and coming home after midnight through London – my first trip to the opera since the war. They had cinemas and drive-ins in Rhodesia, but the drive-ins ceased after a while as the speakers were regularly stolen. There were also complaints about the goings on of some couples in the cars, in front of the children. Still, it was good while it lasted.

Admiring flowers with Alexa

Alexa grew up just fine, of course. Sometimes, when she was a teenager, I thought there were too many parties, but then I remember my own youth and I was not much better. She went to bed late and slept in, but emerged as a beautiful, sensible woman who went on to university and enjoys travel.

When she was about sixteen, she became curious about her father and with Eve's help they succeeded in locating Juan in Panama. He had not seen his daughter since she was six months old and immediately flew out to visit her in the UK, in time to witness her going to her prom. He became very fond of her and they have kept in close contact ever since. Alexa has visited him in Panama twice and they met up in California on another occasion. She enjoyed California so much I would not be surprised if she returns.

I feel Juan must have changed a lot since I first met him in South Africa when he married Eve. I never took him for the type that would take up growing coffee and starting a farm. He has risen in my esteem as a result, as he shares my love of plants and animals.

40. My Mother

On my last visit to Eve's "doll's house", she arranged for my mother to visit at the same time. This was a great reunion: four generations together in one room. My mother had since "gathered" a new boyfriend, Helmut, who was about fifteen years younger than she was. He drove her all the way from Germany by car. When they arrived in Oxted, they could only find parking in a disabled zone and my mother, in spite of her 92 years, was anything but. A Bobby[45] (I miss these old-fashioned chaps around England) told her she was not allowed to park there. She thought he was very sweet and in her broken English she told him so. Her charm worked and he let them offload and get settled in before moving the car.

My mother managed the steep steps to Eve's flat better than I did. Helmut parked the car in the next street, where they were staying in a bed and breakfast. Helmut looked nice and was obviously fond of my mother. A couple of days later we were invited to a barbecue by one of Eve's friends from Zimbabwe. They lived in a huge flat in a mansion, looking after it for most of the year, while the owners (her cousin) lived in Cape Town. When my mother heard of the invitation, she thought the queen had invited her. At long last her offspring had shown some panache!

It was a *braai* in the afternoon, nevertheless my mother got dressed up to the nines. When we got there, Eve's friend was still in the shower and came to the door with a short bath towel wrapped around her torso. Helmut's eyes came out like stalks and for the rest of the afternoon he was most helpful running after Eve's

---

[45] British policeman

friend, although she had her own boyfriend with her. She showed Helmut the garden and I could see my mother fuming more and more.

When we got home that night and separated at our doorstep, my mother and her boyfriend made for the B&B on foot. As soon as they had left, we heard a lot of shouting in the street as my mother gave Helmut hell. The next morning they came for breakfast, Helmut with a black eye. He was all over my mother, kissing and cuddling her. Such is love, or rather such is life.

A couple of years later my mother had a mild stroke and, nearly four years after I saw her last, she had another one. She was lucky to have Helmut staying with her. Norbert was of a different mind, saying Helmut was just after her money.

A couple of weeks after the stroke my mother died, and she was buried in Lüneburg. Moneywise there was nothing left by my mother, but I certainly do not think it all went to Helmut. She left the flat to Norbert's daughter, who was living and working in France and not really interested. On my later enquiries I had been told it had been sold. Eve brought back a couple of ornamental vases and a couple of other decorative items, which my brother generously let her have.

My brother and I kept in touch on a three times yearly phone call basis, Christmas and our birthdays. They never asked me to visit, even when I dropped hints. Norbert has a son who is married – he became a surgeon, and Norbert and his wife Christel visit them often.

41. Life under Mugabe

In Harare, things were slowing down as there was never any money to keep the former sunshine city in the state that it had been known for. In 2002, Mugabe was re-elected president, with a lot of pressure on the other parties. He was less popular with those who lived in towns, which was not a problem as the majority of people in Zimbabwe lived in the country. Most of them did not know any better. My servant, whose home was in the country near Mtoko, a small town or rather a large village, told me a few things.

Mugabe would send his henchmen round the villages to make reluctant people vote in elections – or else. They were either beaten or even sometimes killed, their huts were burned down and they lost their privileges to qualify for the promised bread baskets.

At the last election Mugabe went around himself, mostly accompanied by his wife Grace, dishing out food parcels to the people at the rally and promising them that after the election his supporters would receive one food parcel per family every month. These food parcels consisted of food donated by aid societies. A month after the election a few food parcels were distributed, and that was the end of it.

We never got much information from the Zimbabwe newspaper. There was the *Daily News*, which supported the opposition party. Their office was eventually burned down by a bomb and they refused to give the paper a new concession to start up again. Another newspaper, printed in South Africa, was sometimes found in the streets of Harare, telling us the true stories of Zimbabwe. The street sellers took their lives in their hands selling them. They usually hid them and only got them out if the buyer looked trustworthy. Through this paper we found out (with pictures) that the food aid was stored up to the ceiling in barns, waiting for election day. No wonder the world stopped sending aid. Previously, they had given monetary aid, which landed in the coffers of Mugabe and his cronies.

Mugabe was living in style. His first wife had died and he married his secretary, some 30 years younger. She knew how to spend money. When they started building a mansion in the northern suburbs of Harare, I heard that a whole plane was confiscated in Johannesburg to bring back eight marble baths with gold taps.

I had a friend who was an air hostess for Zimbabwe Airways. When Mugabe wanted to fly anywhere, he always asked for her to be a member of the staff. Mugabe did not have his own plane, so if he wanted to go somewhere, they would cancel one of the passenger flights and confiscate the plane. The passengers had to make alternative arrangements.

Although sanctions were still in place and Mugabe was prevented from entering various countries in Europe and America, somehow he managed to get in, probably to attend NATO meetings – being a member, they could not very well refuse him. These were excellent opportunities for a shopping trip for Grace.

I do not know where the money came from, but it was stated in one of the overseas papers that she had spent over US$100,000 shopping in Paris. This may not sound much for a president's wife, but there was no foreign currency to be had any more in Zimbabwe. Tobacco was still being exported, yet the proceeds certainly never profited the country, nor did copper or diamonds. A lot was sold to China and other countries in Asia on a never-never basis, mostly giving guarantees in the form of land, mines or factories.

They started to persecute the farmers and this became really bad after 2002. Farmers were just given notice, especially the wealthy ones. Compensation was offered which nobody received. Mugabe told them later they should get it from the British government. After all, it was their fault! They started to blame the British for anything that followed, building up hatred amongst the indigenous people. I was once accosted by a drunken youth outside the store, who told me, "Whitey, go home." I told them I was a Zimbabwean citizen, but they told me it was not my country. I quickly got out of sight.

The police were mainly from old stock, who still knew that the whites had treated them well and I found them very polite. Not so the army soldiers, who more and more were roaming the streets. When I was queuing at the till one time, a fat officer plonked himself in front of me. In the bank once a group of them just pushed me aside to get to the counter. Fibian, my gardener, told me they were not much better to their own people.

He was riding a bicycle from town when he got behind a troop of soldiers running in the street. An African tried to overtake them and was pushed off his bike and beaten up. They shouted at Fibian, "Next time we come past, you get off the street!" Fibian quickly pedalled in the opposite direction.

Fibian in the garden, 1997

I was told that they were specially trained in youth camps. They were given dagga to make them fiercer, and were beaten up for the slightest thing. Some were beaten to death to get the others used to violence. They called them the Red Berets, and they were feared even by their own people. They were mostly youngsters, who did not remember the good old times.

When Mugabe came back from a trip, he always received a rousing welcome at the airport, which was highlighted in the newspaper and on TV. I was told they collected people from nearby houses, mainly youngsters and woman, gave them all a T-shirt with Mugabe's image to wear along with Zimbabwean flags and lined them up at the airport.

At election time, they picked up people from their homes and took them by bus to Mugabe's rallies. Also, at football matches when Mugabe was present, although I think they would have come anyhow, seeing they got a free ride. The opposition party never had a chance. There were always roadblocks for their rallies, and people were intimidated to stay away. Their leader, Tsvangirai, found his car and his followers being turned back for some reason or other, and often did not even make it to his own rally. The opposition party hardly got any airtime on the radio or TV, or much footage in the newspaper for election adverts.

There were a lot of car "accidents" in those days, where higher ranks of the opposition perished, and it reminded me of living under Hitler. During the war many old-time soldiers were not happy with Hitler's strategies. They were proud of their tradition. But now, instead of the usual salute between soldiers (hand on cap), they had to lift their hands, arms outstretched, and shout "Heil Hitler". Nothing smart about that. This greeting was not just restricted to the army, but also civilians. Eventually there was (officially) no "Good morning" or "Good bye" any more, only "Heil Hitler".

Anybody who was suspected to be openly or secretly against Hitler was usually despatched in an "accident", like Rommel and Richthofen – mostly in the form of car accidents. Nobody ever found out what really happened. It was just stated that they were killed in action. The same thing happened now in Zimbabwe. Some vanished never to be heard of.

Mugabe was so sure about his latest election in 2008, that he hardly bothered to arrange for the usual stunts, like tampering with the boxes carrying the counted voting forms. He was certain to beat Morgan Tsvangirai and his party. Did he have all the people in his hand? Results later.

Neville and I carried on as usual. We still went to the Orchid Society meetings. A lot of whites were leaving, the ones that had the means to start life anew in another country or those whose qualifications were in demand outside Zimbabwe. Many older people were too poor to leave or had lost all connections with their homelands.

42. Farmers

A few farmers joined the Orchid Society. They had been driven from their land and took up houses in town – at least until they could make new arrangements. We heard a great many stories about the war that was waging between these farmers and the new occupants. A lot of the time, they did not wait for the evictions and just moved in – without permission, of course. The farmers did not want to give up without a fight, but many were killed.

I can understand the reluctance of the farmers to leave. Long ago they, or their forefathers, had saved the money to buy a farm, taken a loan from the bank and made sure their repayments were met with the next harvest. They had developed their land, cultivated it, planted tobacco or kept cattle, and were the mainstay of the economy of the country. Even fruit and flower exports did well.

Now they were supposed to leave their land with no compensation. At first, only farmers and companies with more than one farm were supposed to be affected. Those with only one farm per farmer or organization were permitted. However, the best farms were usually reserved for the big party bosses, who had their eyes on them and made sure they got them, one way or another. Forced, I should really say. Sometimes they gave the farmers 24 hours to vacate the place, sometimes they just moved in, accompanied by a dozen or so soldiers.

Afterwards, when they made a mess of farming, they stated they had been given the wrong farm and applied for another one. Then another farm would be confiscated and another white farmer had to move out. A number of white farmers left for neighbouring countries where their skill was still appreciated.

Some white farmers bought or rented a house in town, still hoping for things to change and to return to their farms. They were not even allowed to take their tractors and other equipment, and, of course, they were never compensated for their losses. The new farmers called themselves farm veterans, having fought in the guerila war. As the war had finished some 30 years ago, they must have been children when they fought, and looking back most of them really were. I heard recently that even the new farmers started fighting among themselves about the best farms, and the farm veterans were not shy about confiscating a farm from their own brothers.

The "new farmers" had it easy. Once they were officially installed on the farm they got a loan from the bank, but not the official banks that did not have any faith in the new settlers without collateral. They had the Landbank (a bank for farmers only). The banks were generous with their loans. If by chance the farmers had succeeded in getting their tractors out (some were driven over the border) before leaving, the government would supply the new farmers with tractors from other farms. (No more imports at that stage.) Sometimes, they had good tractors left on the farms, but these soon broke down as they did not know how to handle or repair them.

When the time for planting seeds came, the new farmers went to the Grain Marketing Board to have seeds issued to them. "INPUT, INPUT[46]" was their favourite slogan. After that they went for fertilizers and when the time came, asked

---

[46] Even today the GMB operates numerous programmes to distribute "inputs" such as seeds and fertilizers

the government to send out someone to do the harvesting. It was so easy. Some did not even bother to farm: when things became scarce, they made more profit out of selling the seeds or fertilizer to more energetic new farmers.

Some made a half-hearted attempt to produce something, but when they showed a bit of profit, they did not endeavour to pay back on the loan or reinvest the money on INPUTs, but rewarded themselves with new cars and, of course, everyone in the family including the children had to have a cell phone. Then there was nothing left for them to do but just sit back and wait for the next INPUT.

A lot of farm workers were loyal to their bosses, the white farmers, and fought on their side. They often had their houses burnt down and I have seen pictures of dogs on the farms that had been butchered.

43. Deterioration

We were much better off in town although things also started to deteriorate. The streets were full of potholes which became so bad it was better to drive on the verge of the road. People started to tell a joke about the police always recognizing whether someone was drunk or not, as sober people just went through the potholes and the drunks tried to avoid them to appear sober.

The streetlamps vanished, one by one. There was one right by a window at the front of our house. I noticed that flowers growing under the light always bloomed earlier. Well, they came, first for the bulbs, later for the lamps and in due course even the poles vanished.

On one train journey we got stuck halfway between Bulawayo and Salisbury, as thieves had stolen the overhead electric wires. While we were waiting for a steam locomotive to take us across the five-kilometre gap, I complained to a fellow passenger about the crime rate. He said "In South Africa they would have stolen the engine as well," and indeed I read in the newspaper a few months later that a whole locomotive had vanished from the railway yard, never to be seen again.

Zimbabwe produces a lot of copper, and many items were made of copper. The telephone wires went first. The first time I went to complain, they said they would fix it if I brought the wire, and then usually they got fixed. Next time, they said they would only come and fix it if we provided a neighbourhood watch. We used to have one, but as this was dependent on volunteers and donations it soon petered out. As a result, I was without a telephone for over two years, right to the end when I left.

So, there was no contact with Eve except through letters, which took three weeks by airmail, if they did not get lost. Eventually I managed to get a cell phone. I was always scared of using them as I was not technically minded, at least not with these "foreign" monsters. I had enough problems learning how to use a remote control for the television and I made a lot of errors at first. However, it was too expensive to use the cell phone for overseas calls.

Luckily, my friend Sue Smith lived in town in an area that housed several ambassadors. They always had a telephone line that was working. Appearances had to be kept up and the outside world must believe all was still rosy in Zimbabwe, so they hardly ever went without electricity, water or telephones. The northern suburbs – more posh areas – did not seem to have as much of a problem either. A lot of houses were occupied by ambassadors' families and those higher up in the Mugabe system. Elsewhere, you were sometimes lucky, if some of Mugabe's cronies happened to live in your area.

In those areas people could afford a decent neighbourhood watch and if there was a breakdown of electricity the generators clicked in straightaway. Sometimes I wondered if Mugabe even knew about these power cuts; he probably never experienced one. He was sitting pretty at Government House, or in his mansion up on the hill with his beloved Grace.

Once in a while I went to visit Sue and made a call to Eve, or she called me there. Sue lived quite a distance from me. She had moved into a townhouse which I found out of this world. And I thought I had a nice house.

Well, we battled on. The crime rate really went up. People were out of jobs and starving. There was no employment for farmers any more. A number of businesses closed down, whites left the country and there were no jobs left in households as a result. The better off blacks usually employed members of their large families, but even if blacks offered a job, their servants were mostly not treated well or paid much.

Fibian told me once he had managed to secure a job for his brother from the country as a gardener, earning far more than Fibian. I was a bit uneasy about the risk of losing my loyal worker. However, after a couple of months Fibian told me that his brother had still not got paid, so his brother left. As he was tall – not short like Fibian – he managed to find a job with a security firm. Security firms sprang up like mushrooms, as there was now much demand for them. A brief training course was all that was required and off they went. Often, they ended up as the thieves, and things vanished.

We just had to tolerate the crime. They made an attempt to steal Neville's car which was parked under the trees between the house and the gate. One morning about 2 a.m. we heard the dogs barking furiously, looked out and saw nothing. The dogs went quiet. A half hour later we were still awake and heard a loud noise like something snapping. When we turned the outside lights on, we saw two of them trying to get into the car. They ran away quickly. We went out, feeling quite scared in case they were waiting for us, Neville ahead with a truncheon, me with a walking stick behind. Well, they had vanished.

Neville had secured a thief lock on the car that went around the steering wheel. As this was pretty thick one would have had to cut through the steering wheel to slip off the thief lock. That was the noise we had heard. From then onwards the car was always parked under our bedroom window.

We wondered why the dogs had gone so quiet. We had about four dogs and they were all vomiting, except the little Lhasa Apso mongrel born from a Pekingese bitch – she was fine. But my Chows started shivering and collapsing. There were no vets available at that time of the night.

Neville had many friends and knew a lot of people through the dog clubs, including one woman who worked at the Society for the Prevention of Cruelty to Animals and lived not too far away. He contacted her and she came out straightaway, with all kinds of medicine, including charcoal. She got this down their throats and they were fine in no time. The dogs had been poisoned, so no wonder they had gone quiet. She left us with emergency rations for future use.

We were now more concerned about the welfare of our dogs, and kept them in the back of the house. We'd had a problem with one of the dogs fighting, and divided the grounds with a fence and gates, which we closed at night.

Not much later the car alarm that Neville had since installed went off. The hood was wide open. This time they were after the car battery, as these were becoming very desirable by then. The would-be thieves gave up and thought it easier to escape through the louvre windows in my living room. As there was so much going on in the area by then we had almost stopped listening to the dogs barking. They neatly lifted the glass out of its casing, and the next day we found four glass panes safely laid out in the lawn near the wall.

Another time, I heard a noise in the lounge and when Neville went to investigate, the thieves vanished back through the window. They had only managed to grab the video recorder and a bottle of whisky which was displayed in a cabinet near the window. I think Neville was more upset about the whisky than the video recorder, as he had started a collection of all kinds of whisky. Well, it was in the early stages of the collapse of the system and video recorders were still in the shops, so we replaced it with a new one.

Some months later, we woke up one morning and I could feel a draft running through the house. The window panes had been removed again, as had our new video recorder. They never went for the television as it was an old-fashioned model and extremely heavy and bulky. Unfortunately, the thieves took the wrong remote control and I could not operate my television any more. We had by then joined Multichoice in South Africa, the equivalent of Sky TV, with about 60 channels or more. It was expensive and, as I had retired, the annual fee was equivalent to two and a half months' pension. Well, I was always good with juggling money and got my priorities right. It was great to watch something other than the one Zimbabwean station, which was full of Mugabe propaganda, and find out what was really going on. Foreign films were only allowed to be shown after midnight and only one a night.

There were no replacements for remotes available in Zimbabwe, but my trusty daughter managed to send us one from the UK. They seemed to have everything in England. When things became worse, Eve sent regular parcels with instant meals, which we had never heard off. By then Zimbabwe was well behind the times. Just add water…

I was very ignorant about modern achievements, and once on the plane to Eve I struggled getting the packaging off the food when it arrived. A little girl sat next to me and said, "Let me show you, Auntie." We had a tin opener, although not the modern variety.

Eve's parcels were sent by air, which took about two or three weeks to arrive. Once she sent me a book by sea that arrived after seven months. Still, we were lucky that it was not stolen on the way. Once I got the wrong parcel from the Post Office, full of baby food, baby bottles and napkins. The parcels were always opened by customs. I got it swapped eventually.

One night the thieves raided our fridge and deep freezer – nothing else. They even took the trays and we found some empties on the lawn the next morning. By then their priority had become food. What good were TVs when there was no electricity?

I think we had given up listening for them at night or the frequent barking of the dogs. Chows can be very fierce; they were the only dogs the vets always muzzled when examining them. The neighbours took notice of them, and told us they were always checking on their side when our dogs barked. They must have been light sleepers. There was so much commotion going around in the neighbourhood we would not have got much sleep if we got up every time.

That was the last time intruders came into the house; they were now busier looking for things outside. One morning, the new wheelbarrow was gone (they left the old one, which lasted for the rest of my stay). They took all the garden tools along with the hosepipe stored in the unlocked shed. After that, we had to make room in the workshop we had built on, which was full of Neville's mechanic's tools. He had a strong lock for that.

They broke into another outside storage place, a wooden cabin we had just put up. One side was left open for my working bench for repotting etc. In the locked section we kept mainly books and old magazines, nothing precious. But they pinched them too. The main loss was some magazines from the Chow Chow Kennel Club in the UK to which I had contributed. I'd had an article on Chows published in it once, and I was very proud of that. Now I had no copy. It was written seen through the eyes of Charlie, our first Chow.

One night they stole all the garden taps. We had four in the garden. Neville had put in two for me in the remote corners of the garden in around 1990, when there was a hosepipe ban and I had to carry watering cans around. I carried buckets for eight years thereafter, I was not too lazy for that, whereas nearly everyone else was using the hosepipes. Some were caught, but I would not take a chance; after all, I was a policeman's daughter and had been taught honesty.

Luckily, when they stole the taps it was already at the stage where there was hardly any water anyhow. We put a stopcock on three of the taps and Fibian dismantled the one next to his *kia* every night and took it inside. As copper was used a lot in Zimbabwe, the taps were copper which could be melted down – there was no demand for actual taps any more.

Domestic workers were getting desperate for food, especially for their families in rural areas, so thieving in the household also grew. Here and there some items vanished, but what is the use in firing them, they all steal. Fibian had worked for me for nearly 30 years by then. A number of Neville's tools vanished and he was not quite as tolerant as me, especially when whisky bottles went missing. Neville complained to me, but as Fibian did not drink, I thought Neville must have miscounted. But eventually when the monetary market collapsed whisky become a good bartering object. When Neville was gone, I wrote down all the bottles and sure enough, a few months later, three were missing. Fibian knew nothing, of course. It could not be anybody else so I locked it up. Two weeks later, a couple more bottles were missing, so I gave the whisky to Sue to lock up at her place. She had no problem with that.

I was a keen reader and over the years I must have collected over a thousand books, mostly paperback novels. I had made a list of the books by my favourite authors, so I would not repeat them. I had around 40 by Catherine Cookson in a line, and noticed that the line was getting shorter. My bookshelves covered two walls in the spare room, so it was a little difficult to keep track of them, but I knew there were some missing. I checked on another shelf and, sure enough, a lot were missing there too. Fibian knew nothing, but he and I were the only ones in the house. So I showed him the shelves of the books I favoured, and told him if he has to steal, at least leave these alone. After so many years he was like family to me and you cannot fire your "family". I sat down with him and gave him a lecture, trying to appeal to his better side, but he just said to me, "Madam, if you gave me higher wages, I would not have to steal from you." Then he gave me long history about his people and the way they were brought up. He said to them stealing is not a crime but a necessity. Well, what could I do, I needed him and clearly he needed me.

In South Africa the servants were just as bad. I once had a nanny working for me. One day I could not find my brassiere. Johnny and I went to the *kia* to confront her, and on opening the suitcase under her bed found lots of my other clothes, which I had not missed as it was the wrong season. Every time we picked up one of my items, she feigned surprise: "Oh, is that yours also?" My bra was not there, but then I took a peep down her neckline, and lo and behold... "This is also yours?" We fired her.

They also stole the petrol out of cars, which was sold in the streets at inflated prices. I went shopping with a friend, and he knew exactly where to find them. They sat by the road, quite innocently, until a car stopped. As per demand they vanished in the bushes to fetch canisters of petrol they had hidden. If, as in rare cases, a police car should come by, the sellers vanished. Some were really enterprising and sold the petrol bottles as cooking oil. Nobody with a brain would touch these bottles.

The petrol queues were getting longer and longer, and sometimes reached a kilometre long. By the time one came to the pump, it was usually dry. Big cars went out of fashion (except for rich people).

They now started to steal the oil out of the transformers. There was one transformer for every 50 houses; once they stole the oil, the transformer exploded, and often we saw the sky lit up. A transformer was worth thousands, but they were only after the oil, which they sold on the street for about Z$60 – it was in demand due to the shortage of petrol. It would keep cars running for a few months but then the engines started to blow up.

By then, foreign money was practically non-existent, and initially it took six months for transformers to be replaced from China. The newspaper stated that over 600 had arrived but nearly 1000 transformers were required. In the meantime, we sat in the dark or candlelight. Neville bought a motor generator that ran on petrol, and it stunk to high heaven. The noise drowned all programmes and it was very expensive to run. So, it was only used for a couple of hours in the evening. We bought a gas plate and a gas cylinder for cooking. The breakdowns steadily got worse, and we did not have electricity for four weeks. We kept things going with the help of friends' fridges and an occasional bath at their place, otherwise it was a wipe down with cold water.

Neville bought a car battery to replace the motor generator, which worked very well. However the car battery had to be charged up continuously, which needed electricity. We had it charged at the garage at first but soon they also run out of electricity. Later on, electricity was rationed and we bought a second battery and a battery charger which we tried to keep topped up in the hours when there was a supply. It gave us at least a few hours of pleasure, although it was very heavy, so Fibian made a trolley that I would pull around when necessary.

Then the electricity went off for just under six months. After four months, and a lot of complaining, they somehow got us half power. I think they connected us to other lines – someone said it was the overland lines. It affected about twenty houses, and the result was that houses nearer to the source had more power than needed (often blowing up electrical appliances in the process), whereas the ones at the end of the line, like us, only had a glimmer of light in the bulbs. It was something. At least we could see again at night, as even candles became hard to find. I played piano a lot at that time as I could play in the dark. Of course, we were still charged for the electricity, both standing charge and minimum usage charges.

The neighbourhood, about 50 families, arranged for a meeting, to which I was invited. I took Fibian along, as I was the only white face amongst them and could not understand their language, or indeed languages. Zimbabwe is split up into a few regions, each with their own language, originating from different parts of Africa. Most of the time they could not even understand each other. Fibian interpreted, in a fashion, but at the end, the head of the meeting, a teacher, spoke to me in English. He explained that he had been told by the electricity authorities, that sometimes you could get a transformer if you were prepared to pay Z$40,000. He appealed to the congregation to club together… but as they were all very poor, it was left to me to fork out the most. Well, money was no good in the bank those days anyhow.

A dozen of us made it to the distribution centre. They insisted I went along, although I felt a bit awkward, with only one other woman in a crowd of men. We set off early and arrived at six in the morning, to be first in the queue. They were supposed to open at nine, but the man in charge only showed up two hours later. He said they had no transformers left, but with a lot of coaxing admitted there was a small, used one somewhere in their yard. However, they had no fuel for the truck; with another Z$10,000 he might be able to get some. We consulted and somehow scraped the money together. However, my African friends knew their mentality and said they would get the diesel and ensure it went into the truck. Four of them stayed till the afternoon and went along with the truck.

Another stipulation was that we would pay for a new hefty door at the generator substation; the Electricity Supply Commission would provide a strong lock. But it was now our duty to arrange for a night watchman, which we duly did… although they would get tired, fall asleep, or decide it was more profitable to steal the oil themselves. Our euphoria at the new supply only lasted a few months anyway, as by then there were power cuts for other reasons.

Then there was the water shortage, or rather nonexistence of water. At first, it went off for a few hours every day and, in the end, we were lucky to get water once every few days. We did not know when this was going to happen, so had to listen for the water coming on. We could not simply leave the tap open, as we had to fill up containers. We had about eight two-litre cans around the place.

The water often came on for a couple of hours at midnight, and we did not get much sleep. There was not much water pressure, as they were supplying so many houses at the same time. To be on the safe side we decided to keep the tap on, running into the bath all the time. So there was not much chance of taking a bath. The water that came out first was always dirty and this we saved for my precious plants.

Either the pumps had broken down or no purifier was available for the town reservoirs. In short: there was no money. A number of people, especially the richer ones, had boreholes, but a lot of them also ran dry as there was not much rain either, or the pumps had been stolen or there was no electricity available. The last year, when I was on my own, I had a huge tank in my lounge (it would not fit anywhere else and one could not leave it outside). Friends who had boreholes filled it up for me.

The Park Meadowlands lounge: plants everywhere

The garden started to degenerate. Fibian found a well across the road where for some reason there was water coming out of a pipe, continuously, not affected by rain or water cuts. A teacher who was a member of the Orchid Society said he used to live and teach in Park Meadowlands, and had heard that there was an aqueduct in the area. Maybe we had struck rich! Fibian went to fetch water from there for my pot plants and orchids, which was the least I could do. He said he even drank it. We also used the water for washing clothes and the water looked cleaner than the water that was supplied by the Water Board, which had a lot of sediment in it. Each week we had to empty the bath as it was gathering all kind of weird things at the bottom. Naturally, we had to pay the water rates as usual or they would come and cut off the last bit of water.

I also got really annoyed at having to pay the full monthly rates for rubbish removal even though we had not seen any dustman for a couple of years. To be sure, some still came over at Christmas to receive their *"bonsella"* (Christmas bonus). I told them what I thought of them. I wrote a letter to the municipality about the payment and I asked them if their workers did not come for years would they still pay them? I even got a reply, saying that the law of the country said, I had to pay. Of course, they could not cut off my removal supply but as they were connected with the water, they could always cut that off as a penalty.

Fibian chucked the waste all across the road onto municipal land – there were quite a few acres of it. Once every so often he struck a match to it. The only snag was he had to be careful not to start a grass fire, although these fires did happen quite regularly – perhaps deliberately – and seemed to be followed by luscious grassland, which the cattle grazing the common land clearly enjoyed.

The people next to the property at the back of us had the habit of burning their rubbish in their yard. Apart from the smoke I also worried about them setting light to the bushes on their side of the property, as we had several trees in our yard. I warned them but they did not take any notice, and one day the bushes caught fire, threatening my trees.

There was no water in our taps otherwise we would have put it out with the hosepipe, so I called the fire brigade. Luckily, they were not far away and a small tank arrived with two firemen within twenty minutes. No fire hose, not even a bucket full of water. They asked if I had water, which I did not. They went to another house and must have found some, as both of them came back with their helmets full of water. They succeeded in getting control of the fire with a great deal of slapping around with branches and using their boots, but it was hilarious.

Writing about this brought back memories from my early days in Rhodesia. Park Meadowlands and most of the outer properties had no connections to public sewerage systems and every property built their own drainage pitch. Only the toilet water went into a special cemented tank in the ground and was regularly emptied by the municipality. The rest of wastage, however, had to be guided into a big underground hole covered by sheeting and grass. As they soon filled up, a new place had to be found in the garden near the drainage pipes. Eventually, the people next door had run out of space and, as there was more space on my side, they built it next to my fence.

They were nice neighbours and I had no objection, especially as they emptied it regularly by pump and manured the lawn. We still had the Collies back then, and one day we heard Cheeky frantically barking by the hole. We went to investigate as we thought it was a snake, only to find poor Chummy hanging onto the edge of the "cesspit" with one paw. We were lucky to get him out alive, smelly as he was.

From time to time a cobra pitched up in the garden and I was always worried about the dogs. On one occasion, my gardener came into the house, stammering there was a snake in the garden. Neville and I took one look and went to fetch an expert. Not far from us we regularly passed a plot that had a big signboard outside: "Snake sanctuary. Beware of snakes".

We called the owner over the fence and told him about the snake. He laughed and said he had nothing to do with snakes. He just put the sign up to keep the crooks away. When we got back to our place the snake had got through to next door's property and the owner and several Africans gave it its last ritual. It was one and a half metres long.

44. Birds

There was a wonderful world of birds in my garden. I counted eighteen different varieties on one day. My favourite were the robins. Not only did they look pretty but were extremely tame. Pecking in the ground next to you when you were digging in the garden, they would come to sit on the *stoep* and produced about twenty different tones. I counted them and wrote down what they sounded like. They seemed to copy every other bird, one sounded like "Fibian, Fibian". The best was one that sounded like "Got a video tape, got a video tape". Unfortunately, I did not have one.

I am not particularly fond of crows as they killed the babies of the birds in my garden, getting right into the bushes or palm trees. Ravens were seldom seen, but once I found a pair digging for crickets; they were very good at that. They flew back and forward, and I saw them land in very tall tree. Right on top, there was a big nest and I could see a head sticking out. They had babies, and it was fascinating to watch them. Unfortunately, the tree was next door and my neighbour sawed half of it down.

I shouted at him, "What are you doing?" He said he was fed up with the crows digging in his lawn. He had no lawn to speak of and I told him he was being stupid. After all, the ravens got rid of the insects, aerated the lawn and manured it afterwards. Too late, the branch came down, nest and all. I could not look. Two of the babies were dead. The third one near our fence also died.

Have you ever heard birds mourn? They say they have no feelings, but the whole next day the parents were lamenting high up in the trees. The day after I saw them digging in the lawn again for their favourite meal. I followed them and there was one baby sitting on the fence. Very wobbly. It came down into our yard. Next thing, the baby bird was sitting on the edge of my small fishpond, swaying precariously. I tried to get him away, scared he might fall into the water, but I was straightaway attacked by the raven parents. Anyhow I called the baby "Moses" as he had landed in the bushes when he fell out of the nest. He moved around the garden for a few days, then took to the tree and next day he was gone. All three came back once more a few days later as if to say goodbye, never to be seen again.

Luckily, I never had to worry about our dogs as they were trained to leave the birds alone. As a matter of fact, sometimes when they were lying on the ground the crows picked on their tail to get nesting material. The dogs just looked at them, got up and moved to another location.

For a couple of years, a tiny bird had also been visiting our lounge almost daily. He did not mind us sitting there talking or the noise of the television. He hopped onto the top of the television to the lampshades or another piece of furniture. We had an indoor garden underneath a huge glass window, full of ferns and other pot plants. He flitted in between the plants, climbed up the curtains, even got behind them and calmly climbed up and back again over the rails. His favourite perch was a red lampshade on a lamp stand and he liked to climb right into it. Maybe he liked the colour!

I looked up the species in my bird book and found him to be an *Apalis thoracica* or plain bar-throated apalis. He was a grey bird, with a black line under his throat and a pert tail.

On one occasion, he sat on the lampshade and chirped his heart out – and lo and behold, another bird joined him on his post. This one did not fancy the lampshade and flew into a fern on a stand in the window box, where it chattered with excitement. They checked out the location over a few days and then they started bringing in nesting material. Eventually the nest took shape. It was a flimsy affair, very transparent. To me, it looked unfinished, but after a few days there was a little basket hanging from the fern, with an entrance on one side, halfway up, and the female bird settled into it.

I thought it was time to give them a name and the Flintstones came to my mind, so Fred and Wilma it was. Next, I noticed that there was an egg in the nest, greenish and speckled and Wilma was spending most of her time on the nest. Once a day or so, Fred came to visit and check out progress, but he did not stay. I did not keep track of the time, but over a week later I noticed both of them flying in and out and carrying food in their little beaks.

The lounge has big glass sliding doors on the opposite side of the window, leading out onto the veranda. It was usually shut and locked at night. That was a problem as the door had to be opened early in the morning, before sunrise, for the birds to go out and about their business. I had to rise at 5.30 a.m. every morning and at night-time I pulled the curtains across the glass door, so they would not knock themselves out trying to get through it. Just before dark, Wilma made her last flight and then settled on the nest. Fred stayed outside somewhere.

One morning I overslept and, to top it all, had forgotten to pull the curtains across the glass door. I found Wilma sitting near the closed door on the curtain. She looked dazed. I picked her up and took her to the veranda and she made it back to the hanging lamp and sat there for about twenty minutes. I was quite worried, but she quickly recovered.

How did I know the difference between the sexes? I didn't really; however, Wilma always made a stop on the lamp hanging from the ceiling before proceeding to the nest. Fred came in at the speed of lighting past my head – I could sometimes feel the draught – straight to the nest. He was so fast that if I blinked, I sometimes missed him going past.

Once, when we had visitors, they had to sit outside so as not to disturb my flying Flintstones. I told them if they had to go through the lounge they would have to duck and we had a lot of fun creeping around. Wilma got a bit excited, chirping at the strangers, but Fred did not mind anything – not even our Chow Chow, who was also not bothered about the birds flying past his head. Even the noise from the vacuum cleaner did not bother them; they just carried on, business as usual.

I noticed the parents did not stay with the babies at night any more. They stayed outside until I opened the door. I took this opportunity to look at the nest and saw a couple of heads with beaks sticking out. I wondered what would happen when they started flying. More about that later.

One time, I came into the lounge and got quite a fright. There was a butcher bird flying around the ceiling, chasing a little bird around in a panic. It turned out to be a sunbird and it flew out eventually. I checked the nest and all looked OK. A couple of days after that episode, there was great excitement between the parents. No food, just a lot of calling from the top of the hanging lamp in the lounge, with a chirping reply from the nest. Then came baby number one, flying a bit awkwardly but making it from the curtains to the lampshade, followed by number two and what was that – there was a third one! We named the first two Bam Bam and Pebbles but had not yet named the last one.

Soon the place felt like the waiting room at the airport. There were birds flying all over the place, from the pictures, sitting on the wall clock, books or even clinging to the wall. The parents were extremely agitated and kept flying in and out of the room. Perhaps they wanted them to go outside, but the chicks were quite happy staying with me. One got behind the curtains and the window and slipped right down. One of the parents went after him and showed him how to climb up the curtains back to the window rail and over the top. It was unbelievable to see the little baby following Fred (it must have been Fred, as he was the cheeky one) up the curtains. I did not get much work done.

After flying about for half an hour, the birds got tired and huddled together on the curtain rail. It was amazing how they found each other. Fred and Wilma were not feeding them again, but after a couple of hours there was a "wake-up call" from the parents with a lot of noise from the lamp post. There was a great deal of "back chat" chirping from the babies, and the flying circus started again. This went on until the evening. Then I noticed that number three, the smallest one was missing, and I found him on the floor unable to get up. Something was wrong with his leg – it was stuck to the wing. I picked him up and disentangled his leg and placed him in his nest, but he lay upside down. I prodded him a couple of times and … he sat up. He started chirping again and Wilma came to feed him. So far, so good.

Night-time came. Normally, the parents would have retired, but the babies were still flying around the lounge, probably because the lights were on, so Fred and Wilma chased them. They got Bam Bam to settle on the fern, but gave up on Pebbles sitting on my red lamp shade, getting roasted. I stroked her little back and she appeared to love it. So, I picked her up and placed her on the fern near their nest. She loved the warm perch of my finger, and I had a job getting her off. Bam Bam joined the little one in the nest. It looked rather crowded, and Pebbles stayed on the fern just outside the nest. Peace at last!

Day two after "take off", I asked a friend of mind to come round with a camera. The "actors" performed well, posing on the picture frames, statues, curtain rails and landing on my arm. They even huddled together for a family portrait.

The lame one – "Pips", short for "Pipsqueak" – survived the night and was trying to get up the curtains to join his siblings but had quite a job to get there. After a few hops he hung from the curtains head down but made it eventually. He definitely had trouble standing up on one leg. He flew a little, but as he landed on the polished floor, I had to pick him up and help him out.

The parents were still feeding the babies but at exercise time they flew in and out of the lounge, probably to show them how to get outside. The chicks however seemed happy in the lounge – and I think safer, too.

Night-time came around again, and Fred and Wilma were now working overtime. Probably still confused with the light on, they got stuck in the kitchen. I turned off the lights and opened the door for them to fly out. I kept the light off for a while until they all settled. This time they found a nice perch at the top of the curtain rail for the night.

Day three after "take off". All was well. Little Pips was still weak and being fed by the parents. He was not always able to follow the others so was often alone chirping for company.

I could see the difference between the chicks. Bam Bam must have been the firstborn, as he looked nearly fully grown. His tail was getting longer. Pebbles must have been the second one, she still had a bit of fluff on her, and then there was Pips. He had most of his fluff and a stump for a tail. Perhaps it had something to do with the eggs being laid on different days.

The evening came and this time I ensured that the lights remained off. (One has to make sacrifices!) Everyone settled for the night.

Day four after "take off". Everything was normal. Pip's wings were not too bad, but he still had trouble with the landing gears. One tyre was flat. I had to keep an eye on him. He got stuck behind the piano, and I noticed his brother Bam Bam was very naughty with him. When Pips wanted to climb up the curtains, Bam Bam would sit on top of him and knock him to the ground, or he would hop behind him and pick on his tail feathers. I suppose that is nature. Survival of the fittest.

The garden was being neglected. Is this what they call "armchair safari"?

The parents had not fed the babies for over an hour. It was lunchtime and the babies were making a racket. I could hardly stand the noise. Fred or Wilma came back without food. The babies were flying up to them. The parents just flew outside to try to encourage the young ones to follow. Eventually, Bam Bam got the message and flew after them. Pebbles was crying louder and louder, and after a long time, one parent came back to get her, so she followed her outside. Then they all vanished into a huge clump of asparagus. There was nothing else I could do for them as nature has taken over. I hoped they were safe. Sadly, Pips did not make it.

45. Hyperinflation

The situation in Zimbabwe was not improving. Still, where would you find so much happiness in the world? We were happy when the lights came back on, happy when the water was on and happy when there was petrol. We still got the sun in the morning and the moon at night.

The money situation was another matter. I think it was about 2006 when I wrote down that the exchange was then Z$12,000,000 to the rand, a loaf of bread was Z$50,000 (still the cheapest food as this was price controlled). At the other end of the scale, fish was now nearly Z$1,000,000 for 600g.

However, prices changed from one day to the next. The funniest thing happened when a friend and I went to a café and we bought one cup of coffee each, it was then Z$40,000 per cup. We finished them and felt like having another cup and asked the waiter to get us one. He said, "Sorry, but the price has just gone up to $45,000." I always said it was best to grab the item in the shop and run like hell to the till, in case the price went up on the way.

Inflation in Zimbabwe hit 500bn%

By **Miles Erwin**

ZIMBABWE'S inflation rate hit a staggering 500billion per cent at its peak, the finance minister confirmed yesterday.

The country's last official figure was 231million per cent last July but the rate soared far beyond that before a power-sharing deal was agreed in February, Tendai Biti revealed.

At the start of last year a loaf of bread cost Z$25million but that leapt to Z$125,000billion by the time a coalition between president Robert Mugabe and opposition rival Morgan Tsvangirai was signed.

However, the economy has started to stabilise and deflation of minus 3.1 per cent was recorded in February, said Mr Biti.

Civil servants are being paid in US dollars and shops are full, he added.

But unemployment remains at 90 per cent after Mr Mugabe's land seizures scared investors away from the southern African country.

Mr Biti, who suffered assault and imprisonment for opposing the 85-year-old president, confirmed yesterday that the country had received a £269million credit line from African states to revive its ailing industries.

Western donors wanted to help the southern African country but this hinged on the government dealing with its 'toxic' issues, he said.

'There are doubts and challenges on political governance and that's what we have to work on.'

Meanwhile, Zimbabwe's government yesterday held its first official meetings with British ministers for nine years.

Foreign secretary David Miliband met Mr Biti in London.

Reforms: Mr Biti

Inflation hits 500,000,000,000% (Metro)

Cheques were no longer being accepted; bank transfers took about a week to clear. If you wanted to buy a more expensive item, they would not accept a cheque. You had to go to the bank and get a signed form to the effect that you had requested the transfer, and you could pick up the items a few days later. Cash was another matter; the queues at the banks stretched for about 100 metres. Cash machines had a shorter queue, but one did not know when they would run dry. It could be the next turn or any time. Not much later, cash machines were shut down, as there was too much vandalism.

There was the same problem with cash in the bank. After queuing for two hours, the bank would often run out of cash money, and that was their quota for the day. One could stand and wait for someone to come in and deposit money, but it did not happen often. Most people kept their money under the bed.

The Reserve Bank could not cope with the printing of new money that people were now hoarding. The paper was mostly imported from Germany, who eventually stopped supplying it, as they were never reimbursed. That is what one means by inflation, when money is printed regardless of reserves, of which the country had none left. Although sanctions had been lifted, they were soon reinforced, due to Mugabe's cruelty to the people. It should not have affected the money side, but if there are no exports, no foreign money is available. There was no more credit, except from China, whose presence was conspicuous in Zimbabwe.

I still do not know why they gave Zimbabwe so much credit. I can only imagine that Mugabe sold them land and industries in exchange. Only a few white farmers were left to produce tobacco. I must say that, here and there, African farmers started to show good results.

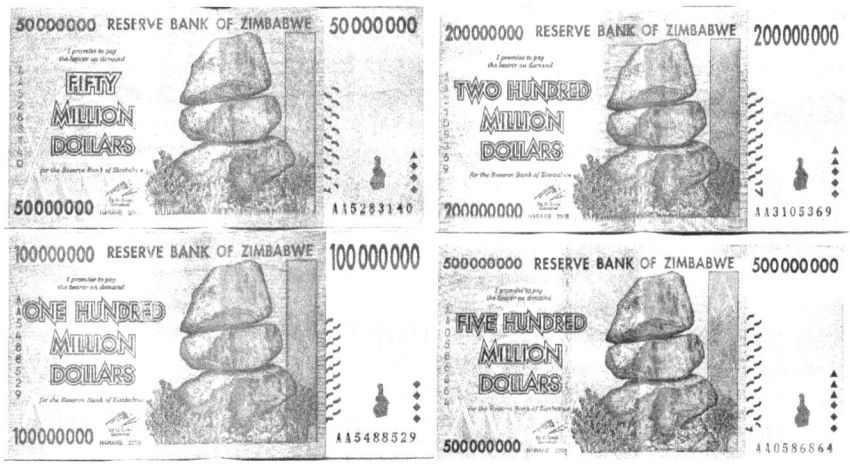

Counting the zeroes on banknotes

In the end, money reached millions and billions. I once saw a woman shopping for a bathroom suite entering the store with two suitcases full of money, carried by a servant. The counting of the money was painful for the cashiers, more waiting around. It took quite a while before some of the bigger shops got hold of cash counting machines.

As a result, the machines at the till could not cope with so many noughts, and the currency was devalued. Over the next three years it was devalued twice, once there were eleven digits knocked off. After that the shopkeepers had to put up a notice "Please add another million to the prices stated".

Lots of people did not know what comes after a million and I must say even I was not sure what came after quadrillion, when it reached that stage. I got confused at times and once put one nought too many on a cheque (when cheques were still accepted). When I went to the bank a week later to withdraw cash, I found my account had been closed. I was desolate. How could that happen to honest Ursula? I decided to see the manager. This was in the morning, and the manager had gone for lunch and would not be back until three in the afternoon.

Garden party at Park Meadowlands

Luckily, I found a seat next to an African lady, also waiting, and getting bored, we started talking. I told her about my problem. This lady asked me if I had any 'forex' on me. Yes, I had US$50 in my purse – I think it was complements of Eve. This African lady concluded I had no worries, "Take your money to Mr So and So at the bank and tell him your story." So, I did. He fixed my overdraft, which had by then gone up from 10 million to 12 million (three days interest on the overdraft), and reinstated my account. I think this is when my crime career started and I joined the foreign exchange smugglers – after all, I had plenty of rand in my account in South Africa, as my pension was being paid in rand, and that was certainly worth something on the black market.

I had originally had the money sent through the bank at a pretty low conversion rate. On the black market, I could get 100 times as much. My financial situation after that was no longer a problem. I was rich by Zimbabwean standards. There was always someone willing to change your rand in South Africa for Zim dollars in Zimbabwe – people that had to import spares for their business, or the like.

It now cost me next to nothing to live well. There were supermarkets with connections to South Africa that were subsidiaries of South African firms. They were the only ones that could still get some goods into the country – otherwise the shops were empty. Africans were lucky to get mealie meal (maize flour), their staple diet, as most of the smaller farmers just grew enough for the use of their families.

I asked Fibian to organize some mealie meal for the dogs. The nearest big shop was the Metro, actually a wholesaler. At first, one had to apply for a card, but that was not much of a problem. They used to get groceries from South Africa about once a month. On the first day any goods came in, the premises were only open to the army and party bosses and their family. So, one queued again early the next day for the leftovers. One time, there was such a storm over the eggs, half of them lay smashed on the floor by the time I got to the empty shelves.

Enjoying the garden

It became a bit more difficult for me to pay with my acquired Zim dollars when the shops started selling their wares in US dollars. But as long as I insisted on having my foreign money paid in cash, I always found someone, somehow – unfortunately now at a lower rate, but still no problem. I was still a rich woman.

46. John and Eve

In March 2006 Eve came with her partner John on a visit to Zimbabwe and we had a lovely time.

Bricks of banknotes

John soon got used to carrying "bricks" around. "Bricks" was the name given to bundles of money sorted out in hundreds of Z$50,000 notes. It was easier to count out your money. If you were lucky you had "bricks" from the bank, still with the Reserve Bank seal, which were accepted at the stated value without counting. For my visitors it was quite an experience; they had to get used to the prices in billions rather quickly. John also took a picture of the queues for petrol. The cars were lined up around three street corners.

Queuing for petrol in Harare, March 2006

They took me to Victoria Falls and I could not get over the fact that here time had stood still and it was still Rhodesia. I had been to the falls before, and it is supposed to be one of the seven natural wonders of the world. As the water was in full flow, it was a sight to behold.

John and Karl at the Balancing Rocks near Harare, March 2006

But what got me was the hotel. No shortages there. Food continued to be cooked in the old style (and boy, did I get stuck in). The waiters wore traditional uniforms and were as friendly as ever. The place was spotless and so was the town. No potholes here. One saw more white faces than blacks. Obviously, everything was geared to show off to the tourists. What a great place Zimbabwe was under Mugabe!

Everything had to be paid in US dollars, and no Zim dollar equivalent was accepted. But we still had a great time. We went to a hotel that had a traditional type of restaurant with an African atmosphere. Most of the food was traditional, such as ostrich meat, kudu meat and mopane worms.

At Victoria Falls

These worms are very much favoured by Africans. They are caterpillars that live on mopane trees. They are quite large, and are served crisply fried with spicy sauces; anybody that volunteered to eat them got a certificate to that effect. John got one. Eve and I declined. In between there were tribal dances, feathers and all, faces painted. We were invited to join in from time to time and we all did. What fun. John paid for my trip. Thank you, John.

It was not the only thing they paid for. Eve and John noticed my primitive bathroom and offered to have it renovated. It was not too expensive when you paid in British pounds sterling at the black-market rate and I had this done shortly after they left. What a difference. Thanks to both of them. Unfortunately, it was the only toilet we had, and when the builders replaced my lavatory we were stuck for the day.

There was an old lavatory next to the servant's *kia*. It flushed OK, but was only a hole in the floor, neatly cemented out. It was the African way and they were used to squatting – even their public toilets were built that way. I had no problem squatting, but unfortunately struggled to get up without putting my hand on the dirty floor. Ugh!

As John and Eve had lots of friends in Harare to visit, they were fully occupied. Neville was helpful as usual, but little did they know that this would be the last time they would see him alive.

47. Neville's last days

Neville had always had trouble with his back. When I originally met him, his back was already scarred from many operations, but otherwise he seemed fit. Somehow, in spite of the pain, he never complained. I always said if I wanted to find out what Neville had been up to, I would ask his friends. He only told me the good things. Perhaps, because he was much younger than me, he had to show off. I once jokingly said to my friends that I had picked a younger chap on purpose, so I would have someone to look after me in my old age.

He suffered from a swollen knee at one time, which the doctors drained. I knew he was on blood pressure pills, but so were a lot of people. However, in the previous couple of years I had noticed he was getting out of breath easily, and when he had to lock the gates every night would come back huffing and puffing. I told him to see the doctor and he said he had been, and the doctor said he was fine.

He lost a lot of weight around the time Eve and John came to visit – twenty kilograms in a couple of months. As he was overweight, one noticed it mainly in his face that started sagging and his trousers starting to slide down. I told him I would go with him to the doctor. As I suspected, he told the doctor about having a cold, not mentioning his breathlessness. They had known one another for twenty years, called each other by their Christian names and chatted about football. I listened to this for a while, until the doctor started prescribing something for Neville's "cold". Then I told him about Neville's real condition. The doctor listened to Neville's chest and asked him to get on a treadmill in the office. All was revealed: his heart was in a bad shape. The doctor prescribed more tablets, asking Neville to return in a couple of weeks' time if there was no improvement.

I think Neville must have started to worry. A week later he came home from work in the middle of the day and said he had to pack night clothes as he was going into hospital. Apparently, that morning his regular doctor had been off and he had seen a new Polish chap. This doctor took one look at him and booked Neville into hospital; the Avenues Clinic. This was a much better hospital than the town hospital, which was cheaper and the conditions matched accordingly. A friend of mine gave us a lift, and I booked him in with a lot of fuss. I had to stand guarantee for his hospital bills.

They gave Neville a blood transfusion, hooked him up to machines and fed him glucose through a needle. An African hospital doctor checked him out, gave him more medicine and a few days later he was home again, feeling much better.

Neville went back to work and looked better for about a month, when he reverted to his old breathless routine. Again, I took him to his usual doctor, who was not so friendly this time. He probably felt usurped by the fact that another doctor had sent Neville to hospital. Neville was, by then, so sick that he had to lie down for over an hour in the waiting room on the bench. There were about thirty patients waiting and although I spoke to the nurses, we had to wait our turn.

As usual, the doctor prescribed different tablets and we took Neville home. A couple of days later, Neville had trouble walking. The next day he could not get out of bed, and I phoned the doctor again (luckily the phone was working for a change. I had told the telephone people about Neville's condition, and they kindly came by and fixed it). The doctor recommended that Neville should be brought into the surgery. I informed them that Neville was immobile and could not even get out of bed. This did not seem to worry the doctor too much.

At this point, I became really angry. I told the doctor that if he did not find a way to get Neville into hospital, I would call the ambulance myself. At last, the doctor responded and said he would book Neville into hospital and arrange for an ambulance.

The ambulance came and Neville was placed on a stretcher. Because of his vast weight they heaved and struggled to get him through the doorways, but eventually managed. I followed by car with a friend. When I was at last allowed to see him, Neville was lying on the hospital bed attached to various devices, a breathing mask, etc. They were just about to take him for X-rays and it was pathetic to see him rolling along on the stretcher attached to all the apparatus, looking white. I really cried then; I thought that would be the last time I would see him.

This time, Neville was sent to the Avondale Clinic which had much better conditions. The surgeon assigned to this hospital was a real honey. I could not see Neville that day, and his doctor told me the next day that Neville's condition was serious. They had taken tests and found his heart was collapsing along with his lungs and liver. He thought he would not last another day and asked if Neville had any other relatives. I told him he had a daughter, and the doctor said it would be advisable to tell her about Neville's condition.

They placed Neville in intensive care and I phoned his daughter Erica, who lived in South Africa. I had only met her once when she came to Harare for business purposes with her husband. Until then, Neville had made no contact with her. Neville had also fallen out with his brothers, and I did not know where they were, apart from somewhere in South Africa. All this happened over the weekend. My friend took me to visit him, as I had given up driving the car years before. He was awake on my next visit, hardly spoke and if he did only in a whisper. When I left, he asked me to put my ear to his mouth and whispered, "I love you." This was the first and only time he ever said that to me.

His daughter came on Monday for the day but had to return to South Africa, but after that called him at the hospital daily. It turned out that she knew more about Neville's condition than the doctor had told me. After all, I was not even married to Neville: I'd only been his partner for three decades.

After ten days in hospital Neville improved and was even walking again although assisted by a stick. The doctor told me I could pick him up and take him home, as long as I ensured he continued to take his many tablets.

Neville felt so good afterwards, he even went back to work. We decided not to go to Neville's previous doctor again and preferred to regularly visit this specialist. Neville had a blood test and they found deficiencies in his blood, enough to kill him. Neville got better, but then got worse. He could not walk and we struggled to get him out of bed to the bathroom. Neville was still heavy, and it was not easy to help him up. We got a bottle for him to pee in which he managed by himself, but we had to get him to the toilet for other business. We were not able to get a wheelchair, so Fibian built a contraption from a low footstool, which he tied to an old lawn mower (no engine). We managed to load Neville on to it. The first time it collapsed, but Fibian strengthened it and, luckily, it worked. I must say the Africans were very inventive with patching up things and shortcuts. So, we could at least push Neville to the bathroom and take him to the living room during the day.

One day, a chap from the dog club came to visit, took one look at Neville and said he had a spare old wheelchair at home as his father had bought a new one. Now we were sorted! It was time for Neville to see his doctor again and off we went by car, wheelchair and all.

The doctor took one look at him and told him he had to go back to the hospital. I started crying. We did not have any more money left. I already owed this doctor US$100 from the last hospital visits. I had run out of money, and Neville's salary just covered the medicine. Neville contributed to the medical aid scheme, but they paid out only a few months afterwards, and we had to pay the doctors first.

When I told the doctor I owed him money, he told me to forget about it and in future he would not charge for any hospital visits either, no matter how often Neville went in. He would also not charge us again for any visits to the surgery. Neville and I were so touched, we both started crying. The doctor even looked round in his cupboard for spare medicine to give Neville to save us buying more.

I asked the doctor, why Neville always felt much better when he left the hospital and then declined: was I doing something wrong? He assured me that I could not provide the machines the hospital used – there was nothing wrong with my nursing.

In October 2007, Neville had come out of hospital so fit that he decided to have a cataract operation, which he badly needed. It was successful and he had no vision problems afterwards.

I was so impressed with his improvement that I decided to have one of my eyes done as well. The difference that made was phenomenal. I had not realized it had been that bad. The first thing I said when the optician took off the bandage was, "I did not know the sky was that blue."

The optician said, "I hope you are not an artist, or you will have to change all your paintings." Well, I was not a painter, but I was doing a lot of hybridizing with my daylilies in those days, and only kept the best ones. The others I gave to my friend. I had not liked the colour at that stage, now they looked beautiful to me with my new eyes.

The last time Neville had been in hospital for one week and this time for ten days. He enjoyed the attention the nurses gave him and was very popular with them. As usual, Neville was fine when he came out, but no longer in any condition to go to work. His boss came to the house with bad news. He was told they had paid him three months' salary while he was ill, but the next three months it would be half pay and after that he was on his own. He suggested it might be better if Neville retired from work. His employers gave him two months' salary and his leave money. In all, it amounted to the Zimbabwean equivalent of about US$600. Neville claimed for some tools that had gone missing while he was away. They agreed and also bought a few of his remaining tools which brought in a similar amount.

To get his money paid out, however, Neville had to go to the bank in person as they would not accept a power of attorney. But Neville could not get out of the car. The escalator was no longer working, and the lift was miles away. I told the teller about this dilemma, and as he knew I was an ex-staff member, he kindly came down to the car for Neville's signature. By then, there was a special entrance for VIPs and as I was a former staff member I qualified for that whenever I had to cash a cheque for myself – otherwise it would have meant at least one hour queuing.

This was the end of October. Nothing more could be done for Neville, so we pushed him around in his wheelchair. As there was no TV at the time due to more power failures, he sat outside in the sun. Sometimes he even managed to dress himself, but otherwise he lay in bed listening to music on his cassette player. Only later did I find out that he had recorded about ten tapes with my favourite songs and even wrote the names on the labels.

Life went on. I was grateful for Fibian's help; no wonder I forgave him all his trespasses. He had by now met a priest of some sect and became a senior member. I once said to him, "Funny religion that allows you to steal."

Neville and I lived together for 30 years, more like friends than as lovers, which suited me as I had never been one for sex and was glad he hardly made any demands on me. He was never one for complaining, and as I mentioned before, he was very helpful. He was simply good to have around.

He did not earn much, so he just paid for food. As my house was paid for, I managed the rest. He was a friend in need for everyone – rough on the outside but soft as butter in the inside. He never complained to the end, which came very suddenly.

One morning in December 2007, I was talking to one of Neville's co-workers, the only one from work to visit and call regularly. He asked if he could talk to Neville, and I asked him to hang on while I go and check that he had made it up. When I got to Neville's bedroom (I had since moved him into the spare room, as he liked it better that way), he lay sprawled on the bed, fully dressed, mouth open and his eyes already glazed. I told the chap on the phone I thought Neville had died, hung up and immediately phoned the doctor. The specialist suggested that in this case I would have to phone his practitioner. They told me it was no more a matter of their concern and I had to contact the police.

In tears, I phoned some of our friends, who rushed over. I phoned the police and they said they would send an ambulance to take Neville to the police morgue as it was now a police matter. The police were there within twenty minutes (a record) and carried Neville on a stretcher to the wagon. I shall never forget the sight of that.

They said I had to be at the police mortuary the next day and they opened at 8.00 a.m. Unfortunately, it was just before Christmas and most of my best friends were on holiday somewhere out of the country. Nourrish, Shirley's son, said he would take me, but was not the most reliable of chaps and pitched up very late the next day. By the time we got there they told us the mortician had left as he only worked from eight to nine in the morning and I was to return the next day.

The next day, this fellow told me they could not release the body as they had to do a postmortem because Neville had died at home without a doctor present. He said to come back in a week's time. I phoned Neville's specialist, who said he would speak to this person. In no time had he sorted this out – medical jargon was passed between him and the police mortician. In the end, they were satisfied that Neville had died from a heart attack and his body was released and collected by a mortuary in town. The doctor promised to let me have a certificate to confirm Neville's heart condition and issue a death certificate.

Neville had contributed to a funeral policy and there was nothing outstanding. They placed him somewhere to wait for an opportunity to cremate his body, as the crematorium had run out of special oil for the incinerator, and they were waiting for supplies.

As we could not bury Neville, I arranged for a funeral service to be held in a chapel at the earliest opportunity between Christmas and New Year. Shirley had just come back from holiday and took me to the service. Nourish pitched up only when we were on the way out after the event. Hardly any of Neville's fellow workers came, not even his former boss, but the dog club members were there in full force. Many of our African neighbours also came, and all visited the house, one after the other, to give me their condolences. I had brought along a big photo of Neville and placed it on the podium amongst flowers, and wrote a nice speech, but broke down halfway so someone else read the rest.

After that, life had to go on. I waited for news about the cremation and went to see them a couple of times to pressure them, but it was no use. I heard that the bodies were piling up in the mortuaries; apparently they had to have a special gas. Once the television showed a picture of a mortuary in Harare with bodies lying on shelves, like the images of wartime concentration camps. It was horrible. Poor Neville, just lying there.

It was April, four months after Neville's death, when the mortician phoned and told me that they had at long last found a crematorium in a nearby city that had now enough gas to cremate the 40 or so bodies that had piled up since. He asked me if I wanted to come and collect the ashes. I was not very keen to have his ashes mixed with 40 others, obviously. I pictured all these souls howling in my garden – and told him to forget about it.

48. Life after Neville

After Neville died, I was alone in the house with Fibian sleeping in his *kia*, but I still had the dogs.

The Pekingese Max was the first one to go. Long ago, at one stage Neville had been given an unwanted male Pekingese, already six years old. He did not look as good as the Pekingese we had seen at the dog shows when I first noticed them. They were so cute. A lot of people do not like them, thinking they are ugly, but I loved their little monkey faces, especially when they had a black mask over their face. I had loved Max; he was adorable.

Chows are still the best dogs for me, but they are very aloof, more catlike. They would fall over themselves to greet you when you got home, and then ignore you for the rest of the day. Except when they wanted food, then they would sit in front of you with hungry eyes.

Pekingese on the other hand just want your love all the time. Chows would never sit on your lap, even as puppies, and it was so lovely to have something to warm your lap and that one could cuddle. Max was special. He used to come to the settee when I was watching television, get up on his hind legs and tap me gently on my knee, as if he was asking "May I?" Only when I patted the place beside me and said "come" would he jump up and curl up on my lap. I also found that Pekingese are the only dogs with such pliable bodies, like a pyjama dog – soft and cuddly.

Max

We had a number of mishaps with Max. He was a fighter and, although he got on well with the Chows, he would not take any nonsense from them. He used to sleep on top of them at night when all the dogs slept outside. But from time to time, he got stroppy. The first fight he had with one of them, the Chow must have bitten him in the face and his eye popped out. I mean, it was not out completely out, but halfway. As usual this happened in the evening, when the vets were closed and there was only one place in town open, staffed by university graduates.

We rushed Max there, but the vet said he could not do anything and I had to take him to my own vet in the morning. The next day my vet said that if they had put the eye back the night before he might have been OK. Now it was so swollen, it was a job to get it back in. The vet succeeded at last, but the eye went blind. Well, better one eye than no Max. His eye still looked normal, and nobody would have noticed it.

However, about a year later there was another fight and the other eye popped out. The vet put it back within an hour, but told us there was something wrong with his tear ducts, which meant his eye would dry out eventually. The vet also said the eye would go blind in time anyhow, and the special tear drops required were not available in Zimbabwe. In the meantime, Max would always be in pain.

Neville and I did not know what to do, but we both thought it would be better not to let the little chap go on suffering and it was perhaps better to have the vet put him to sleep. When we arrived at the surgery, the vet was beaming and said, "Look what I've got for you." He had made enquiries with other vets in Harare and found one that had a few bottles of the required tear drops, he had obtained as samples.

Nobody in Zimbabwe ever looked at "Best Before" dates, if there were any. Once in a while I could see that a tin of peas had expired a year ago. By that time, we were not fussy any more. So, of course, Max was saved. After a month, we had a second miracle. The tear ducts were working normally again without the drops. He slowly lost his eyesight, but this gave him time to get used to it and he had no problem getting around. At least his fighting days were over. His eyes both looked normal and we sometimes said we would put him in the show ring and fool the judges (blind dogs would be disqualified). So we loved Max even more.

When Neville got sick, Max never left his side and slept on Neville's bed all the time. When Neville died, Max spread himself out by the front door and would not budge. The next morning, Max was dead. He had a bit of a weak heart, but he must have known something was wrong and given up.

Now I had only Teddy, the red Chow, and Misty, the grey blue one. They were both over eleven years old, but still fit. Not for long, however, as two months later Teddy started coughing a lot and when we took him to the vet, he found Teddy had cancer of the throat. They operated on him and we hoped for the best. The next month, Misty developed a huge lump on her neck. It was also cancer and non-operable. So I had to say goodbye to Misty.

A month later, Teddy was choking and the vet told us his cancer had spread. There was no option but to put him to sleep, as I could not see him suffer. This was, perhaps, one of the worst days of my life when I had to take him to the vet. I just could not stop crying. I think everything that had happened over the past months really hit me. It was too much. Practically all my connection to life with Neville and the Chows was now over.

Everyone told me to get another dog, but I did not want to hear about it. In any case, there were no Chows or Pekingese to be had in the country any more. My friends kept on trying, and Sue Smith asked me to go with her to a small private kennel just to look around. There were about two dozen dogs there, all looking well-fed, but all picked up from the street and pretty wild (never mind ugly). Then they said they had a red cocker spaniel in a separate run, together with a bulldog. The spaniel had been left by a woman going on holiday six months previously who never came back, although she still paid something towards the upkeep for the first few months. Her son had come to pick the dog up, but said she was hopeless and unapproachable. After a month, the poor dog was back in the kennels.

Well, no harm looking. The kennel boy was trying to coax out a bedraggled looking dog from under the kennel. In the end, he had to reach down and drag her out. The poor dog simply wanted to go back again. But by that time, I felt sorry for this dog, and said I would give it a go. He dragged her to the car and dumped her in the back seat. She did not struggle much, just cowered in the corner, shivering and trembling. We had trouble getting her into the house and then she crept into a corner and did not move. If I went near her, she growled. I had to put the food under her nose, and she only ate when I was far enough away.

Well, I gave up and left her alone, ignoring her completely. Eventually, she came out of the corner and lay down in the middle of the lounge, just glaring or staring at me. I continued to ignore her. About 24 hours later, she got up, jumped up on me and started to perform as if I was her long-lost friend. She cried, I think with happiness, and licked my hand and tried to lick my face. She had decided I was not so bad after all. I kept her until I left Zimbabwe. She was at least a living thing around me and slept in my bedroom at night.

Talking about leaving Zimbabwe. I had no intention of doing so, in spite of all the hardship. I always said I would never leave my precious house; they would have to carry me out feet first.

49. Passports

My Zimbabwean passport had expired in 2003, although shortly before that I tried to get an extension. After three futile visits to the passport office, and a separate place for application forms, I was back again, as more documents were required. I then had to get these and go back again… only to find that these documents needed authentication by an advocate or the police, so off I went again. It was at this point that they told me I had lost my Zimbabwean nationality in 2002.

I vaguely remembered hearing about having to go to the registration office in order to have my rights to my original birth country renounced, which I had overlooked. So, they told me I had to start from scratch again, getting my citizenship back first.

Now, this was not a short queue at the passport office. There were about 100 people lined up every time. People queued the night before, and the next day they were given numbers and about 40 were seen, the rest were told to come back. No way could I stand there for that long. I tried once, but after four hours I had moved two feet forwards, so I gave up. People told me that because I was by then 81, I should just push through to the front. In the end, I did that every time. Very reluctantly, the (mostly) African people let me through. Once I made it to the front of the queue and was stopped by old people, who said they were also waiting. I asked them whether there was anybody over 81 there, and if so, they were welcome to stand in front of me. They shut up.

In the end, I had seen eighteen authorities before my passport application was finally accepted. Every time I managed to get another document, it had to be authenticated by a commissioner at the police station, which meant more queuing.

I paid for the price of the passport, which was not cheap, but I never received it. A year later I enquired, and they said they were running two years behind. Then they ran out of the special passport paper, and after that the paper for the covers and then they probably ran out of ink as well. They never ran out of excuses, though.

Never fear, Eve was here. She suggested I should get my old British passport reinstated, which I had obtained on my marriage to Will, her father. It had expired some time ago, as I was then using the South African passport that my second husband had insisted on, as he was very patriotic. I think I mentioned before that he had adopted my children and insisted that their names be changed to la Cock, something they never thanked me for, as they would have rather kept their old name, Johnstone. Eve had at least changed her name when she got married. Richie changed his back to Johnstone by deed poll. I liked my name. Sometimes I told people it should have been "la Hen". It was very easy for Africans in Zimbabwe to remember as they had used the cock as their party's symbol and all were familiar with this.

I had trouble with transport to the British Consulate in Harare, but Eve had already spoken to someone at the Home Office in London. She explained the situation and about my age and they were most helpful.

Shortly after Neville died, I got a phone call from the British Embassy in Harare telling me that they had been contacted by their office in London and volunteered their assistance. They said they were sending the application in the post and not to worry about bringing a photograph or authentication of copies of the required certificates. They would make copies, and everything else was done in their office.

Only someone who has lived in Zimbabwe can appreciate that. No queuing for photocopies in one place, having your photo taken at another, or at the police to have documents authenticated. Not to mention the trouble I would have usually had of getting the application form in the first place. Besides, they only asked me for a couple of documents in comparison to the Zimbabwe authorities. Luckily, I still had my old expired British passport and they could obtain a lot of information from that.

I received the forms in the mail a few days later. (The official envelope probably helped to speed things up. Eventually, the Post Office would no longer deliver letters and one had to pick them up at an office three kilometres away.) The application only ran to about four pages instead of the Zimbabwean twelve pages.

I had no problem filling it in. A lady from the Orchid Society also wanted to see the British Embassy about a two-yearly renewal on the British evacuation list for British subjects in Zimbabwe in case of emergency. Highly organized people, the British. So, this lady took me. There were only a couple of people in front of me and all was completed within ten minutes.

There was a slight snag with the payment though. I had spoken to them on the phone just before the New Year and the cost was then £200, cash, which I had brought, but the price had now gone up to £420, which I did not have. The lady at the embassy asked if I was in a hurry to get the passport. Being at the age of 82, I would not have to pay anything if I was prepared to wait three to four weeks for the application to be sent to the UK.

Good gracious me! What were they talking about? After waiting donkey's years for my first Zimbabwean passport, and still waiting for my second one, I had not even expected to get the passport back for a few months at best. So I was £200 richer.

They phoned me over three weeks later, apologizing for the delay, but I now had my British passport again and could travel anywhere with ease. With a Zimbabwe passport it was not easy to get around, always having to apply for visas for certain countries, and even for a return visa to Zimbabwe. Otherwise they would not let you back into the country, even though you lived there. More queues. Well, no more of that.

50. Cars

As you will have noticed I had many friends in Zimbabwe, who kindly drove me to places in their cars. It was not always easy for them to find enough petrol to accommodate me. As I mentioned before, I had stopped driving ten years previously. I had an old Volkswagen (Gertie), which started to show its age by breaking down in the most impossible places and occasions. Neville was always there to help. If I broke down, it took half an hour to find a phone that was still working in that area, and then I would sit in the road waiting for Neville. Sometimes he would sit behind the wheel and the car started after a few coughs. How embarrassing. Sometimes, he got a tow car from work and towed my car to his workshops. I spent hours by the side of the road. Only once did I get help from a passer-by.

This was quite a funny occasion. I was returning from a visit to my friend Marina, when about five kilometres from home, my car started hopping over the tarmac. I thought it was the engine again and decided to carry on until it came to a standstill, hopefully nearer to home. I jerked along for about a kilometre when poor Gertie made a grating noise on one side, so I stopped. I noticed one tyre was lying about 100 metres behind in the road and realized that my poor car had a puncture. It had had all kinds of "illnesses" before but never a puncture, so I knew nothing about how to deal with it.

An African chap came up to me and asked if I had a jack, I did not know what that was, so I said no. This chap then went around various premises and came back with a borrowed jack. He asked where my spare wheel was and again, I did not have a clue, but he soon found it, and also found I'd had a jack all along. He fixed the tyre in no time. The tyre was a bit flat, and poor Gertie limped home.

Where were the good days when I still had a company car which was serviced regularly? I could have had a space in the underground parking at our bank, but I was too scared to drive down the narrow ramp, which ran around two bends and was two floors down. What do you do if a car comes from the front and one has to reverse downwards around the corner? I was never a confident driver. In Johannesburg, I took the bus into town. Once, when my second husband, Johnny, had a broken wrist after one of his accidents and asked me to pick him up in town, I quickly went out at lunchtime to check out the streets around my office, making sure I only had to take left-hand turns, without having to cross the road.

In Harare when I was working, I parked my car a few streets down from the office – parking was free. One time, I came back and could not find my car. I thought I must have parked it round the corner. No, it had been stolen. The company claimed from the insurance and gave me another car, no problem.

I did see the car again at the police depot when I was asked to identify it two months later. It had been sold to a garage near the border of Zimbabwe and Zambia, who in turn sold it to a schoolteacher. This schoolteacher was honest – a lot of people would have found falsified registration papers. One could even get forged passports on the black market, or a driving licence. As long as you had foreign money, you could buy the world. Anyhow, this teacher got caught with the stolen car when he tried to register it. Unfortunately for him, he never got the money back he had paid. The insurance had already paid out, and my bank was no longer interested in the car, although it still looked the same. Anyhow, by the time Neville died I had given up on driving long ago. I had sold my old car for next to nothing and then relied on my friends, who had also been Neville's friends.

Neville's best friend was Brian. They had met at the dog club. Brian showed bull terriers, one breed I could not stand. Neville became a frequent visitor, but

Brian was not popular amongst my other friends. He had the kindest heart, but never took any interest in his appearance. He wore the same shirt, day after day, and as he had a beard, he was not very good at aiming his food when eating. He never took any notice of my scolding him like a schoolboy. In the end, I got him a new shirt and kept it at home. Every time he came to visit, I made him change and put his old shirt back on when he left. He never complained, probably happy about the motherly attention he got. He had no problem with money, just could not be bothered to tidy up himself, although his house was always clean and tidy. Neville persuaded him to buy two new shirts on one of their trips to South Africa. Both of these ended up decorating his wardrobe – they were never worn.

Brian was small and a bit plump, and when I met him again in the UK, he had not changed at all. However, on one of our more recent meetings he looked very presentable, with his beard neatly trimmed, it now being white, and it did look quite good. He even had a clean shirt on. He had also lost weight and did not spill any food. Perhaps he has a girlfriend?

When he stayed with us the month before he moved to the UK my servant refused to wash his underwear, so I still see Brian standing by a bucket of water placed on a bench in the garden merrily washing his underwear, or what was left of it. Funnily enough, he never took offence, but now, looking back, I think I was a little cruel. But he took all my criticisms in his stride.

Brian's brother suffered from some kind of illness and decided to leave Harare with his wife for the UK. Brian missed him a great deal and soon after he also decided to emigrate. He was going to give Neville his small car, when he left, but it got stolen beforehand and he bought himself a Volkswagen Combi which he was going to leave Neville. While he was staying with us during the last month, he still used the Combi.

One day I was standing in the garden watering the plants when I heard a small explosion in the street in front of me. Next thing, there is smoke coming over the wall. When I looked, it was Brian's Combi on fire. Luckily, I was there with the hosepipe in my hands and soon put it out, but the engine and front seat were burnt out. We pushed it into the yard and Neville sold it to some Africans.

Brian also left Neville his savings book with Z$15 and gave him authority to draw on it, as he was expecting Z$3 every month to be paid into the account. Brian sold his house and bought a flat in Harrow, for cash. However, his money was worthless in the end and we did not bother about his savings book.

51. Rising costs

My friend Sue Bewes was even worse off with her husband's pension. He used to work at the Railways and when he died, he left Sue a small pension – still not enough for her to live on. She had her own house, but was talked into selling it after her husband's death and moved in with one of her sons. They converted the garage into a small room, a tiny bedroom and even tinier bathroom and kitchen. No wonder Sue never invited me to her place. Once, when Neville and I were dropping something off at her house, she reluctantly asked us to come in for a cup of coffee. The lounge was not too bad, but the rest of the space together would have fitted into my servant's quarters. It was very clean but overrun by six Giant Schnauzers, her favourite breed, which she used to show at dog shows, where Neville had first made her acquaintance.

Sue's pension dwindled over the years through inflation and they never gave increases anyhow. She had to queue up monthly for her pension at the Railways, but when it went down to fifteen cents a month she gave up. The money from her house, which she had invested with the building society to draw on as supplementary income, became worthless. Luckily, Sue had three sons in Harare and one in Cape Town, who all clubbed together every month to give her money. She also had a daughter in Australia, who was not in a financial position to contribute, but she sent Sue a ticket to Australia every couple of years.

Still, it can't have been very nice for her to rely on them. She had a car, which her sons also filled up with petrol for her as needed and as I had no transport, she was a lifeline for me. She lived only about five kilometres from me and regularly picked me up on her way to the suburban supermarket not far away. It took her a bit out of the way, but she would have come to my place afterwards anyway. I also contributed by filling up her car with petrol from time to time, and often told them in the shop to put her shopping on my tab. She only bought the bare necessities anyhow. In later years, her children thought she was spending too much money, also on petrol. She perhaps kept quiet about my contributions, so they decided to buy the food for her and deliver it to her house once a week according to her shopping list, slightly revised.

However, as I paid towards the petrol, she still picked me up. She was always hungry for fruit and now, living in the UK where I have fruit every day, I always think of her. I never bothered with fruit before, sometimes not for months. I'd rather spend my money on cheese, which I could eat three times a day. Neville would bring me tea and a slice of toast with cheese every morning. I think he enjoyed having the kitchen to himself and would get stuck into an enormous breakfast he cooked himself every morning – probably making up for my poor cooking in the evening.

Sue was one of my friends that I saw most of. She would pitch up at the doorstep at least every other day during the week. I liked unexpected guests, you offer them whatever you've got, instead of a big invitation when they always expected something special. I cooked nearly every time Sue came, or rather opened a tin, and sometimes Sue cooked to show me how it was done. The first time she came to my house I made the tea and introduced her to the kitchen and said that now she knew where everything was, next time it was her turn. After that it was her turn every time and she would march straight into the kitchen and put the kettle on.

Even now when Eve comes to visit sometimes with John or Alexa, I always say, "What would you like? Cappuccino I will make, tea you make yourselves." I find it too much of a fuss to make tea for other people, it is either too strong, too weak, too much milk, too cold… I think that is why I do not like cooking; I feel completely inadequate. Not to mention that I am lazy, too. Once, when Neville was still alive, we had a big *braai*. Neville and the men did all the cooking, but Fibian was off that day and I could see myself being landed with washing the empty dishes. So, when the guests started to break up, I shouted, "Nobody leaves until the dishes are washed." It was great fun. Everyone chipped in and there was a lot of laughter coming from the kitchen.

Sue Bewes was also the one that introduced me to the cell phone. In the UK they call it a mobile, whereas in Zimbabwe a mobile is what here you call a cordless handset. Sue was an expert at using it and forever on the phone. Remember, we had no landline most of the time. At first, it looked too complicated for me. She loved it, even if this old second-hand make was as big as a TV remote. But she said at least she could see the numbers and find it in her bag. I never really wanted a new one. I already had trouble learning how to handle a remote control for my TV. I found if I restricted myself to just the necessary steps, I was fine, even though sometimes it would get lost.

However, I was intrigued by the cell phone and thought I would give it a go. By that time, one could only buy them for US$, but there were plenty advertised in the local newspaper. I looked up one of the advertisers and found he had a stall in a backyard. The chap told me the price in the newspaper was from two days ago, it had since gone up. I had the same problem buying a new TV when mine packed up. It was advertised for US$160 (second-hand, of course). When I got there, it was US$165. I went outside to scratch in my bag for more money. When I came back, he told me it had just gone up another US$5. Eventually, he settled for a few British coins I had left from previous trips to the UK.

I managed the cell phone in due course, but it was very expensive to phone Eve. When she phoned me, we could not understand a thing, the connection was too bad. Even local calls were expensive and it intrigued me to see the poor Africans riding on a bicycle or walking past talking into a cell phone. I think it was more important to them than food.

Sue Bewes was an ardent Jehovah's Witness and after Neville died, she said she now felt better visiting me, as their religion forbids making friends with someone living in sin. She never tried to convert me; she knew me. Sometimes we had a bit of a friendly argument, when somehow, she spoke about the life thereafter when all "righteous" ones would be reborn. I always asked her where all the righteous millions of people would fit on earth, going back over the last century. And at what age would they be, not much fun me waking up with wrinkles and meeting my first love again who died when I was nineteen. She somehow talked herself out of that. Evolution was another subject. About the earth being created in a couple of days. Well, the Bible says so, but how do you explain that in practical terms? We never fell out with each other. She said her prayers at the table, I listened, and we both said "Amen".

Sue Bewes was a great help after Neville's death. Even while he was still alive, she never hesitated to take him to hospital or me to visit him. Luckily, I did not have to go to the doctor too often myself.

Then there was Sue Smith and her husband Joss, who lived at first in Borrowdale, in a lovely house with a swimming pool, tennis court, borehole, waterfall, the lot. We had first met her father just after we started out with the Chows and were looking for a black stud. Her father left for Johannesburg and then Australia, and we lost touch with him. Years later, we met Sue and Joss when they had returned to Rhodesia and were into showing Chows, and we soon became friends. We visited each other regularly, about every couple of months.

Then there was Dieuwe and her husband Piet, the Dutch couple we'd met at the Orchid Society and with whom we had an instant rapport. Both were painters, Dieuwe, I think the better one, so Piet concentrated more on making frames. Sometimes they were lucky and sold some. I especially liked her watercolours. The trouble with their paintings was that they were the old style, painting as it is seen, mostly of African animals and landscapes. Nowadays, people are not interested in that style any more. I was into decking out my room in zebra style stripes in the UK and looking for a picture of a zebra to go with it. All one could find was a few stripes painted on the canvas and a huge eye in the middle. I ordered one from them eventually, all the way from Zimbabwe, and they enclosed a watercolour of my Pekingese Max. He now hangs over my bed and still brings tears to my eyes.

They also struggled, although they had a small pension. Still, that did not stop them from having beautiful orchids to swap with me. They lived in the richer northern suburbs, where there was still water except when rationed, but as they were living high up on a hill, the pressure was by then not strong enough to reach them. In the last years, they had to pay US$100 or more every month to get someone with a bowser to fill up the swimming pool, which was then used to water the plants or for washing. Another friend in need. They also sold their house after I left and are now in South Africa at the seaside. I am still in touch with them.

It was really getting quite embarrassing to ask people to ferry me to and fro. But buses had ceased to operate years ago, I cannot remember seeing any taxis around, which would have been unaffordable as everything had now to be paid in forex, even the commuter buses that had sprung up like mushrooms once the regular buses disappeared. If you wanted to be nostalgic, one could see the carcass of buses in the scrapyard, or even some at old bus depots still hoping for spare parts. Maybe one day? Miracle over miracle, they had somehow started a commuter train between the largest African township and Harare station. However, this was not anywhere near me and operated went on a "maybe" system.

The commuter buses, as they were called, were actually twelve-seater mini buses, but they managed to fit at least two dozen people into them. They came past whenever there were enough people to start the journey and went past mostly full. Sometimes one had to wait up to 30 minutes. I braved it a few times, although it was difficult, and I hardly ever saw any other elderly people on the bus. There were no small steps up to the bus, just one giant leap. No one ever helped or offered me a seat, and I stood, squashed amongst the dozens of smelly bodies.

My bus stop was not far away, just round the corner in front of the few shops that still existed. Once there had been five shops, one of which had stocked a nice selection of groceries, more like a mini market. It had been run by a Chinese couple, who were very friendly and sometimes popped over for a chat. Their son ran a Chinese restaurant in the town. The name "Bamboo Inn" springs to my mind. This son invited Neville and me once for a meal. As we could not make up our mind what to choose, the Chinese owner said that he would bring us one of whatever was available. We really had a feast.

Where once this mini market had been, in Park Meadowlands, there was only a bottle store left, run by Africans and selling mainly African brewed beer. There was a bakery that only baked one kind of bread, which contained sawdust and sweepings off the floor but nevertheless seemed popular. In later years, I developed an allergy, mainly to white bread, and this was the only bread available to me as it contained everything except white flour!

Another tiny shop sold mainly mealie meal (whenever they were lucky to find some), sugar (seldom) and margarine (once in a blue moon). But there was always baby food for sale. The Africans did not mind going around in tatters, but their baby clothes were always the best. (I am talking about the ones that still had a job. But African men were always smartly dressed when they went to work.) One thing I never could get Neville to do was to wear long trousers or a tie. Except on the few occasions, when he represented either the Flower or Utility Club, when he looked really smart.

I doubt the younger generation can still remember milk deliveries. Now, milk was not even available in the shops. We found a farm about three kilometres away, selling milk while you waited for the cows to be milked – the first few gallons always being kept for special customers, like hotels. Fibian spent hours queuing up, yet sometimes they ran out before his turn. Luckily, he had a bicycle.

In the supermarkets, prices were still displayed as e.g. US$3.56, but as there was no change you had to look for something to make up the balance to the nearest five dollars. Prices kept rising as usual – not so much in US$, but certainly in Zim Dollars. Banks had at long last got some money printed again so were operating in Zim Dollars, but the queues for cash were long: the bank closed the door and the rest had to wait outside. If you were lucky, someone would arrive to deposit cash, but people tended to hang onto it. Luckily, someone told me there were special privileges for the elderly in a back room, which I took advantage of straightaway. I gave them a cheque, waited a while, then a clerk went to the back of the till and extracted the money for me. Great! However, as I usually went to the bank when one of my friends also had to go, I generally had to wait a couple of hours for them. At least I could sit.

I've still got a diary from 2008 where I see the following entries:

	US$1	**£1**	**SA R1**
13 June 2008	Z$3 billion	Z$6 billion	Z$400 million
31 July 2008	Z$69 billion	Z$138 billion	Z$9.5 billion

The black-market rate was always about four times higher.

To make it possible for the bank to record these huge figures in their computers, they were shown in millions with a note saying "Please add six noughts". Even shops marked their goods that way. The black market was simpler; they always had cash. No wonder the banks had run dry.

Shops had begun to sell their goods in US$ quite slowly. It started first in the backstreets, where you were vetted by the manager in a back room. He would hand you a paper saying you were OK, and you would then select the goods. Luxuries appeared that we had not seen for years, like baked beans, tinned meat and sardines – even a frozen section with poultry, and one for my favourite cheeses.

The shops were mainly larger stores, often subsidiaries of South African chains. They were mostly found in parts of town occupied by the "elite", which included all the big party bosses. Unfortunately, I lived on the "wrong" side of town and they were hard to get to, especially as I did not have a car.

However, the people of Zimbabwe were very enterprising, and eventually "runners" were employed who went to South Africa and bought goodies for rand before returning to Harare. With a bit of bribery, they managed to get through customs at the border, although as usual they had to queue, sometimes for a whole day.

Sue Bewes's daughter-in-law was one of the "runners" and from then on, I just put in an order for whatever I wanted, made sure the money had been transferred from my bank in South Africa to the right places and waited for her return. As Sue visited me anyhow, she brought the goodies along.

I found an order noted in my diary for September 2008, which included: 2 kilograms sugar, 500 grams Cremora[47], 250 grams Nescafé Ricoffy[48], 4 packets of candles and matches. Another order was for toilet paper, orange squash, washing-up liquid, potatoes, salt and other items. You can see from this where our shortages lay. Most of these things were not even available in the local supermarkets. Unfortunately cheese was not possible as the trucks were not refrigerated, so for cheese and margarine or butter there was another runner specializing in such items, with whom Sue Smith had a connection. She organized those items for us whenever she ordered some for herself.

With the arrival of the US dollar things looked brighter, but there was now another snag. One could buy the items cheaply enough in South Africa, but by the time the runners added their transportation costs, salaries and profits, the expense just about doubled, and my paltry R2000 per month did not cover much anymore. The benefits I had from the black market crashed and I really worried how I would manage. The electricity, water etc. also had to be paid in US$ and the domestic workers started to demand their wages in forex.

The equivalent of my monthly pension was about £200 sterling, and as Fibian's wages would have been the equivalent of £30, I could only afford to give him a minimum. It was better than nothing for him. At least he still had his little stretch of vegetable and mealies in my garden, some of which he took home to his family in the country. There were not many gardening jobs left. With no water, what was the point of a garden?

Fibian, always inventive, found a little sideline. One day, when he was off work, I heard my (petrol operated) lawn mower running a couple of houses away. I caught him sneaking it into the workshop that night. He had not even asked me. I was not against helping the neighbours, but spares were not available and the neighbours did not have lawns, just grass a metre high. So he got an old one started, using the spares from some broken-down ones.

---

[47] Coffee creamer
[48] Sweet instant coffee infused with chicory

52. Health

I was still covered by medical aid, which my bank paid for as part of my pension deal. However, getting payments back from the local medical aid societies could be a lengthy process, if I managed at all.

Zimbank opened a special clinic for all staff and pensioners, even those who had South African pensions, as they were refunded by the South African bank. A few nurses and one sister were operating out of ten rooms (including the waiting room and a dispensary). A doctor came once a week for a few hours to deal with serious cases. The queues were not too bad, and it was handy for prescriptions to be fulfilled and for minor accidents.

Luckily, there was not too much wrong with my health and I think I must elaborate a little on my medical history. My first visit to a hospital had been in East Prussia, when I was eleven years old and had to have an operation on one ear; a little piercing of the drum to get rid of accumulated pus. I was in for only a couple of days, but will never forget my first meal there; a crispy pigeon. All I could see were my lovely pigeons at home, where they followed my father around the room, so I threw up.

The next operation I had was in Harare, a few years after Ronnie and Eve were born, when I had an infection in my ovaries. I had non-stop periods and the doctor decided to remove one ovary. I said to him, "While you are at it, what about removing the other one as well?" He was sympathetic and removed a bit on the other side too. Great! No more pregnancies.

At some point, I had back trouble and the doctors decided to operate on my neck as a nerve was pinching there, due to degeneration, and they "welded" three vertebrae together. For that, they had to chop off a bit of my hipbone. The operation did not give me a pain in the neck, but my hip was very sore and I could not walk on it without the support of the nurse. I soon fixed that. I got hold of one of the tea trolleys next to my bed, and made my way to the bathroom leaning on the trolley. It soon caught on, and I noticed other patients following my example. I don't think the nurses were too pleased!

I developed tinnitus around the age of 50. One morning after "the drums" had been playing all night, I woke up with this buzzing in my ear, but also the rhythm of the drums going through my head in a repeat performance. The doctor said there was nothing that would cure tinnitus and prescribed tranquillizers, shaking his head when I told him about the music in my ear. As I was worried he might certify me insane, I did not pursue the matter. I stopped taking the tranquillizers, as they just made me sleepy, and I had to get used to the buzzing, which sometimes stopped for a few hours, but started again as soon as I fell asleep. No lunchtime naps any more. As the years went on, I did not even know any more if it was there, unless I listened.

The music took some getting used to, as it always repeated the first bar of a song I had heard last. When I got landed with the Zimbabwe national anthem, which was played on television at about eleven o'clock each night, I made sure to switch off before that. My friends used to tease me. "What songs are playing now?" Like all unpleasant things in my life, this was pushed into my subconscious.

I had a bit of stomach trouble for a year, but nobody found out what it was. I went to all kinds of specialists, and one professor, who even had a clinic named after him, said I should let him know if I ever found out what the problem was. At one stage they decided to do some scans and I had to drink six glasses of water first. After five, I told the nurse that if I had another one, I'd throw up, and she replied, "Just do that and we'll start with number one again." I kept it in, but with no results, and eventually the pain disappeared.

I had seen the same doctor for about fifteen years (the same one as Neville), with just a cough or cold here and there. I was about 70 when I went to see him about a sore throat and he was off that day, so a fairly new Polish doctor attended to me. First he took my blood pressure, which nobody had bothered about for as long as I could remember.

I told him he would have trouble finding it, as from sneaking looks at my chart when I was in hospital, I had noticed it was so low they had to draw lines at the bottom of the chart. He looked down the scale and could not find it, then shouted, "Good God, your blood pressure is over 190. Have you never bothered about any signs?" I told him I suffered a lot from hot flushes, but I thought I was still in the menopause. "At your age?" he said. Well, what did I know? I was then past 70. Anyhow, he soon fixed that with a tablet for water retention. (I remember my mother used to take some before she went to parties, apparently it made her look six kilograms lighter.)

I considered myself fairly fit, but it was an accident that changed my whole life and made me come to my senses.

Over the years, especially after Neville died, Eve kept on and on about it being time for me to pack up and come to England. She was genuinely worried about me, especially getting older, but I had always said, I would only leave my house feet first. The situation was bad, but I had achieved so much over the years and was proud of it. Somehow, I would cope.

On Sunday, 5 October 2008, there was an Orchid Society visit to Bertha's place in Helensvale, a posh suburb in the north of Harare, where there were a lot of embassy residences, and grand houses being built for the higher ups in Mugabe's regime. As I mentioned before, Bertha was an African lady with a white husband.

She was the best cook I ever met. Perhaps being married to a German, she cooked more the German way. Her *Schwarzwälder Kirschtorte* was famous. She had a great many orchids, as money was no object at that stage. An Orchid Society visit to Bertha's was always very welcome, especially as there would be a cocktail party afterwards. The meeting and party took place at the bottom of the garden, which was terraced on quite steep ground.

No, I was not drunk when I had the accident. There was a drive up to the house and from there three flights of steps to the meeting place. The steps were made from rough rocks, very uneven. On the first flight, the heel of my shoe got caught between the rocky steps and I tumbled. I was losing my balance, but still tried to carry on with the momentum down the steps, hoping I would find my equilibrium somewhere along the line. It carried me over the first flight and the second flight, but on the next landing I fell. One more flight and I would have landed in the swimming pool, which would have been softer, but I bumped my head on the rocks, blood dripping down my eyes and my arm in an awkward position. The first thing I asked was if my sunglasses were OK, but they had shattered.

Everyone else was more worried about the blood gushing from my scalp. I understand it always flows more freely from the head. Someone suggested an ambulance and hospital, but everyone agreed it would not be financially possible. Everything had to be paid up front – in forex. Still, by placing ice on my head, the bleeding stopped in fifteen minutes and I made it to the meeting place. My arms were terribly sore, but as I could move my fingers, everyone assured me nothing was broken.

I carried on with the meeting and stayed for the cocktail party, as I had to wait for the people who had given me a lift and I did not want to spoil their day. I got home OK. The bleeding had stopped, but my left arm and hand were useless. I could not bend it nor move it. Fibian had to help me get undressed and to bed.

The next day was even worse. I was as stiff as a board and had trouble getting around. My left leg was also black and blue. Sue Smith phoned and said no way could I stay there on my own and, on Monday, she picked me up to stay at her home. I was well looked after, but not very fond of Joss doing the cooking, which was always pasta and swimming in cooking oil. Sue had to go to work.

The good thing was I could phone Eve from there, as they had no trouble with the telephone lines. Eve again insisted I should sell up and come to England. I spoke to her on Tuesday night and said, "No way." By Wednesday, worried about the dogs and my home, I just wanted to go back to my house. Joss said he would take me home. On the way I said perhaps I should visit the doctor's, which was not too far away. Joss could not find the way, but we went past a clinic and decided to go in there. Normally, I would have expected a big queue, but I was the only patient there. A couple of nurses were reading books, another one at the reception knitting.

When I asked to see the doctor, they asked for US$500 cash up front, just to see him. I did not have that much money and I left.

Then I remembered the Zimbank Clinic. The sister there attended to my arm, said nothing was broken, bandaged it up neatly and put my arm in a sling. A couple of painkillers and that was that. However, while I was waiting, I started talking to an African woman next to me. She told me about having to pay the ambulance upfront, and the hospital demanding US$1,000 a night. She said her daughter had been in a car accident. In this case the ambulance had to pick her up off the street, and she was admitted to hospital, but the doctor would not even come and look at her unless she paid US$500 upfront and also another US$1,000 for further treatment. She rushed around her friends and relatives to get the money together, which took her two days. By the time she returned to the hospital with the money, her daughter had died.

It was then it hit me. What would happen to me in the future? After all, I was now 83 years old. I went back with Joss to his house and phoned Sue to ask her to put my house on the market. Sue Smith was working for a property agency so she soon got the ball rolling. In the evening, I phoned Eve and told her my house was up for sale, and I would come to the UK as soon as it was sold.

53. Leaving Zimbabwe

Joss took me home the next day. My arm was still out of action and painful, but I told Fibian to look for buyers for my furniture etc. I would keep the bare essentials, which I would then give to Fibian in gratitude for his many years of service. He was good at this: he already had a number of connections from selling all the other items he had pilfered.

Anyway, I sorted things out, put prices on them – all in US$ of course – and it was amazing where all the poor Africans got their forex from. Nearly every family in that area had a son or daughter working in the UK and sending home money. One woman visited her daughter in the UK, stayed for a year, came back, sold her house, then moved there for good. No wonder the UK was flooded with 'immigrants' (whereas I, of course, was merely a 'returning resident'!).

Fibian did well, selling things. I was selling items for next to nothing as I was in a hurry. My plants were in demand – my potted ones too, which surprised me, when I could only see mealies in their gardens. Even the ornaments went. They also bought my big two-sided fridge: one side was a freezer, the other a normal fridge, leaving the top as a working space. I never saw one like that again in my life. The smaller one was bought by friends. It was so small it would even operate on the inverter Eve had brought me from the UK.

I sold the bedroom suite with the king-size bed and moved into the spare room, which was furnished with a single bed. At least I had somewhere to sleep till the last day, and then Fibian could do with it as he liked. His plain *kia* in the tribal trust lands must have looked like a king's castle to the poor parishioners.

All my lovingly acquired objects and achievements were practically given away. For instance, over a thousand books: I sold bundles of two dozen for US$3 each. Gardening and dog books, which nobody wanted, I left behind. Probably someone's children somewhere are now cutting out the pictures. Another thing I could not sell were my dozens of tapestries.

What a pleasure it had been at one time, when for ten years, while I was still working, I stitched them in my spare time. It was wonderful to see the pictures slowly developing. These were not just cross stitch, but fine stitches on material imported from Germany as kits together with embroidery cotton. I liked mostly the "Old Masters", and my tapestries looked like Rembrandt's paintings.

I also did Sara Moon[49] tapestries on very fine cloth. Once the women from the Orchid Society came to a meeting at my place and came in to look at my tapestries. One woman liked the tapestries but not the Sara Moon ones. She said she was not interested in 'photographs' of paintings. She could not believe it when I told her to look a little closer.

They had been quite expensive, especially the framing, never mind the work. I had so many of them I had run out of wall space, but no one wanted to buy them. I always found it unfair, as I would spend a month on a tapestry, whereas a chap at work told me that his wife took two hours to paint a picture and had no trouble selling it for good money. In any case, almost all of my buyers were Africans and had no use for such nonsense, so I gave them away and left the rest behind. Sue's daughter-in-law said she would take twenty and try and sell them, but I never heard any more. In the end, I took two tapestries with me, a Sara Moon one with two Collies and an "Old Master"; a child and her dog and a music album with Viennese songs, which is now my favourite.

She did however pay me US$400 for the rest of my orchids – 250 of them along with some other plants. I had tried to sell them to members of the Orchid Society, who offered US$2 each, but I said I would rather give them away. They paid better for my collection of bromeliads, but my bestseller was my collection of cycads and palm trees.

My biggest buyer was Manfred, Karl's German ex-business partner, who had been after these plants for years, as he now specialized in these and already had hundreds of them, which he hoped to propagate and sell. He paid US$300 for one

---

[49] pseudonym/brand of Iranian artist, Bijan Djamalzadeh; q.v. sara-moon.com

cycad alone. I did not set the price: he simply told me that was its worth and what he would pay.

I liked Manfred, as I found him easier to talk to than Karl. We had more in common as he also liked plants and dogs. I remember one time when we visited him, he had brought twelve brand-new tennis balls from Durban. Remember, good stuff was not readily available in the country. The tennis court had always been very popular and as usual there was a crowd of young chaps playing around. Manfred had to go to town and when he came back, he found there were only three balls left. He got cross, plonked himself in the middle of the tennis court and shouted, "No more playing until all twelve balls are found." He did not move from the spot. There was a frantic search in the bushes around, and they found thirteen balls eventually.

His girlfriend Geraldine was greatly into showing her Dobermann at the Harare showgrounds and we became closer. Manfred was more interested in palm trees and cycads, even then, and he became chairman of the Zimbabwe Cacti and Aloe Society, which included palm cycads. The beautiful garden Eve had helped plan was now overshadowed by huge potted palms – even the tennis court and swimming pool. He became very friendly with Neville as Manfred also fixed and rebuilt old cars and antiques, which were mostly acquired by foreign embassy staff, so he had no problem getting foreign currency.

When Neville died, Manfred picked me up once in a while to take me to his Cacti and Aloe Society shows. I am still in touch with him, or rather Geraldine. I find men are not that keen on communicating, on the whole.

The tools, what was left of them, went mainly to Nourrish, who was always helpful in times of need. He often popped in for a chat and his daughter was crazy about the piano, which was in the lounge and it was often annoying when she would not stop hammering away on it. But Nourrish had sent his children to the schools still available, and he told me proudly that the teacher kept finding his daughter sneaking into the music room to play the piano and he should try to get her one. So, my beloved piano went to him for a token price. I also gave him my piles of music books. My biggest regret, when I got to the UK, was that I had not brought at least some of them with me.

I did not think I would have room enough for a piano, but when I got a keyboard, I thought longingly of my books. I tried everywhere, even on the internet, to find them again, but to no avail. There were plenty of books and sheet music to be had, even of the old times, which I preferred, but they were not the same. The setting is different, and my fingers are still adjusted to the old ones. I realized I could have easily brought some of them with me, because it turned out that I had plenty of room left in my suitcase.

I was worried about my luggage being overweight and felt I had got rid of everything. I even left the majority of my photos behind. I just took some photos out of the albums here and there. Well, I had about twenty albums of the dog years alone and a few of the years before. I only kept my first photo album intact. I think I was in a daze.

Selling the house was another problem. Sue Smith sent one couple over soon after it went on the market, as they had seen a photograph of it at the estate agent, which Sue's staff had taken. They even made a firm offer and signed papers, but a week later they dropped out as they could not get a big enough loan from the bank.

My property was another item that went for next to nothing. Number one, I was in a hurry, and I would also only sell it in US$. White people already had a property or were thinking of selling theirs as well to leave the country. Another couple came, liked it, but had to sell their property first. A few more came during the first month, then nothing. However, there was a lot of interest in the neighbourhood from people who had found out from Fibian that the house was for sale.

I mentioned before that nearly all of them had relatives working in the UK who had been saving to return for good and buy a house of their own. They were in and out, most of them were not interested in the house (I must say it had started to look rather neglected as there had not been any money for repairs or painting). What they were most interested in was the grounds, plenty of space to plant mealies, they had no interest in my beautiful flower garden. Mind you, it did not look its best any more either, with the water shortage and short rainy season in Zimbabwe. I had cut down on flower beds and planted more grass, as the grass was like a miracle grass, always green. Well, the weeds in between helped, giving the luscious appearance when cut.

One person came from a church with his delegation and wanted it badly, he was going to build a church in the back garden. It should have been heartbreaking for me to learn the possible future of my garden, but I think I was numb. They begged me not to sell the house to anybody else; they were going to get money from the church in the UK and USA. When I left, they were still interested.

I decided to leave anyhow, whether the house was sold or not, and leave it in the hands of the agents. Fibian would move in to look after it. I booked my ticket for 28 December 2008.

It was again Fibian who sold the house for me. I had given him Eve's inverter to sell and he was at the shops across the street, trading with someone, when another African gentleman saw him and wanted it. They agreed on the price and this gentleman asked if I had anything more to sell. Fibian brought him to the house and he bought a lot of the more expensive items. He then asked if I was selling the house and was straightaway keen on buying it.

He had a daughter outside the country working at the bank, so there would be no problem about the transaction. I must mention here that it was kind of illegal to sell a house in any other currency than Zimbabwean, but who cares? There were ways and means. Most people sold their house at a loss, and I should have got at least four times as much. This was one of the reasons white people were reluctant to leave the country, as they could not get the right price for their properties.

This was in the second week of December. Sue Smith was on holiday in the UK, so I contacted the agent to handle the whole business on my behalf. People told me I should get a solicitor, handle it myself and save the agency fees, but it was too complicated for me, so they took over. In no time the papers were drawn up, the deposit arranged and everything ready for the solicitor to make it legal. Unfortunately, by then it was Christmas and nobody was working.

It was a good thing I had instructed the agents, as they found a solicitor who would come to his office and we could all meet him on Boxing Day. All went well, and I sold the house for trillions of Zimbabwe dollars; the official conversion was something like US$40,000. The new owners were in no hurry to move in, wanting to redecorate the house first and later let it until one of their siblings returned from overseas. Fibian was staying on to look after it. It was a bit like putting the goat in charge of the garden, but that was not my business any more.

Fibian did his best. I had given him my cell phone along with some money to top up the phone and he sent me a message in the UK from time to time. The new tenants moved in, put Fibian in charge of the garden, and after a few months, he texted me that the property was now overrun by chickens – even the house. He was not happy with the way they treated him and missed me a lot. He was not very good on the cell phone and must have got his preacher friend to text me for him. Eventually, all I received was a text from time to time: "I miss you".

My one suitcase, containing my whole life in Zimbabwe for 50 years, was packed, weighed and I waited for Sue Bewes and her son and daughter-in-law, who had offered to take me to the airport. I had said goodbye to my other friends long before, as they were nearly all away for the holidays.

We got to the airport, which was crowded with passengers, big queues as usual. There were no seats available, and no benches anywhere in any case, probably already burnt as firewood. I stood for nearly three hours, got to the front, and was then told I was in the wrong queue, as I only had a standby ticket – this was news to me. When I had bought it, they never said anything, and I had not looked too closely, indeed probably would not even have noticed it (one had to read between the lines).

I nearly collapsed then. My friends had refused to go home and Sue's daughter-in-law, who had always been the most enterprising, looked for a wheelchair. I really thought I would feel stupid, but she got hold of one and, I must say, I was most relieved. Once I was in the wheelchair, everything went like clockwork. An air attendant took me around wherever I still had to go, no more waiting. I said goodbye to my friends and was off to the aeroplane.

Arrival at Gatwick, 28 Dec 2008

When I got to the steps of the plane, they asked if I wanted to wait for a ramp, but I feared delays and said I would try to make it up the steps. My performance would have put Elizabeth Taylor to shame. I asked someone to carry my hand luggage and dragged myself up the steps. When I reached the top everyone was fussing around me, and when the plane neared Gatwick the air hostess asked if she should contact the airport to arrange for a wheelchair. No way was I going to wait for a wheelchair – I was in too much of a hurry. I said thank you very much, but the rest on the plane had done me good, I felt much better and would make it on foot. Luckily, there were no steps from the plane to the ground, so I could skip my performance.

I am glad they could not see me charging down the long corridor to the exit.

My flight had been uneventful except that, on taking off from Harare, the realization struck me for the first time that I was leaving a whole life behind me, and I shed a few tears.

Part 7: NEW BEGINNINGS

54. Oxted (2008–2010)

At Gatwick, I went to the luggage collection point and had trouble getting change for a trolley. Never fear, a gentleman next to me showed me how to get change from a machine, collected my luggage for me and made sure I was delivered to my "reception committee".

There they were! My daughter had hardly changed, my granddaughter Alexa, whom I had not seen for about six years, had developed into a beautiful teenager and last but not least, John, my daughter's partner of a few years, were all waiting for me. He reminds me of Richard Gere and is a fantastic chap – not just his looks but his nature. I think Eve hit the jackpot this time.

I had warned Eve that I had no winter clothes, and I arrived wearing sandals. Luckily, I had a jacket that I had bought the last time I was in the UK. Zimbabwe never got really cold. In the short spells of winter, I just put a cardigan on and sat under a blanket. So, I arrived with a suitcase full of summer clothes, which I hardly got round to wearing again. Eve had told me that the car was parked under cover, something one never saw in Zimbabwe, and after a great and passionate reunion, we were off to Oxted in Surrey, where Eve had rented a house.

When I stepped over the threshold, I thought, whenever one door shuts another one opens, and a new life began for me.

The house was small by Zimbabwe standards, but nicely furnished and laid out. Eve had made space for me, by emptying a small spare room, which was used normally as Alexa's storeroom. Alexa had her own room, big by UK standards, but she had trouble with hoarding her belongings. There was a built-in wardrobe, but still some space left for my few clothes. It was comfortable, with everything I required, and there was also a small room for me to use as my living room which had a settee and, most important of all, a television. What else did I need?

Eve is a very good organizer and next day we went straight to the doctor for me to register, although I had brought a big supply of the only medicine I needed, my blood pressure pills. I could not get over the speedy attention and almost instant registration. This was new for me. I also applied for a free bus pass in Surrey, although the buses were not very convenient. It was not far to the town shopping centre, and if I had been younger, I could have walked it easily. It became a bit of a nuisance, having to depend on Eve's trips to town, still I no longer had to queue for things.

The shops were another revelation, full of anything one needed. But to this date, I still stock up once my supplies are down to half. I also fill the kettle with water every time after use. It was fantastic to open a tap and have hot water coming out – even cold water would have been a surprise. When you pressed a switch, electricity came on; and the toilets flushed. People do not know how much they have to be grateful for.

My room was on the first floor and I was a bit weary of the stairs. Ever since my fall I'd been a bit paranoid about steps, if they had no railing to hang on to. Two years later, I still used the lifts in the shops going down, instead of the escalator. I tried once and fell backwards, but luckily there was a gent standing behind who caught me. Still, I am getting better, I think.

There was no queuing at the bank to have my account opened. Everything was so easy. Well, almost. I did not think too much of the doctors, though. They study your records on the computer, without looking directly at you, enquire about the problem and then search for the answer online. I once said to the doctor I might just as well talk to the computer in the first place. Give me the Zimbabwe doctors anytime. They greeted you like a long-lost friend, asked questions to your face, looked at the problem if necessary and usually had the answers in their head. They even carried out small operations themselves, and only as a last resort did they send you to a specialist. The snag was, of course, that there one had to queue for hours. Here you only have to wait a couple of weeks for your next appointment and a few months for the specialist. Well, at least it's free.

Eve cooked the main meal, otherwise we helped ourselves, which suited me perfectly. After a couple of weeks, they tried to get me to do some cooking, but it only lasted a week or so before I was "fired". They were used to spicy meals, a lot of pasta, and I always cooked plain. The only spices I knew were salt and pepper. Still, it was OK for me to do the vacuum cleaning and wash the dishes, sort of. I had not used a vacuum cleaner for the last 40 years. When there was electricity, my servant did all that, also the washing up. Give me the gardening any time (or a book, or television). I just cannot cotton on to housework.

I have since learnt that gardening in this country is rewarding but not easy. Most of the time the soil is so hard one has to use a pick to make a tiny hole. We had sandy soil in Zimbabwe in my garden, and the spade went right to the bottom. Eve had a small garden attached to the house and was very proud of it. She had been looking forward to my advice, but she had managed very well on her own with the layout. I also did not know much about the seasonal conditions, which were very different to South Africa, where things grow all year round.

She was looking forward to showing me the garden in spring as it was now winter, but shortly after I arrived, the owners of the house gave us notice to leave. He was a colonel in the army and ready for retirement and settling back in his own house.

I saw some of her hard labour when spring came and had already started ordering plants for my own requirements to be put into containers. But at the beginning of May we had to move out, together with my pot plants. As usual, they took up more space in the removal van than my suitcases.

It was exiting to look for new accommodation and I was surprised at some of the old houses. How could anybody live with low ceilings, having to duck at every door. But there were nice ones too. I especially liked one with open planning, large windows and a view over a valley. However, they found the place too isolated and it had not much of a garden either. Eventually they found a "mansion" in Ballards Lane in Limpsfield, near Oxted. It had enormous rooms and plenty of them, and most of all a swimming pool, which was a big plus, especially for Alexa. It was enormous and Eve was worried about the cost of heating it, likewise the big rooms. Still, when the rent was reduced to nearly half, they decided to take it.

The garden was really large, but the owners had made arrangements for a gardener to come in once a week. I noticed something about gardeners in the UK. They are not keen on pulling out weeds or even digging too much. They just like to push the lawn mower and trim the hedges. But there was plenty of space for me to put up lots of containers and it was easy to order plants with all the beautiful catalogues. It was not so easy for me to get to a garden centre unless I got a lift with Eve.

Another thing I noticed was that in the UK you can get any plant you desire. At first, I was sad to leave my tropical plants behind, but when one could pick up orchids in the supermarket, cheaper than a lot of other plants, I brightened up. The phalaenopsis, which everyone at the Orchid Society in Zimbabwe had been crazy about, grew well on my windowsill, flowered more and better than in Africa and without any coddling. Even my beloved hibiscus that I had struggled to keep alive in Zimbabwe, the Hawaiian ones, I now have growing and flowering on my windowsill. And the varieties! So, I hardly miss my garden in Zimbabwe.

The new house had a side entrance to a large room connected to a smaller room (I think it was originally a converted garage), which had been described as a pool room. Just perfect for me, nearly a granny flat and on the ground floor. I think John was rather disappointed as he had visualized this as a perfect study for him and Alexa would have loved the pool room for table tennis etc. Sorry guys, it's mine!

I bought furniture, cheap but new, used the big room – one half as bedroom the other as sitting room for my television, typewriter and desk etc. Buying these took a big chunk of my savings, but what were they for otherwise? I had committed myself to sharing the cost of the rent, thinking I would get it back from the housing benefit, but I had slightly miscalculated there.

I now had to get serious with my pension credit application and apply for housing benefit, but found out that none of my applications would be even looked at until I had my National Insurance number. A few weeks after my application, a lady representing the National Registration Department came to visit me at home, probably to make sure I existed, and was most helpful in filling in the application forms, all I had to do was sign. Great country this!

After a month or so I was fixed up with payments from Pension Credit. I had declared the £250 I got from South Africa monthly and they topped up the difference to the maximum entitlement. However, the housing benefit was a disappointment, it was still classified as shared accommodation as I did not have my own kitchen and bathroom. However, I had plenty of money left in my savings to help top up most of the difference on my rent payments. It did not count that I did a lot of cooking for myself, had my own fridge and kettle and only had the main meal with the rest of the family.

I joined a coach travel company and once every couple of months I booked to "go places" – mostly garden shows, exhibitions etc. My favourite trip was the one to the Orchid Extravaganza at Kew Gardens in February, and I said to the other passengers that I'd like to live nearby. Dreams sometimes come true. In the meantime, I was very happy in my accommodation at the mansion.

My friend Sue Smith from Harare came to visit me with her son Julian, who lived and worked in Woking. Sue had two sons and daughter living in the UK, so there was hope of seeing her once in a while.

I was settled in nicely, but when it came near to renewing the lease Eve and John decided otherwise. They had got a bit fed up with the high bills for rent and electricity, and thought it would be far more advantageous to spend that money on their own property. They had enough for a deposit and started looking in the London area. John worked in London and it was a rather long journey by train to work. The winter had been exceptionally harsh, with snow and ice, and as a result we were effectively "snowed in" at times, as we had no chance of getting the car down the icy road. John walked to the station in Oxted for his train to London a couple of times and noticed all the cars lined up on the side of the road.

Not having to go outside, I did not feel the cold as much. The house was heated and there was always my trusted hot water bottle. I had since acquired some warm clothes and good, practical shoes. I was surprised that the cold weather in England did not bother me as much as I had thought it would. But if one has transport, it is really no problem. On the other hand, it was exciting to see snow again after fifty years. Alexa was also enjoying the cold, getting together a few more friends and making snowmen, having snowball fights. Everyone was outside taking photographs.

Eve and John started looking for houses or flats for sale in the south of London, but they were not only expensive but also not attractive. They took me along once, and I found parts of it very dreary and even the adjoining areas not very appealing.

Their search took them to Surbiton, near Kingston, where Eve had friends. The previous Christmas, we had been to Kingston on a shopping tour. I loved Kingston, with the convenient shopping malls, closed off from the traffic. But they thought Surbiton had a better connection of trains to London and restricted their search to there.

In the meantime, I also looked in the property newspapers for a one-bedroom flat, but found that my finances would not stretch that far, so I started looking for somewhere cheaper. I had been to Redhill with Eve a couple of times and liked the inner town, not so much the living areas, but it was within my reach and it was at least a little nearer to Surbiton than Oxted. Then, one day, John visited his stepmother in Weymouth, and as I knew a lady from Harare called Jean who lived in Bournemouth, practically on the way, I thought it might be an opportunity to visit her and check out the town.

Neville knew Jean's daughter from Zimbabwe Airways, where he had worked for a couple of years – the air hostess previously mentioned. She and her mother were also friends of Shirley (the one that died) and I had met them there a couple of times. Jean loved gardening, and in Zimbabwe we soon started casual visits to each other.

They paid cabin crew well in foreign currency on their flights, and the daughter always brought things home for her mother, from bread-making machines to a flatscreen TV (electrical items were a rarity in Zimbabwe). Perhaps that was their downfall.

One evening, at about 8 p.m., Jean heard someone rattling her garden gate, and assumed it was her daughter returning from a flight. As she went to the gate, she saw someone standing outside, and just as Jean thought of returning to the house, another person sprang at her from behind and threw her onto the ground. He turned her face down and sat on her back. The other ransacked the house – really there was not much left in the end. They threatened her if she got up, then jumped over the fence and took off in their car.

Jean got back to the house. I don't remember if she phoned the police, who would not have come anyway, but shortly after that her daughter arrived home. This whole experience left Jean extremely traumatized and the doctors did not know how to help. Jean had relatives in Bournemouth and they asked her to stay with them for a while. Her ticket cost her nothing, as her daughter got free flights.

I wish Neville had stayed at the airways. In fact, while working for the airways, Neville took advantage of his free flight to Frankfurt in Germany to get a second-hand TV. It was then summer in Zimbabwe, and Neville forgot about the winter there and arrived in Frankfurt in a short-sleeved shirt, no jacket and shorts. This was most embarrassing. He did get the TV, by the way, which lasted ten years.

Jean stayed in Bournemouth for nearly a year, hated it, but at least she had nothing to worry about there. She insisted on returning to Harare, where she had been happy, but her fears started to overpower her again, and she decided to move to Bournemouth. She sold me a number of her plants, not cheap, but she had some rare plants not available in Zimbabwe, as her daughter had brought them from her trips. I was sorry to see her go, as I was just getting to know her better. Her daughter also moved to the UK. Their house was left to Jean's other son, who owned half.

I heard about her from time to time and learnt she still was not happy and missed Zimbabwe. I thought this was an opportunity to look her up, while John and Eve carried on to Weymouth. Jean was really pleased to see me and we had a chat about the good old times. I told her I was quite happy in the UK, but Jean just could not stop complaining. She had a flat in the suburbs, within walking distance from the sea. I thought I would be glad to have a place like hers. No garden, but a driveway stacked full of containers plants. Jean and her daughter suggested I should look for a place to live there, and I made enquiries. The rent was similar to Oxted.

55. Kingston (2010–2025)

Eve and John had found a flat in Surbiton (in a "mansion" again), with high ceilings and huge rooms. There were only two bedrooms, one to be occupied by Alexa, when back home on her holidays from the university.

I preferred Kingston, and Eve and I went there to check out the market. We went first to some estate agents, who put down my name. When we came to the third one, the agent told me of a flat that had just come onto the market, and had a garden. This interested me.

We went with the agent straightaway to this property, which was within walking distance of the station, a bit far for me, but I sometimes managed it. I took one look at it and said I would take it. Eve did not like it too much as it had no window in the sitting room.

The main entrance door was at the back of the property and led directly into the sitting room. I preferred to use it as such – walking into a bedroom was not such a good idea to me. The bedroom was a nice size with a big window towards the street. The lounge door had frosted glass panels, but looked straight into my portion of the garden, which was pretty big by local standards. The top floor was occupied by another couple and kids. They were not keen gardeners, but my side was a mess. The last owners had had no interest in gardening at all. Still there was evidence of a lawn and a few nice big conifers near the house with signs of days gone by. I had plenty of plans.

I found later that this area was very much in demand, being so close to the station and yet relatively quiet from traffic. I think it was the only house that was split into two, having been renovated the year before. Any other house in that area would have been beyond my means. As it is, I offered slightly less and told the agents I was a keen gardener and would make something of this one. They agreed, the lease was signed, and I moved in at the beginning of April 2010. Eve and her family moved to Surbiton at the beginning of May.

I was happy as a lark. I was to be independent again, with my own bathroom and a kitchen, even if very small. Once I had organized everything, it looked nice, to me at least. It had a washing machine as well, which I had to learn to use. In Zimbabwe, we only had the two-legged ones. I had wanted to throw all my underwear away when I came to this country, as it had that grey look. Eve put it into the washing machine and it came out snow-white. Well almost.

I found out about a bus going past the end of the street every ten minutes, and there was also one just about opposite the house, "hail and ride", which would stop anywhere. It only went every hour, but was convenient for coming back from Kingston with heavy parcels. It was a real family bus and I got to know a lot of women, all about my age, perhaps a little younger. We chatted, even across the bus, and the bus driver was called by his Christian name.

Eve always encouraged me to make friends, but it was difficult. Although people were very friendly, at least I found them so, they never hinted on visiting at home, although I did so at first. I think in the UK one has to have an invitation, and there is less dropping in. Perhaps in time, but everyone had been there for years and had enough friends and relatives to keep them busy. Previously, it had always been Neville that had made friends first.

I did not miss that, as I was always busy. Eve was in Surbiton, ten minutes' drive away, and dropped in at least once a week, while Ronnie had by now settled in Portsmouth with one of his sons.

After their divorce, Ronnie had left Driekie the house and moved into a flat in Ermelo. Driekie returned to South West Africa and later remarried. At first, their sons stayed with Driekie, then Richie moved to the UK. In the meantime, his half-brother Calvin and half-sister Charmaine were already working in the UK, so he had an anchor, but at first he kept on going forward and back to his mother. He missed Africa very much, but is now settled in England.

I had met Richie at Eve's on one of my previous visits, but he was very shy. I also met Charmaine and Calvin on one of these visits, but they were really strangers to me and they must have felt the same way. We were having a *braai* at one of these open-air functions. They had brought their friends, we had ours, and somehow we did not mix.

When I came to the UK for good, Eve told me that she had now made better contact with them and they were looking forward to meeting me again. Two months later was my birthday, the same day as Charmaine's. Incidentally, Calvin was born on Ronnie's birthday. They said they had planned it that way – I'd like to know how. Charmaine had married in the meantime and had a daughter about three years old then. They invited us to her birthday in Enfield, where they then lived.

I must say here again, I was not used to giving and receiving so many presents. Anyhow, I gave Charmaine one of the two tapestries I had brought with me from Zimbabwe, although I now realize people do not go for that type of thing any more. They showered me in presents and I was highly embarrassed.

They had a nice flat and laid on a big spread. Charmaine is a very good cook and more the style I was used to from Africa. Mekayla, their daughter, and I got on well together. I am only good with children of that age for one hour at the most, and as we did not stay too long, they did not notice my shortcomings. I soon lose patience, especially when they start showing off by playing pranks.

All went so well, that when they later moved to Darlington and I was looking for a town to make my home in, they suggested I should move there, as flats were cheaper. It was too far away from London for me, and too cold. I preferred Bournemouth as I thought it was warmer than Oxted, but later found out that London is about the warmest place in the UK. What luck!

The next Christmas I received a parcel from them. I did not know people sent gifts here; more embarrassment. Now between Eve and Charmaine they pulled out all the stops to get Ronnie over as well. He had had enough of Ermelo and was ready to move. We all clubbed together and sent Ronnie a ticket. It was now up to him. He was still hedging.

On my next birthday (and Charmaine's), I was invited to Darlington. Calvin and his girlfriend Carmella were also going and picked me up in Oxted. On the way they made a detour to Gatwick Airport. I found this strange, but thought maybe they had found a special café to show me or had other business there. Only once we were sitting down did they tell me they were waiting for Ronnie's arrival. I could not believe it. They had not seen Ronnie since they were very small, and relied on me to recognize him. I had not seen him for ages either and picked out the wrong person at first, but Ronnie was close behind and was not to be mistaken. It was a great reunion and off we went to Darlington, where Ronnie was going to stay with Charmaine and her family.

The reception was great as usual, but I was on tenterhooks not to get carried away with Mekayla, who was at a mischievous age. They had decided that Ronnie would stay with them for free but look after Mekayla while they went to work. It did not work out that way: it turned out Ronnie held similar views to mine when it came to discipline, preferring a firm hand, but Charmaine did not agree. He lost his temper one day and smacked Mekayla's bum, resulting in furore all around.

I returned to Kingston and Ronnie remained, but he was full of complaints and within a few days had booked his return; Charmaine was going to help pay for his ticket. Reason prevailed, however, and it was decided in the end that he would stay on a bit longer. Richie, who was now living and working in Portsmouth, offered to take his father in, but had to wait a few weeks for his flatmate to move out. Meanwhile, Ronnie stayed in Darlington.

In the end, he came and stayed with me for about a week. I had just moved into Kingston so we had to rough it a bit, but managed OK and Ronnie eventually moved in with Richie, where he is to this day. He is not happy, but resigned to life in the UK. He has plenty of opportunity to visit me, and finds a patient ear to listen to his problems.

We all have our problems, at least he can talk to me openly about his health. And I must say I also try to get rid of my accumulated complaints as nobody else wants to listen. I find the women on the bus are much more open about their aches and pains, perhaps because they are also older now and have more or less the same problems. I always feel it helps me to talk about it sometimes. I do not expect any help, just a patient ear.

My body is starting to feel its age, my face looks older, but my spirit is still that of a teenager. I continue to enjoy every minute of each day. In the evening, I look forward to the next day and in the morning I look forward to what the day might bring. There is always something to do and, so far, I have never been bored.

I've got a London Freedom Pass and can travel anywhere free by train or Tube, with buses are on my doorstep. Since moving to Kingston, I am on the bus about three times a week (weather permitting). If it rains there is always my television, my laptop, my books (I also joined the library), my keyboards and Sudoku.

I regularly visit Kew Gardens (remember I wanted to live close to it?), Wisley Gardens once in a while (it's a bit awkward to get there, I need a new pair of legs and feet for that) or London. I sometimes walk along the River Thames or take a boat trip to Hampton Court or Richmond. I love the shopping centre in Kingston; it's so easy to walk around with no interference of cars or buses. I could go on longer trips, but do not trust my body.

I miss perhaps the coach trips from Oxted. I had become quite a regular on them, trips to an Ice Show in Brighton, Christmas market in Winchester, exhibitions, etc. I could do that from here, but it was so much easier to let someone else make the arrangements. I wish the days had longer hours.

So what does it matter if I am sitting in a small lounge with no window compared to my wall-to-wall windows in Park Meadowlands? When I open the door, my garden is in front of me. Does it matter that when I look out of the front room, a comfortable bedroom, instead of wide-open spaces there are buildings opposite, and the street, instead of trees, is full of cars? Poor Neville, in spite of my one-acre property, he was never allowed to keep more than two cars.

The carpet is part of the flat and I have to be careful not to leave it too dirty. Ronnie said to me the other day that I had changed. Now I ask him to take his shoes off when he comes in. In Zimbabwe, I never bothered – he was even allowed to put his feet on the table when watching TV as we did not have footstools. Of course, it was all mine and, on top of that, I had my trusted servant to clean up.

I soon learnt about the shoe business in this country. Eve introduced me to it. "Take your shoes off." As I said before, she was now the mother and I the daughter. What would I have done without her? She taught me a new life – including how to use a laptop.

I bought a portable typewriter when I came to the UK. I tried using her computer, but I was useless on it. However, when my brand-new typewriter broke down, I got my money back – in Zimbabwe you would forget about such things – and seeing an advert for a kid's school laptop, I ordered it. Eve and John had been pestering me to give it a go. I thought you cannot teach an old dog new tricks. But here it goes.

It took about a full day to learn how to open the damn thing. I was just about ready to throw the beast against the wall, when I must have pressed the right button by accident. Open Sesame! Unfortunately, I did not know why it had opened suddenly – I do not think it was just the threat. So I had to take more time learning about the opening business.

John had set it up for me nicely, with a lot of explaining, of which I did not remember one thing. Eve was helping too, but I think she did not realize that my brain could not take in more than one item at a time. She told me do this, or that, or the other. All roads lead to Rome, but my wheels were not spinning, although my head did. Eventually, I wrote down every step (no shortcuts or detours please). At last, I learnt how to switch it on. I was scared to press the wrong button, in case the laptop would just disintegrate in front of my eyes.

I had written emails to my friends in Zimbabwe, on Eve's computer, after she set it up for me. All I had to do was type and I was proud when I even found out how to send them. All by myself. Big deal, you say? All of you were brought up with this technology, while to me, it was completely alien. I was proud when at last I was able to send emails. They started to show me other miracles one can perform on the computer.

John took me around the globe on Google Earth and showed me my house in Park Meadowlands from the satellite, along with many other places. It was awesome. He ordered items for me over the internet, more miracles.

I typed letters, although I still cannot find the tab setting and just hop along on the space bar. It will come one day. After a lot of teaching by them, I also managed to look for properties on the internet, when we decided to move from Oxted. Every step was a giant step for mankind. I hated to keep asking them when I got stuck, as they were always busy, so sometimes I ventured a couple of steps on my own and with a great deal of trial and error I succeeded. Gosh, I even order books on the internet, all by myself now and I learnt how to print these pages on my printer. (It reminds me, must ask John to come and change my cartridge for me, should know by now, must write it down next time.)

Calvin and Charmaine installed Facebook for me. Charmaine at least knew what my brain could digest and neatly wrote down for me step by step how to use it, also other things. No detours or shortcuts, just one straight line. I do not like Facebook, it's full of uninteresting things. I look at it from time to time to see how certain people are doing – like Charmaine.

Next thing was Skype. I did not like showing my picture on the screen and was glad when it packed in. Now I can see Ronnie and talk to him without feeling self-conscious. (Hold on, I must just brush my hair, put some decent clothes on, etc.)

I bought a book, *PCs for Dummies*. I wish I hadn't, I do not even qualify as a "dummy". So, back to trial and error. One time, it just would not shut up – I mean shut down. I had to phone a friend to help me find the "panic" button. Anyhow, there is now something else to keep me entertained.

I still miss my friends from Zimbabwe, but continue to work at making friends in this country. Frankly, I never feel lonely and Zimbabwe – I have only to look at all the interesting possibilities to forget my previous life. Like my granddaughter says, "It is so yesterday!"

Life is good.

56. Afterword

After completing her memoirs in 2011, at the age of 86, Ursula has continued to live a happy life in Kingston-Upon-Thames. She finally mastered the art of using her smartphone and fully embraced technology, getting to grips with the internet, Google and Facebook.

Living within a London borough meant that she qualified for a free bus, train and Tube pass which she has exploited to the full. With her new-found energy and enthusiasm, she mastered stairs, and even escalators were now "a piece of cake".

With her annual membership to Kew Gardens, she visits every month. She looks up places of interest on Google Maps, checks the directions and heads off the next day via trains and buses. She then takes photos and happily uploads them, together with reviews.

She's travelled to many of the London parks and loves Regent's Park. She likes to go to the dances held each month at the Festival Hall on the Southbank, where she made many friends, while she's also been able to meet up with many old friends from her time in Rhodesia.

Avril (former neighbour), Ursula, Eve and Lana

In June 2018, Ursula finally travelled, together with her daughter Eve, son-in-law John and granddaughter Alexa, back to Allenstein (now Olsztyn in Poland), the town where she grew up. The last time she had been there was in 1944 during the war.

This time she was able to visit the house where she grew up, her grandfather's house and the Seestern restaurant that he once owned, where she had so many happy memories.

She also visited the town hall, where they were able to provide a copy of her original birth certificate (for one euro), which she had never seen before.

Revisiting Poland

One day, when she was 90 years old, she discovered a hat which she thought was rather cute. She then made her first selfie video, of herself dancing, which she uploaded to her YouTube channel, and subsequently added more. You can find her at https://www.youtube.com/@ursulalacock3791. Her greatest success so far is the Jerusalem Dance she did in 2020 when she was 95, which has had over 41,000 views.

Unfortunately, in 2022 she had a mild heart attack but subsequently recovered well. More recently, at the age of 99, she had to go into hospital to have her pacemaker checked. They said everything was OK and to make another appointment for seven years' time!

She continues to live independently in her rented garden flat. She still walks to the shop around the corner and cooks for herself, does her own laundry and even a bit of cleaning now and again.

She enjoys watching TV, doing Sudoku, keeping up with her family and friends on Facebook (https://www.facebook.com/ursula.lacock) and tending her beloved garden when the weather is fine. Eve and John live in Surbiton, which isn't far away, so they visit her regularly. Her son Ronnie still lives in Portsmouth and also calls her regularly. She remains full of fun, laughter and mischief!

Original birth certificate

Ursula's motto and advice for living to an old age is simple: ***"Don't worry, be happy"***. Hence comes the title of this book… which was published to share her amazing life with a wider audience, but also to help her celebrate her 100th birthday, 27 February 2025.

Other publications from Ōzaru Books

Ōzaru Books is a boutique publisher based in the Thanet village of St Nicholas-at-Wade. Our primary focus is on books with a local connection, ranging from creative writing by East Kent authors to (occasionally niche) scholarly tomes about Kentish history, but we have a secondary interest in works in translation, particularly from Eastern languages, and also tales from East Prussia as shown on the following pages. Some of our profits go to support gorilla charities, which is the origin of the name Ōzaru ('Great Ape') and our logo.

Reflections in an Oval Mirror
Memories of East Prussia, 1923–45
Anneli Jones

8 May 1945 – VE Day – was Anneliese Wiemer's twenty-second birthday. Although she did not know it then, it marked the end of her flight to the West, and the start of a new life in England.

These illustrated memoirs, based on a diary kept during the Third Reich and letters rediscovered many decades later, depict the momentous changes occurring in Europe against a backcloth of everyday farm life in East Prussia (now the north-western corner of Russia, sandwiched between Lithuania and Poland).

The political developments of the 1930s (including the Hitler Youth, 'Kristallnacht', political education, labour service, war service, and interrogation) are all the more poignant for being told from the viewpoint of a romantic young girl. In lighter moments she also describes student life in Vienna and Prague, and her friendship with Belgian and Soviet prisoners of war. Finally, however, the approach of the Red Army forces her to abandon her home and flee across the frozen countryside, encountering en route a cross-section of society ranging from a 'lady of the manor', worried about her family silver, to some concentration camp inmates

ISBN: 978-0-9559219-0-2

Also available on Kindle

German translation (with colourized photographs) available as ISBN 978-1-915174-00-0

Skating at the Edge of the Wood
Memories of East Prussia, 1931–1945...1993
Marlene Yeo

In 1944, the twelve-year old East Prussian girl Marlene Wiemer embarked on a horrific trek to the West, to escape the advancing Red Army. Her cousin Jutta was left behind the Iron Curtain, which severed the family bonds that had made the two so close.

This book contains dramatic depictions of Marlene's flight, recreated from her letters to Jutta during the last year of the war, and contrasted with joyful memories of the innocence that preceded them.

Nearly fifty years later, the advent of perestroika meant that Marlene and Jutta were finally able to revisit their childhood home, after a lifetime of growing up under diametrically opposed societies, and the book closes with a final chapter revealing what they find.

Despite depicting the same time and circumstances as *"Reflections in an Oval Mirror"*, an account written by Marlene's elder sister, Anneli, and its sequel *"Carpe Diem"*, this work stands in stark contrast partly owing to the age gap between the two girls, but above all because of their dramatically different characters.

ISBN: 978-0-9931587-2-8

Also available on Kindle

German translation (with colourized photographs) available as ISBN 978-1-915174-01-7

Carpe Diem
The Ongoing Journey of an East Prussian Exile
Anneli Jones

This sequel to *Reflections in an Oval Mirror* describes Anneli's life after arrival in northern 'West Germany'. At first, as a refugee she moves rapidly from one job to the next — interpreter for military government, secretary, hotel receptionist... Finally she finds work as a journalist, and ends up assisting *The Observer*'s foreign correspondent in Berlin, just at the time when the Marshall Plan and Russian blockade are starting. Forced to flee again in the Berlin airlift, she is then asked to become a mother's help for the original Swallows and Amazons at Lake Coniston, before beginning her own family in Kent, and enjoying weekends with the Astors at Cliveden. But the adventures continue until finally, after the fall of the Iron Curtain, she is able to revisit her childhood home once more.

The author had drawn up an initial draft for *Carpe Diem* already before *Reflections* was published in 2008 — but died in 2011 before it could be completed. Her family then worked on it for fifteen years, teasing out details from her countless letters, diaries, and thousands of annotated photographs, to compile them into a coherent narrative.

The original book was published on Anneli's 85th birthday; this sequel was published on what would have been her 100th birthday.

ISBN: 978-0-9931587-3-5

www.ingramcontent.com/pod-product-compliance
Lightning Source LLC
Chambersburg PA
CBHW041303240426
43661CB00010B/1000